RUPA

Published by
Rupa Publications India Pvt. Ltd 2023
7/16, Ansari Road, Daryaganj
New Delhi 110002

Sales centres:
Bengaluru Chennai
Hyderabad Jaipur Kathmandu
Kolkata Mumbai Prayagraj

P-ISBN: 978-93-5702-601-7
E-ISBN: 978-93-5702-603-1

Second Impression 2024

10 9 8 7 6 5 4 3 2

Printed in India

Contents

Introduction

In the heart of the ancient Indian epic, the Mahabharata, lies a conversation that transcends time, space, and culture—a discourse that delves into the very essence of human existence, purpose, and ethics. This timeless dialogue, known as the Bhagavad Gita, has captivated the minds and hearts of seekers, philosophers, and spiritual enthusiasts for centuries. Its teachings, profound and intricate, offer a guide to navigating life's challenges, dilemmas, and complexities while unraveling the deeper mysteries of existence.

Imagine the scene—a battlefield set to witness a devastating war between two factions of the same royal family. Amidst the clash of swords and the tension of impending battle, the great warrior Arjuna stands bewildered and paralyzed by doubt. In this moment of moral crisis, he turns to his charioteer, Krishna, who is not merely a divine friend but the embodiment of the supreme consciousness. What follows is a conversation that transcends the boundaries of time and delves into the realms of duty, righteousness, devotion, and the nature of reality itself.

The Bhagavad Gita is no ordinary dialogue. It is a philosophical and spiritual treasure trove that addresses the fundamental questions that have haunted humanity for ages. Who are we? What is our purpose? How do we navigate the ethical intricacies of life? How can we find inner peace in the midst of outer chaos? These inquiries, relevant in any era, find resonance in the verses of the Gita, offering insights that have the potential to transform our understanding of the world and our place within it.

The Significance of the Bhagavad Gita:

To label the Bhagavad Gita as a mere philosophical discourse or a spiritual text would be an understatement. It is a multifaceted gem that holds the power to elevate human consciousness, providing guidance not only for spiritual seekers but also for individuals grappling with the challenges of daily existence. Its teachings touch upon myriad aspects of life—personal, societal, ethical, and metaphysical—offering a holistic framework for understanding and navigating the complex tapestry of reality.

At its core, the Bhagavad Gita is an exploration of dharma—often translated as duty or righteousness. The text delves into the nuances of duty, the ethical dilemmas one faces, and the concept of selfless action. Through its verses, the Gita asserts that embracing one's duty without attachment to outcomes is the key to liberation and spiritual growth. It introduces the idea of "Karma Yoga," the path of selfless action, which advocates performing one's duties with dedication while relinquishing attachment to the fruits of those actions.

Furthermore, the Bhagavad Gita is a treatise on the nature of reality and the self. It introduces concepts like the eternal soul (Atman), the transient body, and the distinction between the material and spiritual realms. The teachings of the Gita encourage self-awareness and self-realization, urging individuals to recognize their divine nature and strive for self-mastery.

The Journey Within:

As we embark on this journey through the Bhagavad Gita, we will traverse its eighteen chapters, each presenting a unique facet of wisdom that contributes to the holistic understanding of life. We will delve into the depths of concepts such as yoga—understood not just as physical postures but as a means to unite with the divine—and the various paths to spiritual realization, including Bhakti Yoga (the path of devotion), Jnana Yoga (the path of knowledge), and Dhyana Yoga (the path of meditation)

This exploration will also lead us to the heart of the Gita's teachings: the concept of detachment. Detachment, as presented in the Gita, is not an aloofness from the world but a state of mind that allows us to engage with life's experiences without being ensnared by their fleeting nature. It is through detachment that we can find equilibrium amidst the dualities of pleasure and pain, success and failure.

Relevance in the Modern World:

The Bhagavad Gita's wisdom is not confined to the annals of history or the boundaries of a particular culture. Its teachings resonate across cultures, faiths, and times, offering profound insights that can guide individuals in their pursuit of a meaningful and purposeful life. In an age characterized by technological advancements, rapid changes, and an increasing sense of disconnection, the Gita's message of inner harmony, ethical integrity, and spiritual growth holds a mirror to our contemporary dilemmas and offers a path toward resolution.

As we navigate the complexities of the modern world, the Bhagavad Gita stands as a lighthouse, illuminating our journey with the light of timeless wisdom. It reminds us that while the external circumstances may change, the fundamental questions of human existence remain unchanged. It encourages us to look within, to discover the reservoir of strength, wisdom, and serenity that resides in the depths of our own being.

Conclusion:

The Bhagavad Gita is not just a philosophical discourse frozen in time; it is a living, breathing guide that continues to offer solace, guidance, and inspiration to all who seek answers to life's most profound questions. In the pages that follow, we will embark on a transformative journey through its verses, unraveling its intricate teachings and applying its timeless wisdom to the challenges and aspirations of the present day. As we do so, may we find ourselves drawn deeper into the ocean of insight that is the Bhagavad Gita, discovering within its verses the keys to unlocking a life of purpose, fulfillment, and inner freedom.

Chapter 01

The Armies on the Battlefield of Kuruksetra

ᘓ 1 ᘐ

धृतराष्ट्र उवाच ।
धर्मक्षेत्रे कुरुक्षेत्रे समवेता युयुत्सवः ।
मामकाः पाण्डवाश्चैव किमकुर्वत सञ्जय ।।

dhrtarastra uvaca
dharma-ksetre kuru-ksetre samaveta yuyutsavah
mamakah pandavas caiva kim akurvata sanjaya

Dhritarashtra said: O Sanjaya, after assembling in the place of pilgrimage at Kuruksetra, what did my sons and the sons of Pandu do, being desirous to fight?

ᘓ 2 ᘐ

सञ्जय उवाच ।
दृष्ट्वा तु पाण्डवानीकं व्यूढं दुर्योधनस्तदा ।
आचार्यमुपसङ्गम्य राजा वचनमब्रवीत् ।।

sanjaya uvaca
drstva tu pandavanikam vyudham duryodhanas tada
acaryam upasangamya raja vacanam abravit

Sanjaya said: O King, after looking over the army gathered by the sons of Pandu, King Duryodhana went to his teacher and began to speak the following words:

☙ 3 ❧

पश्यैतां पाण्डुपुत्राणामाचार्य महतीं चमूम् ।
व्यूढां द्रुपदपुत्रेण तव शिष्येण धीमता ।।

pasyaitam pandu-putranam acarya mahatim camum
vyudham drupada-putrena tava sisyena dhimata

O my teacher, behold the great army of the sons of Pandu, so expertly arranged by your intelligent disciple, the son of Drupada.

☙ 4 ❧

अत्र शूरा महेष्वासा भीमार्जुनसमा युधि ।
युयुधानो विराटश्च द्रुपदश्च महारथः ।।

atra sura mahesv-asa bhimarjuna-sama yudhi
yuyudhano viratas ca drupadas ca maha-rathah

Here in this army there are many heroic bowmen equal in fighting to Bhima and Arjuna; there are also great fighters like Yuyudhana, Virata and Drupada.

ങ 5 ഇ

धृष्टकेतुश्चेकितानः काशिराजश्च वीर्यवान् ।
पुरुजित्कुन्तिभोजश्च शैयश्च नरपुङ्गवः ।।

dhrstaketus cekitanah kasirajas ca viryavan
purujit kuntibhojas ca saibyas ca nara-pungavah

There are also great, heroic, powerful fighters like Dhrstaketu, Cekitana, Kasiraja, Purujit, Kuntibhoja and Saibya.

ങ 6 ഇ

युधामन्युश्च विक्रान्त उत्तमौजाश्च वीर्यवान् ।
सौभद्रो द्रौपदेयाश्च सर्व एव महारथाः ।।

yudhamanyus ca vikranta uttamaujas ca viryavan
saubhadro draupadeyas ca sarva eva maha-rathah

There are the mighty Yudhamanyu, the very powerful Uttamauja, the son of Subhadra and the sons of Draupadi. All these warriors are great chariot fighters.

❧ 7 ❧

अस्माकं तु विशिष्टा ये तान्निबोध द्विजोत्तम ।
नायका मम सैन्यस्य संज्ञार्थं तान्ब्रवीमि ते ।।

asmakam tu visista ye tan nibodha dvijottama
nayaka mama sainyasya samjnartham tan bravimi te

O best of the brahmanas, for your information, let me tell you about the captains who are especially qualified to lead my military force.

❧ 8 ❧

भवान्भीष्मश्च कर्णश्च कृपश्च समितिञ्जयः ।
अश्वत्थामा विकर्णश्च सौमदत्तिस्तथैव च ।।

bhavānbhīṣhmaśhcha karṇaśhcha
kṛipaśhcha samitiñjayaḥ
aśhvatthāmā vikarṇaśhcha
saumadattis tathaiva cha

They are: Your venerable self, Bhisma and Karna, and Krpa who is ever victorious in battle; Asvatthama, Vikarna, Saumadatti and Jayadratha.

˜ 9 ™

अन्ये च बहवः शूरा मदर्थे त्यक्तजीविताः ।
नानाशस्त्रप्रहरणाः सर्वे युद्धविशारदाः ।।

anye cha bahavaḥ śhūrā madarthe tyaktajīvitāḥ
nānā-śhastra-praharaṇāḥ sarve yuddha-viśhāradāḥ

There are many heroes who have dedicated their lives for my sake, who possess various kinds of weapons and missiles, (and) all of whom are skilled in battle.

˜ 10 ™

अपर्याप्तं तदस्माकं बलं भीष्माभिरक्षितम् ।
पर्याप्तं त्विदमेतेषां बलं भीमाभिरक्षितम् ।।

aparyāptaṁ tadasmākaṁ balaṁ bhīṣhmābhirakṣhitam
paryāptaṁ tvidameteṣhāṁ balaṁ bhīmābhirakṣhitam

Therefore, our army under the complete protection of Bhisma and others is unlimited. But the army of these (enemies), under the protection of Bhima and others is limited.

☙ 11 ❧

अयनेषु च सर्वेषु यथाभागमवस्थिताः ।
भीष्ममेवाभिरक्षन्तु भवन्तः सर्व एव हि ॥

ayaneṣhu cha sarveṣhu yathā-bhāgamavasthitāḥ
bhīṣhmamevābhirakṣhantu bhavantaḥ sarva eva hi

However, venerable sirs, all of you without exception, while occupying all the positions in the different directions as allotted (to you respectively), please fully protect Bhisma in particular.

☙ 12 ❧

तस्य सञ्जनयन्हर्षं कुरुवृद्धः पितामहः ।
सिंहनादं विनद्योच्चैः शङ्खं दध्मौ प्रतापवान् ॥

tasya sañjanayan harṣhaṁ
kuru-vṛiddhaḥ pitāmahaḥ
siṁha-nādaṁ vinadyochchaiḥ
śhaṅkhaṁ dadhmau pratāpavān

The valiant grandfather, the eldest of the Kurus, loudly sounding a lion-roar, blew the conch to raise his (Duryodhana's) spirits.

௸ 13 ஜ

ततः शङ्खाश्च भेर्यश्च पणवानकगोमुखाः ।
सहसैवाभ्यहन्यन्त स शब्दस्तुमुलोऽभवत् ।।

tataḥ śhaṅkhāśhcha bheryaśhcha
paṇavānaka-gomukhāḥ
sahasaivābhyahanyanta sa
śhabdastumulo "bhavat

Just immediately after that conchs and kettledrums, and tabors, trumpets and cow-horns blared forth. That sound became tumultuous.

௸ 14 ஜ

ततः श्वेतैर्हयैर्युक्ते महति स्यन्दने स्थितौ ।
माधवः पाण्डवश्चैव दिव्यौ शङ्खौ प्रदध्मतुः ।।

tataḥ śhvetairhayairyukte
mahati syandane sthitau
mādhavaḥ pāṇḍavaśhchaiva
divyau śhaṅkhau pradadhmatuḥ

Then, Madhava (Krishna) and the son of Pandu (Arjuna), stationed in their magnificent chariot with white horses attached to it, loudly blew their divine conchs.

∞ 15 ∞

पाञ्चजन्यं हृषीकेशो देवदत्तं धनञ्जयः ।
पौण्ड्रं दध्मौ महाशङ्खं भीमकर्मा वृकोदरः ।।

pāñchajanyaṁ hṛiṣhīkeśho
devadattaṁ dhanañjayaḥ
pauṇḍraṁ dadhmau mahā-śhaṅkhaṁ
bhīma-karmā vṛikodaraḥ

Hrsikesa (Krishna) blew the conch Pancajanya; Dhananjaya (Arjuna) (the conch) Devadatta; and Vrkodara (Bhima) of terrible deeds blew the great conch Paundra;

∞ 16 ∞

अनन्तविजयं राजा कुन्तीपुत्रो युधिष्ठिरः ।
नकुलः सहदेवश्च सुघोषमणिपुष्पकौ ।।

anantavijayaṁ rājā kuntī-putro yudhiṣhṭhiraḥ
nakulaḥ sahadevaśhcha sughoṣha-maṇipuṣhpakau

King Yudhisthira, son of Kunti, (blew) the Anantavijaya; Nakula and Sahadeva, the Sughosa and the Manipuspaka (respectively).

ॐ 17 ॐ

काश्यश्च परमेष्वासः शिखण्डी च महारथः ।
धृष्टद्युम्नो विराटश्च सात्यकिश्चापराजितः ।।

kāśhyaśhcha parameṣhvāsaḥ
śhikhaṇḍī cha mahā-rathaḥ
dhṛiṣhṭadyumno virāṭaśhcha
sātyakiśh chāparājitaḥ

And the King of Kasi, wielding a great bow, and the great chariot-rider Sikhandi, Dhrstadyumna and Virata, and Satyaki the unconquered;

ॐ 18 ॐ

द्रुपदो द्रौपदेयाश्च सर्वशः पृथिवीपते ।
सौभद्रश्च महाबाहुः शङ्खान्दध्मुः पृथक् पृथक् ।।

drupado draupadeyāśhcha
sarvaśhaḥ pṛithivī-pate
saubhadraśhcha mahā-bāhuḥ
śhaṅkhāndadhmuḥ pṛithak pṛithak

Drupada and the sons of Draupadi, and the son of Subhadra, (Abhimanyu) the mighty-armed all (of them) together, O king, blew their respective conchs.

꧁ 19 ꧂

स घोषो धार्तराष्ट्राणां हृदयानि व्यदारयत् ।
नभश्च पृथिवीं चैव तुमुलो नुनादयन् ।।

sa ghoṣho dhārtarāṣhṭrāṇāṁ hṛidayāni vyadārayat
nabhaśhcha pṛithivīṁ chaiva tumulo nunādayan

That tremendous sound pierced the hearts of the sons of Dhrtarastra as it reverberated through the sky and the earth.

꧁ 20 ꧂

अथ व्यवस्थितान्दृष्ट्वा धार्तराष्ट्रान् कपिध्वजः ।
प्रवृत्ते शस्त्रसम्पाते धनुरुद्यम्य पाण्डवः ।
हृषीकेशं तदा वाक्यमिदमाह महीपते ।।

atha vyavasthitān dṛiṣhṭvā
dhārtarāṣhṭrān kapi-dhwajaḥ
pravṛitte śhastra-sampāte
dhanurudyamya pāṇḍavaḥ
hṛiṣhīkeśhaṁ tadā
vākyamidamāha mahī-pate

O king, thereafter, seeing Dhritarashtra's men standing in their positions, when all the weapons were ready for action, the son of Pandu (Arjuna) who had the insignia of Hanuman on his chariot-flag, raising up his bow, said the following to Hrsikesa.

೧ 21 ೨

अर्जुन उवाच ।
सेनयोरुभयोर्मध्ये रथं स्थापय मेऽच्युत ॥

arjuna uvācha
senayor ubhayor madhye rathaṁ sthāpaya me "chyuta

Arjuna said: O Acyuta, please place my chariot between both the armies.

೧ 22 ೨

यावदेतान्निरीक्षेऽहं योद्धुकामानवस्थितान् ।
कैर्मया सह योद्धव्यमस्मिन् रणसमुद्यमे ॥

yāvadetān nirīkṣhe "haṁ yoddhu-kāmān avasthitān
kairmayā saha yoddhavyam asmin raṇa-samudyame

And keep it there until I survey these who stand intent on fighting, and those who are going to engage in battle with me in this impending war.

☙ 23 ❧

योत्स्यमानानवेक्षेऽहं य एतेऽत्र समागताः ।
धार्तराष्ट्रस्य दुर्बुद्धेर्युद्धे प्रियचिकीर्षवः ।।

yotsyamānān avekṣhe "haṁ
ya ete "tra samāgatāḥ
dhārtarāṣhṭrasya durbuddher yuddhe
priya-chikīrṣhavaḥ

These who have assembled here and want to accomplish in the war what is dear to the perverted son of Dhritarashtra, I find them to be intent on fighting.

☙ 24 ❧

सञ्जय उवाच ।
एवमुक्तो हृषीकेशो गुडाकेशेन भारत ।
सेनयोरुभयोर्मध्ये स्थापयित्वा रथोत्तमम् ।।

sañjaya uvācha
evam ukto hṛiṣhīkeśho guḍākeśhena bhārata
senayor ubhayor madhye sthāpayitvā rathottamam

Sanjay said: O scion of the line of Bharata (Dhrtarararastra), Hrsikesa, being told so by Gudakesa (Arjuna), placed the excellent chariot between the two armies.

☙ 25 ❧

भीष्मद्रोणप्रमुखतः सर्वेषां च महीक्षिताम् ।
उवाच पार्थ पश्यैतान्समवेतान्कुरूनिति ।।

bhīṣhma-droṇa-pramukhataḥ
sarveṣhāṁ cha mahī-kṣhitām
uvācha pārtha paśhyaitān
samavetān kurūn iti

In front of Bhisma and Drona as also all the rulers of the earth, and said, 'O Partha (Arjuna), see these assembled people of the Kuru dynasty.'

☙ 26 ❧

तत्रापश्यत्स्थितान् पार्थः पितॄ नथ पितामहान् ।
आचार्यान्मातुलान्भ्रातॄ न्पुत्रान्पौत्रान्सखींस्तथा ।
श्वशुरान्सुहृदश्चैव सेनयोरुभयोरपि ।।

tatrāpaśhyat sthitān pārthaḥ
pitṝin atha pitāmahān
āchāryān mātulān bhrātṝinputrā
npautrān sakhīṁs tathā
śhvaśhurān suhṛidaśh chaiva
senayor ubhayor api

Then Partha (Arjuna) saw, marshalled among both the armies, (his) uncles as also grandfathers, teachers, maternal uncles, brothers (and (cousins), sons, grandsons, as well as comrades and fathers-in-law and friends.

27

तान्समीक्ष्य स कौन्तेयः सर्वान्बन्धूनवस्थितान् ।
कृपया परयाविष्टो विषीदन्निदमब्रवीत् ।।

tān samīkṣhya sa kaunteyaḥ
sarvān bandhūn avasthitān
kṛipayā parayāviṣhṭo
viṣhīdann idam abravīt

The son of Kunti (Ajuna), seeing all those relatives arrayed (there), became overwhelmed by supreme compassion and said this sorrowfully:

૦૩ 28 ౭૦

अर्जुन उवाच ।
दृष्ट्वेमं स्वजनं कृष्ण युयुत्सुं समुपस्थितम् ।।

arjuna uvācha
dṛiṣhṭvemaṁ sva-janaṁ kṛiṣhṇa
yuyutsuṁ samupasthitam

Arjuna said: O Krishna, seeing these relatives and friends who have assembled here with the intention of fighting, my limbs give way and my mouth becomes completely dry.

૦૩ 29 ౭૦

सीदन्ति मम गात्राणि मुखं च परिशुष्यति ।
वेपथुश्च शरीरे मे रोमहर्षश्च जायते ।।

sīdanti mama gātrāṇi mukhaṁ cha pariśhuṣhyati
vepathuśh cha śharīre me roma-harṣhaśh cha jāyate

And there is trembling in my body, and there are cold shivers; the Gandiva (bow) slips from the hand and even the skin burns intensely.

☙ 30 ❧

गाण्डीवं स्रंसते हस्तात्वक्चै व परिदह्यते ।
न च शक्नोम्यवस्थातुं भ्रमतीव च मे मनः ।।

gāṇḍīvaṁ sraṁsate
hastāt tvak chaiva paridahyate
na cha śhaknomy avasthātuṁ
bhramatīva cha me manaḥ

Moreover, O Kesava (Krishna), I am not able to stand firmly, and my mind seems to be whirling. And I notice the omens to be adverse.

☙ 31 ❧

निमित्तानि च पश्यामि विपरीतानि केशव ।
न च श्रेयोऽनुपश्यामि हत्वा स्वजनमाहवे ।।

nimittāni cha paśhyāmi viparītāni keśhava
na cha śhreyo "nupaśhyāmi hatvā sva-janam āhave

Besides, I do not see any good (to be derived) from killing my own people in battle. O Krishna, I do not desire victory, nor even a kingdom nor pleasures.

ൽ 32 ൾ

न काङ्क्षे विजयं कृष्ण न च राज्यं सुखानि च ।
किं नो राज्येन गोविन्द किं भोगैर्जीवितेन वा ।।

na kāṅkṣhe vijayaṁ kṛiṣhṇa na
cha rājyaṁ sukhāni cha
kiṁ no rājyena govinda
kiṁ bhogair jīvitena vā

I desire not victory, O Krishna, nor kingdom, nor pleasures. Of what avail is dominion to us, O Krishna, or pleasures or even life?

ൽ 33 ൾ

येषामर्थे काङ्क्षितं नो राज्यं भोगाः सुखानि च ।
त इमेऽवस्थिता युद्धे प्राणांस्त्यक्त्वा धनानि च ।।

yeṣhām arthe kāṅkṣhitaṁ no
rājyaṁ bhogāḥ sukhāni cha
ta ime "vasthitā yuddhe
prāṇāṁs tyaktvā dhanāni cha

Those for whose sake we desire kingdom, enjoyments and pleasures, stand here in battle, having renounced life and wealth.

॥ 34 ॥

आचार्याः पितरः पुत्रास्तथैव च पितामहाः ।
मातुलाः श्वशुराः पौत्राः श्यालाः सम्बन्धिनस्तथा ।।

āchāryāḥ pitaraḥ putrās
tathaiva cha pitāmahāḥ
mātulāḥ śhvaśhurāḥ pautrāḥ
śhyālāḥ sambandhinas tathā

Teachers, fathers, sons and also grandfathers, maternal uncles, fathers-in-law, grandsons, brothers-in-law and other relatives.

॥ 35 ॥

एतान्न हन्तुमिच्छामि घ्नतोऽपि मधुसूदन ।
अपि त्रैलोक्यराज्यस्य हेतोः किं नु महीकृते ।।

etān na hantum ichchhāmi ghnato "pi madhusūdana
api trailokya-rājyasya hetoḥ kiṁ nu mahī-kṛite

O Madhusudana, even if I am killed, I do not want to kill these even for the sake of a kingdom extending over the three worlds; what to speak of doing so for the earth!

☙ 36 ❧

निहत्य धार्तराष्ट्रान्नः का प्रीतिः स्याज्जनार्दन ।
पापमेवाश्रयेदस्मान्हत्वैतानाततायिनः ।।

nihatya dhārtarāṣhṭrān naḥ kā prītiḥ syāj janārdana
pāpam evāśhrayed asmān hatvaitān ātatāyinaḥ

O Janardana, what happiness shall we derive by killing the sons of Dhritarashtra? Sin alone will accrue to us by killing these felons.

☙ 37 ❧

तस्मान्नार्हा वयं हन्तुं धार्तराष्ट्रान्स्वबान्धवान् ।
स्वजनं हि कथं हत्वा सुखिनः स्याम माधव ।।

tasmān nārhā vayaṁ hantuṁ
dhārtarāṣhṭrān sa-bāndhavān
sva-janaṁ hi kathaṁ hatvā
sukhinaḥ syāma mādhava

Therefore, it is not proper for us to kill the sons of Dhritarashtra who are our own relatives. For, O Madhava, how can we be happy by killing our kinsmen?

☙ 38 ❧

यद्यप्येते न पश्यन्ति लोभोपहतचेतसः ।
कुलक्षयकृतं दोषं मित्रद्रोहे च पातकम् ।।

yady apy ete na paśhyanti lobhopahata-chetasaḥ
kula-kṣhaya-kṛitaṁ doṣhaṁ mitra-drohe cha pātakam

O Janardana, although these people, whose hearts have become perverted by greed, do not see the evil arising from destroying the family and sin in hostility towards, friends,

☙ 39 ❧

कथं न ज्ञेयमस्माभिः पापादस्मान्निवर्तितुम् ।
कुलक्षयकृतं दोषं प्रपश्यद्भिर्जनार्दन ।।

kathaṁ na jñeyam asmābhiḥ
pāpād asmān nivartitum
kula-kṣhaya-kṛitaṁ doṣhaṁ
prapaśhyadbhir janārdana

yet how can we who clearly see the evil arising from destroying the family remain unaware of (the need of) abstaining from this sin?

☙ 40 ❧

कुलक्षये प्रणश्यन्ति कुलधर्माः सनातनाः ।
धर्मे नष्टे कुलं कृत्स्नमधर्मोऽभिभवत्युत ।।

kula-kṣhaye praṇaśhyanti
kula-dharmāḥ sanātanāḥ
dharme naṣhṭe kulaṁ
kṛitsnam adharmo "bhibhavaty uta

From the ruin of the family are totally destroyed the traditional rites and duties of the family. When rites and duties are destroyed, vice overpowers the entire family also.

☙ 41 ❧

अधर्माभिभवात्कृष्ण प्रदुष्यन्ति कुलस्त्रियः ।
स्त्रीषु दुष्टासु वार्ष्णेय जायते वर्णसङ्करः ।।

adharmābhibhavāt kṛiṣhṇa praduṣhyanti kula-striyaḥ
strīṣhu duṣhṭāsu vārṣhṇeya jāyate varṇa-saṅkaraḥ

O Krishna, when vice predominates, the women of the family become corrupt. O descendent of the Vrsnis, when women become corrupted, it results in the intermingling of castes.

☙ 42 ❧

सङ्करो नरकायैव कुलघ्नानां कुलस्य च ।
पतन्ति पितरो ह्येषां लुप्तपिण्डोदकक्रियाः ॥

saṅkaro narakāyaiva kula-ghnānāṁ kulasya cha
patanti pitaro hy eṣhāṁ lupta-piṇḍodaka-kriyāḥ

And the intermingling in the family leads the ruiners of the family verily into hell. The forefathers of these fall down (into hell) because of being deprived of the offerings of rice-balls and water.

☙ 43 ❧

दोषैरेतैः कुलघ्नानां वर्णसङ्करकारकैः ।
उत्साद्यन्ते जातिधर्माः कुलधर्माश्च शाश्वताः ॥

doṣhair etaiḥ kula-ghnānāṁ
varṇa-saṅkara-kārakaiḥ
utsādyante jāti-dharmāḥ
kula-dharmāśh cha śhāśhvatāḥ

Due to these misdeeds of the ruiners of the family, which cause intermingling of castes, the traditional rites and duties of the castes and families become destroyed.

44

उत्सन्नकुलधर्माणां मनुष्याणां जनार्दन ।
नरकेऽनियतं वासो भवतीत्यनुशुश्रुम ।।

utsanna-kula-dharmāṇāṁ
manuṣhyāṇāṁ janārdana
narake "niyataṁ vāso
bhavatītyanuśhuśhruma

O Janardana, we have heard that living in hell becomes inevitable for those persons whose family duties get destroyed.

45

अहो बत महत्पापं कर्तुं व्यवसिता वयम् ।
यद्राज्यसुखलोभेन हन्तुं स्वजनमुद्यताः ।।

aho bata mahat pāpaṁ kartuṁ
vyavasitā vayam
yad rājya-sukha-lobhena
hantuṁ sva-janam udyatāḥ

What a pity that we have resolved to commit a great sin by being eager to kill our own kith and kin, out of greed for the pleasures of a kingdom!

☙ 46 ❧

यदि मामप्रतीकारमशस्त्रं शस्त्रपाणयः ।
धार्तराष्ट्रा रणे हन्युस्तन्मे क्षेमतरं भवेत् ।।

yadi mām apratīkāram aśhastraṁ śhastra-pāṇayaḥ
dhārtarāṣhṭrā raṇe hanyus tan me kṣhemataraṁ bhavet

If, in this battle, the sons of Dhritarashtra armed with weapons kill me who am non-resistant and unarmed, that will be more beneficial to me.

☙ 47 ❧

सञ्जय उवाच ।
एवमुक्त्वार्जुनः सङ्ख्ये रथोपस्थ उपाविशत् ।
विसृज्य सशरं चापं शोकसंविग्नमानसः ।।

sañjaya uvācha
evam uktvārjunaḥ saṅkhye rathopastha upāviśhat
visṛijya sa-śharaṁ chāpaṁ śhoka-saṁvigna-mānasaḥ

Sanjaya narrated: Having said so, Arjuna, with a mind afflicted with sorrow, sat down on the chariot in the midst of the battle, casting aside the bow along with the arrows.

Chapter

02

Sankhya Yoga Teachings of Gita condensed

☙ 1 ❧

सञ्जय उवाच ।
तं तथा कृपयाविष्टमश्रुपूर्णाकुलेक्षणम् ।
विषीदन्तमिदं वाक्यमुवाच मधुसूदनः ।।

sañjaya uvācha
taṁ tathā kṛipayāviṣhṭamaśhru pūrṇākulekṣhaṇam
viṣhīdantamidaṁ vākyam uvācha madhusūdanaḥ

Sanjaya said: To him who had been thus filled with pity, whose eyes were filled with tears and showed distress, and who was sorrowing, Madhusudana uttered these words:

☙ 2 ❧

श्रीभगवानुवाच ।
कुतस्त्वा कश्मलमिदं विषमे समुपस्थितम् ।
अनार्यजुष्टमस्वर्ग्यमकीर्तिकरमर्जुन ।।

śhrī bhagavān uvācha
kutastvā kaśhmalamidaṁ viṣhame samupasthitam
anārya-juṣhṭamaswargyam akīrti-karam arjuna

The Blessed Lord said: O Arjuna, how has this infatuation overtaken you at this odd hour? It is shunned by noble souls; neither will it bring heaven, nor fame to you.

☙ 3 ❧

क्लैब्यं मा स्म गमः पार्थ नैतत्त्वय्युपपद्यते ।
क्षुद्रं हृदयदौर्बल्यं त्यक्त्वोत्तिष्ठ परन्तप ॥

klaibyaṁ mā sma gamaḥ
pārtha naitat tvayyupapadyate
kṣhudraṁ hṛidaya-daurbalyaṁ
tyaktvottiṣhṭha parantapa

O Partha, yield not to unmanliness. This does not befit you. O scorcher of foes, arise, giving up the petty weakness of the heart.

☙ 4 ❧

अर्जुन उवाच ।
कथं भीष्ममहं सङ्ख्ये द्रोणं च मधुसूदन ।
इषुभिः प्रतियोत्स्यामि पूजार्हावरिसूदन ॥

arjuna uvācha
kathaṁ bhīṣhmam ahaṁ sankhye
droṇaṁ cha madhusūdana
iṣhubhiḥ pratiyotsyāmi
pūjārhāvari-sūdana

Arjuna said: O Madhusudana, O destroyer of enemies, how can I fight with arrows in battle against Bhisma and Drona who are worthy of adoration?

ଓ 5 ଃ

गु:नहत्वा हि महानुभावान् श्रेयो भोक्तुं भैक्ष्यमपीह लोके ।
हत्वार्थकामांस्तु गु:निहैव भुञ्जीय भोगान् रुधिरप्रदिग्धान् ।।

gurūnahatvā hi mahānubhāvān
śhreyo bhoktuṁ bhaikṣhyamapīha loke
hatvārtha-kāmāṁstu gurūnihaiva
bhuñjīya bhogān rudhira-pradigdhān

Rather than killing the noble-minded elders, it is better in this world to live even on alms. But, by killing the elders we shall only be enjoying here the pleasures of wealth and desirable things drenched in blood.

ଓ 6 ଃ

न चैतद्विद्मः कतरन्नो गरीयो यद्वा जयेम यदि वा नो जयेयुः ।
यानेव हत्वा न जिजीविषाम स्तेऽवस्थिताः प्रमुखे धार्तराष्ट्राः ।।

na chaitadvidmaḥ kataranno garīyo
yadvā jayema yadi vā no jayeyuḥ
yāneva hatvā na jijīviṣhāmas
te "vasthitāḥ pramukhe dhārtarāṣhṭrāḥ

We do not know this as well as to which is the better for us, (and) whether we shall win, or whether they shall conquer us. Those very sons of Dhritarashtra, by killing whom we do not wish to live, stand in confrontation.

☙ 7 ❧

कार्पण्यदोषोपहतस्वभावः पृच्छामि त्वां धर्मसम्मूढचेताः ।
यच्छ्रेयः स्यान्निश्चितं ब्रूहि तन्मे शिष्यस्तेऽहं शाधि मां त्वां प्रपन्नम् ॥

kārpaṇya-doṣhopahata-svabhāvaḥ
pṛichchhāmi tvāṁ dharma-sammūḍha-chetāḥ
yach-chhreyaḥ syānniśhchitaṁ brūhi tanme
śhiṣhyaste "haṁ śhādhi māṁ tvāṁ prapannam

With my nature overpowered by weak compassion, with a mind bewildered about duty, I pray to You. Tell me for certain that which is better; I am Your disciple. Instruct me who have taken refuge in You.

8

न हि प्रपश्यामि ममापनुद्याद् यच्छोकमुच्छोषणमिन्द्रियाणाम् ।
अवाप्य भूमावसपत्नमृद्धं राज्यं सुराणामपि चाधिपत्यम् ।।

na hi prapaśhyāmi mamāpanudyād
yach-chhokam uchchhoṣhaṇam-indriyāṇām
avāpya bhūmāv-asapatnamṛiddhaṁ
rājyaṁ surāṇāmapi chādhipatyam

Because, I do not see that which can, even after acquiring on this earth a prosperous kingdom free from enemies and even sovereignty over the gods, remove my sorrow (which is) blasting the senses.

9

सञ्जय उवाच ।
एवमुक्त्वा हृषीकेशं गुडाकेशः परन्तप ।
न योत्स्य इति गोविन्दमुक्त्वा तूष्णीं बभूव ह ।।

sañjaya uvācha
evam-uktvā hṛiṣhīkeśhaṁ guḍākeśhaḥ parantapa
na yotsya iti govindam uktvā tūṣhṇīṁ babhūva ha

Sanjaya said: Having spoken thus to Hrsikesa (Krishna), Gudakesa (Arjuna), the afflicter of foes, verily became silent, telling Govinda, 'I shall not fight.'

☙ 10 ❧

तमुवाच हृषीकेशः प्रहसन्निव भारत ।
सेनयोरुभयोर्मध्ये विषीदन्तमिदं वचः ।।

tam-uvācha hṛiṣhīkeśhaḥ prahasanniva bhārata
senayorubhayor-madhye viṣhīdantam-idaṁ vachaḥ

O descendant of Bharata, to him who was sorrowing between the two armies, Hrsikesa, mocking as it were, said these words:

☙ 11 ❧

श्रीभगवानुवाच ।
अशोच्यानन्वशोचस्त्वं प्रज्ञावादांश्च भाषसे ।
गतासूनगतासूंश्च नानुशोचन्ति पण्डिताः ।।

śhrī bhagavān uvācha
aśhochyān-anvaśhochas-tvaṁ
prajñā-vādānśh cha bhāṣhase
gatāsūn-agatāsūnśh-cha
nānuśhochanti paṇḍitāḥ

The Blessed Lord said: You grieve for those who are not to be grieved for; and you speak words of wisdom! The learned do not grieve for the departed and those who have not departed.

ℭ 12 ℵ

न त्वेवाहं जातु नासं न त्वं नेमे जनाधिपा ।
न चैव न भविष्यामः सर्वे वयमतः परम् ।।

na tvevāhaṁ jātu nāsaṁ na tvaṁ neme janādhipāḥ
na chaiva na bhaviṣhyāmaḥ sarve vayamataḥ param

But certainly (it is) not (a fact) that I did not exist at any time; nor you, nor these rulers of men. And surely it is not that we all shall cease to exist after this.

ℭ 13 ℵ

देहिनोऽस्मिन्यथा देहे कौमारं यौवनं जरा ।
तथा देहान्तरप्राप्तिर्धीरस्तत्र न मुह्यति ।।

dehino "smin yathā dehe kaumāraṁ yauvanaṁ jarā
tathā dehāntara-prāptir dhīras tatra na muhyati

As are boyhood, youth and decay to an embodied being in this (present) body, similar is the acquisition of another body. This being so, an intelligent person does not get deluded.

ʗ 14 ʖ

मात्रास्पर्शास्तु कौन्तेय शीतोष्णसुखदुः खदाः ।
आगमापायिनोऽनित्यास्तांस्तितिक्षस्व भारत ।।

mātrā-sparśhās tu kaunteya
śhītoṣhṇa-sukha-duḥkha-dāḥ
āgamāpāyino "nityās tans-titikṣhasva bhārata

But the contacts of the organs with the objects are the producers of cold and heat, happiness and sorrow. They have a beginning and an end, (and) are transient. Bear them, O descendant of Bharata.

ʗ 15 ʖ

यं हि न व्यथयन्त्येते पुरुषं पुरुषर्षभ ।
समदुःखसुखं धीरं सोऽमृतत्वाय कल्पते ।।

yaṁ hi na vyathayantyete puruṣhaṁ puruṣharṣhabha
sama-duḥkha-sukhaṁ dhīraṁ so "mṛitatvāya kalpate

O (Arjuna, who are) foremost among men, verily, the person whom these do not torment, the wise man to whom sorrow and happiness are the same he is fit for Immortality.

ଓ 16 ଛ

नासतो विद्यते भावो नाभावो विद्यते सतः ।
उभयोरपि दृष्टोऽन्तस्त्वनयोस्तत्वदर्शिभिः ।।

nāsato vidyate bhāvo nābhāvo vidyate sataḥ
ubhayorapi dṛiṣhṭo "nta stvanayos tattva-darśhibhiḥ

Of the unreal there is no being; the real has no nonexistence. But the nature of both these, indeed, has been realized by the seers of Truth.

ଓ 17 ଛ

अविनाशि तु तद्विद्धि येन सर्वमिदं ततम् ।
विनाशमव्ययस्यास्य न कश्चित्कर्तुमर्हति ।।

avināśhi tu tadviddhi yena sarvam idaṁ tatam
vināśham avyayasyāsya na kaśhchit kartum arhati

But know That to be indestructible by which all this is pervaded. None can bring about the destruction of this Immutable.

☙ 18 ❧

अन्तवन्त इमे देहा नित्यस्योक्ताः शरीरिणः ।
अनाशिनोऽप्रमेयस्य तस्माद्युध्यस्व भारत ।।

antavanta ime dehā nityasyoktāḥ śharīriṇaḥ
anāśhino "prameyasya tasmād yudhyasva bhārata

These destructible bodies are said to belong to the everlasting, indestructible, indeterminable, embodied One. Therefore, O descendant of Bharata, join the battle.

☙ 19 ❧

य एनं वेत्ति हन्तारं यश्चैनं मन्यते हतम् ।
उभौ तौ न विजानीतो नायं हन्ति न हन्यते ।।

ya enaṁ vetti hantāraṁ
yaśh chainaṁ manyate hatam
ubhau tau na vijānīto
nāyaṁ hanti na hanyate

He who thinks of this One as the killer, and he who thinks of this One as the killed both of them do not know. This One does not kill, nor is It killed.

20

न जायते म्रियते वा कदाचि नायं भूत्वा भविता वा न भूयः ।
अजो नित्यः शाश्वतोऽयं पुराणो न हन्यते हन्यमाने शरीरे ।।

na jāyate mriyate vā kadāchin
nāyaṁ bhūtvā bhavitā vā na bhūyaḥ
ajo nityaḥ śhāśhvato "yaṁ purāṇo
na hanyate hanyamāne śharīre

Never is this One born, and never does It die; nor is it that having come to exist, It will again cease to be. This One is birthless, eternal, undecaying, ancient; It is not killed when the body is killed.

21

वेदाविनाशिनं नित्यं य एनमजमव्ययम् ।
कथं स पुरुषः पार्थ कं घातयति हन्ति कम् ।।

vedāvināśhinaṁ nityaṁ ya enam ajam avyayam
kathaṁ sa puruṣhaḥ pārtha kaṁ ghātayati hanti kam

O Partha, he who knows this One as indestructible, eternal, birthless and undecaying, how and whom does that person kill, or whom does he cause to be killed!

☙ 22 ❧

वासांसि जीर्णानि यथा विहाय
नवानि गृह्णाति नरोऽपराणि ।
तथा शरीराणि विहाय जीर्णा
न्यन्यानि संयाति नवानि देही ।।

vāsānsi jīrṇāni yathā vihāya
navāni gṛihṇāti naro "parāṇi
tathā śharīrāṇi vihāya jīrṇānya
nyāni sanyāti navāni dehī

As after rejecting worn-out clothes a man takes up other new ones, likewise after rejecting worn-out bodies the embodied one unites with other new ones.

☙ 23 ❧

नैनं छिन्दन्ति शस्त्राणि नैनं दहति पावकः ।
न चैनं क्लेदयन्त्यापो न शोषयति मारुतः ।।

nainaṁ chhindanti śhastrāṇi
nainaṁ dahati pāvakaḥ
na chainaṁ kledayantyāpo
na śhoṣhayati mārutaḥ

Weapons do not cut It, fire does not burn It, water does not moisten It, and air does not dry It.

ଓ 24 ଥ

अच्छेद्योऽयमदाह्योऽयमक्लेद्योऽशोष्य एव च ।
नित्यः सर्वगतः स्थाणुरचलोऽयं सनातनः ।।

achchhedyo "yam adāhyo "yam akledyo "śhoṣhya eva cha
nityaḥ sarva-gataḥ sthāṇur achalo "yaṁ sanātanaḥ

It cannot be cut, It cannot be burnt, cannot be moistened, and surely cannot be dried up. It is eternal, omnipresent, stationary, unmoving and changeless.

ଓ 25 ଥ

अव्यक्तोऽयमचिन्त्योऽयमविकार्योऽयमुच्यते ।
तस्मादेवं विदित्वैनं नानुशोचितुमर्हसि ।।

avyakto "yam achintyo "yam avikāryo "yam uchyate
tasmādevaṁ viditvainaṁ nānuśhochitum arhasi

It is said that This is unmanifest; This is inconceivable; This is unchangeable. Therefore, having known This thus, you ought not to grieve.

☙ 26 ❧

अथ चैनं नित्यजातं नित्यं वा मन्यसे मृतम् ।
तथापि त्वं महाबाहो नैवं शोचितुमर्हसि ॥

atha chainaṁ nitya-jātaṁ nityaṁ
vā manyase mṛitam
tathāpi tvaṁ mahā-bāho
naivaṁ śhochitum arhasi

On the other hand, if you think this One is born continually or dies constantly, even then, O mighty-armed one, you ought not to grieve thus.

☙ 27 ❧

जातस्य हि ध्रुवो मृत्युर्ध्रुवं जन्म मृतस्य च ।
तस्मादपरिहार्येऽर्थे न त्वं शोचितुमर्हसि ॥

jātasya hi dhruvo mṛityur dhruvaṁ
janma mṛitasya cha
tasmād aparihārye "rthe na
tvaṁ śhochitum arhasi

For death of anyone born is certain, and of the dead (re-) birth is a certainty. Therefore, you ought not to grieve over an inevitable fact.

☙ 28 ❧

अव्यक्तादीनि भूतानि व्यक्तमध्यानि भारत ।
अव्यक्तनिधनान्येव तत्र का परिदेवना ।।

avyaktādīni bhūtāni vyakta-madhyāni bhārata
avyakta-nidhanānyeva tatra kā paridevanā

O descendant of Bharata, all beings remain unmanifest in the beginning; they become manifest in the middle. After death, they certainly become unmanifest. What lamentation can there be with regard to them?

☙ 29 ❧

आश्चर्यवत्पश्यति कश्चिदेन माश्चर्यवद्वदति तथैव चान्यः ।
आश्चर्यवच्चैनमन्यः शृणोति श्रुत्वाप्येनं वेद न चैव कश्चित् ।।

āśhcharya-vat paśhyati kaśhchid enan
āśhcharya-vad vadati tathaiva chānyaḥ
āśhcharya-vach chainam anyaḥ śhṛiṇoti
śhrutvāpyenaṁ veda na chaiva kaśhchit

Someone visualizes It as a wonder; and similarly indeed, someone else talks of It as a wonder; and someone else hears of It as a wonder. And someone else, indeed, does not realize It even after hearing about It.

☙ 30 ❧

देही नित्यमवध्योऽयं देहे सर्वस्य भारत ।
तस्मात्सर्वाणि भूतानि न त्वं शोचितुमर्हसि ।।

dehī nityam avadhyo "yaṁ dehe sarvasya bhārata
tasmāt sarvāṇi bhūtāni na tvaṁ śhochitum arhasi

O descendant of Bharata, this embodied Self existing in everyone's body can never be killed. Therefore, you ought not to grieve for all (these) beings.

☙ 31 ❧

स्वधर्ममपि चावेक्ष्य न विकम्पितुमर्हसि ।
धर्म्याद्धि युद्धाच्छ्रेयोऽन्यत्क्षत्रियस्य न विद्यते ।।

swa-dharmam api chāvekṣhya
na vikampitum arhasi
dharmyāddhi yuddhāch chhreyo
"nyat kṣhatriyasya na vidyate

Even considering your own duty you should not waver, since there is nothing else better for a Ksatriya than a righteous battle.

♈ 32 ♉

यदृच्छया चैपपन्नं स्वर्गद्वारमपावृतम् ।
सुखिनः क्षत्रियाः पार्थ लभन्ते युद्धमीदृशम् ।।

yadṛichchhayā chopapannaṁ
swarga-dvāram apāvṛitam
sukhinaḥ kṣhatriyāḥ pārtha
labhante yuddham īdṛiśham

O son of Partha, happy are the Ksatriyas who come across this kind of a battle, which presents itself unsought for and which is an open gate to heaven.

♈ 33 ♉

अथ चेतत्वमिमं धर्म्यं संग्रामं न करिष्यसि ।
ततः स्वधर्मं कीर्तिं च हित्वा पापमवाप्स्यसि ।।

atha chet tvam imaṁ dharmyaṁ
saṅgrāmaṁ na kariṣhyasi
tataḥ sva-dharmaṁ kīrtiṁ cha
hitvā pāpam avāpsyasi

On the other hand, if you will not fight this righteous battle, then, forsaking your own duty and fame, you will incur sin.

☙ 34 ❧

अकीर्तिं चापि भूतानि कथयिष्यन्ति तेऽव्ययाम् ।
सम्भावितस्य चाकीर्तिं मरणादतिरिच्यते ॥

akīrtiṁ chāpi bhūtāni
kathayiṣhyanti te "vyayām
sambhāvitasya chākīrtir
maraṇād atirichyate

People also will speak of your unending infamy. And to an honoured person infamy is worse than death.

☙ 35 ❧

भयाद्रणादुपरतं मंस्यन्ते त्वां महारथाः ।
येषां च त्वं बहुमतो भूत्वा यास्यसि लाघवम् ॥

bhayād raṇād uparataṁ mansyante
tvāṁ mahā-rathāḥ
yeṣhāṁ cha tvaṁ bahu-mato
bhūtvā yāsyasi lāghavam

The great chariot-riders will think of you as having desisted from the fight out of fear; and you will into disgrace before them to whom you had been estimable.

ଓଃ 36 ୬୦

अवाच्यवादांश्च बहून्वदिष्यन्ति तवाहिताः ।
निन्दन्तस्तव सामर्थ्यं ततो दुःखतरं नु किम् ॥

avāchya-vādānśh cha
bahūn vadiṣhyanti tavāhitāḥ
nindantastava sāmarthyaṁ
tato duḥkhataraṁ nu kim

And your enemies will speak many indecent words while denigrating your might. What can be more painful than that?

ଓଃ 37 ୬୦

हतो वा प्राप्स्यसि स्वर्गं जित्वा वा भोक्ष्यसे महीम् ।
तस्मादुत्तिष्ठ कौन्तेय युद्धाय कृतनिश्चयः ॥

hato vā prāpsyasi swargaṁ jitvā
vā bhokṣhyase mahīm
tasmād uttiṣhṭha kaunteya
yuddhāya kṛita-niśhchayaḥ

Either by being killed you will attain heaven, or by winning you will enjoy the earth. Therefore, O Arjuna, rise up with determination for fighting.

☙ 38 ❧

सुखदुःखे समे कृत्वा लाभालाभौ जयाजयौ ।
ततो युद्धाय युज्यस्व नैवं पापमवाप्स्यसि ।।

sukha-duḥkhe same kṛitvā lābhālābhau jayājayau
tato yuddhāya yujyasva naivaṁ pāpam avāpsyasi

Treating happiness and sorrow, gain and loss, and victory and defeat with equality, engage in battle. Thus, you will not incur sin.

☙ 39 ❧

एषा तेऽभिहिता साङ्ख्ये बुद्धिर्योगे त्विमां शृणु ।
बुद्ध्या युक्तो यया पार्थ कर्मबन्धं प्रहास्यसि ।।

eṣhā te "bhihitā sānkhye
buddhir yoge tvimāṁ śhṛiṇu
buddhyā yukto yayā pārtha
karma-bandhaṁ prahāsyasi

O Partha, this wisdom has been imparted to you from the standpoint of Self-realization. But listen to this (wisdom) from the standpoint of Yoga, endowed with which wisdom you will get rid of the bondage of action.

☙ 40 ❧

नेहाभिक्रमनाशोऽस्ति प्रत्यवायो न विद्यते ।
स्वल्पमप्यस्य धर्मस्य त्रायते महतो भयात् ।।

nehābhikrama-nāśho "sti
pratyavāyo na vidyate
svalpam apyasya dharmasya
trāyate mahato bhayāt

Here there is no waste of an attempt; nor is there (any) harm. Even a little of this righteousness saves (one) from great fear

☙ 41 ❧

व्यवसायात्मिका बुद्धिरेकेह कुरुनन्दन ।
बहुशाखा ह्यनन्ताश्च बुद्धयोऽव्यवसायिनाम् ।।

vyavasāyātmikā
buddhir ekeha kuru-nandana
bahu-śhākhā hyanantāśh cha
buddhayo "vyavasāyinām

O scion of the Kuru dynasty, in this there is a single, one-pointed conviction. The thoughts of the irresolute ones have many branches indeed, and are innumerable.

❧ 42 ❧

यामिमां पुष्पितां वाचं प्रवदन्त्यविपश्चितः ।
वेदवादरताः पार्थ नान्यदस्तीति वादिनः ।।

❧ 43 ❧

कामात्मानः स्वर्गपरा जन्मकर्मफलप्रदाम् ।
क्रियाविशेषबहुलां भोगैश्वर्यगतिं प्रति ।।

yāmimāṁ puṣhpitāṁ vāchaṁ
pravadanty-avipaśhchitaḥ
veda-vāda-ratāḥ pārtha
nānyad astīti vādinaḥ

kāmātmānaḥ swarga-parā
janma-karma-phala-pradām
kriyā-viśheṣha-bahulāṁ
bhogaiśhwarya-gatiṁ prati

O son of Partha, those undiscerning people who utter this flowery talk which promises birth as a result of rites and duties, and is full of various special rites meant for the attainment of enjoyment and affluence, remain engrossed in the utterances of the Vedas and declare that nothing else exists; their minds are full of desires and they have heaven as the goal.

ଓ 44 ଽ

भोगैश्वर्यप्रसक्तानां तयापहृतचेतसाम् ।
व्यवसायात्मिका बुद्धिः समाधौ न विधीयते ।।

bhogaiśwvarya-prasaktānāṁ tayāpahṛita-chetasām
vyavasāyātmikā buddhiḥ samādhau na vidhīyate

One-pointed conviction does not become established in the minds of those who delight in enjoyment and affluence, and whose intellects are carried away by that (speech).

ଓ 45 ଽ

त्रैगुण्यविषया वेदा निस्त्रैगुण्यो भवार्जुन ।
निर्द्वन्द्वो नित्यसत्वस्थो निर्योगक्षेम आत्मवान् ।।

trai-guṇya-viṣhayā vedā nistrai-guṇyo bhavārjuna
nirdvandvo nitya-sattva-stho niryoga-kṣhema ātmavān

O Arjuna, the Vedas [Meaning only the portion dealing with rites and duties (karma-kanda)] have the three Gunas (modes of Prakriti) as their object. You become free from worldliness, free from the pairs of duality, established in the Eternal Existence (God), without (desire for) acquisition and protection, and self-collected.

ꕥ 46 ꕥ

यावानर्थ उदपाने सर्वतः सम्प्लुतोदके ।
तावान्सर्वेषु वेदेषु ब्राह्मणस्य विजानतः ।।

yāvān artha udapāne sarvataḥ samplutodake
tāvānsarveṣhu vedeṣhu brāhmaṇasya vijānataḥ

A Brahmana with realization has that much utility in all the Vedas as a man has in a well when there is a flood all around.

ꕥ 47 ꕥ

कर्मण्येवाधिकारस्ते मा फलेषु कदाचन ।
मा कर्मफलहेतुर्भूर्मा ते सङ्गोऽस्त्वकर्मणि ।।

karmaṇy-evādhikāras te
mā phaleṣhu kadāchana
mā karma-phala-hetur bhūr mā
te saṅgo "stvakarmaṇi

Your right is for action alone, never for the results. Do not become the agent of the results of action. May you not have any inclination for inaction.

☙ 48 ❧

योगस्थः कुरु कर्माणि सङ्गं त्यक्त्वा धनञ्जय ।
सिद्ध्यसिद्ध्योः समो भूत्वा समत्वं योग उच्यते ।।

yoga-sthaḥ kuru karmāṇi
saṅgaṁ tyaktvā dhanañjaya
siddhy-asiddhyoḥ samo
bhūtvā samatvaṁ yoga uchyate

By being established in Yoga, O Dhananjaya (Arjuna), undertake actions, casting off attachment and remaining equipoised in success and failure. Evenness of mind is called Yoga.

☙ 49 ❧

दूरेण ह्यवरं कर्म बुद्धियोगाद्धनञ्जय ।
बुद्धौ शरणमन्विच्छ कृपणाः फलहेतवः ।।

dūreṇa hy-avaraṁ karma
buddhi-yogād dhanañjaya
buddhau śharaṇam anvichchha
kṛipaṇāḥ phala-hetavaḥ

O Dhananjaya, indeed, action with a self-motive is far inferior to the yoga of wisdom. Take resort to wisdom. Those who thirst for rewards are pitiable.

ᏨᏒ 50 ᏧᏩ

बुद्धियुक्तो जहातीह उभे सुकृतदुष्कृते ।
तस्माद्योगाय युज्यस्व योगः कर्मसु कौशलम् ॥

buddhi-yukto jahātīha
ubhe sukṛita-duṣhkṛite
tasmād yogāya yujyasva
yogaḥ karmasu kauśhalam

Possessed of wisdom, one rejects here both virtue and vice. Therefore, devote yourself to (Karma) yoga. Yoga is skilfulness in action.

ᏨᏒ 51 ᏧᏩ

कर्मजं बुद्धियुक्ता हि फलं त्यक्त्वा मनीषिणः ।
जन्मबन्धविनिर्मुक्ताः पदं गच्छन्त्यनामयम् ॥

karma-jaṁ buddhi-yuktā hi
phalaṁ tyaktvā manīṣhiṇaḥ
janma-bandha-vinirmuktāḥ
padaṁ gachchhanty-anāmayam

Because, those who are devoted to wisdom, (they) becoming men of Enlightenment by giving up the fruits produced by actions, reach the state beyond evils by having become freed from the bondage of birth.

52

यदा ते मोहकलिलं बुद्धिर्व्यतितरिष्यति ।
तदा गन्तासि निर्वेदं श्रोतव्यस्य श्रुतस्य च ।।

yadā te moha-kalilaṁ
buddhir vyatitariṣhyati
tadā gantāsi nirvedaṁ
śhrotavyasya śhrutasya cha

When your mind will go beyond the turbidity of delusion, then you will acquire dispassion for what has to be heard and what has been heard.

53

श्रुतिविप्रतिपन्ना ते यदा स्थास्यति निश्चला ।
समाधावचला बुद्धिस्तदा योगमवाप्स्यसि ।।

śhruti-vipratipannā te yadā sthāsyati niśhchalā
samādhāv-achalā buddhis tadā yogam avāpsyasi

When your mind that has become bewildered by hearing will become unshakable and steadfast in the Self, then you will attain Yoga that arises from discrimination.

☙ 54 ❧

अर्जुन उवाच ।
स्थितप्रज्ञस्य का भाषा समाधिस्थस्य केशव ।
स्थितधीः किं प्रभाषेत किमासीत व्रजेत किम् ।।

arjuna uvācha
sthita-prajñasya kā bhāṣhā
samādhi-sthasya keśhava
sthita-dhīḥ kiṁ prabhāṣheta
kim āsīta vrajeta kim

Arjuna said: O Kesava, what is the description of a man of steady wisdom who is Self-absorbed? How does the man of steady wisdom speak? How does he sit? How does he move about?

☙ 55 ❧

श्रीभगवानुवाच ।
प्रजहाति यदा कामान्सर्वान्पार्थ मनोगतान् ।
आत्मन्येवात्मना तुष्टः स्थितप्रज्ञस्तदोच्यते ।।

śhrī bhagavān uvācha
prajahāti yadā kāmān sarvān pārtha mano-gatān
ātmany-evātmanā tuṣhṭaḥ sthita-prajñas tadochyate

The Blessed said: O Partha, when one fully renounces all the desires that have entered the mind, and remains satisfied in the Self alone by the Self, then he is called a man of steady wisdom.

☙ 56 ❧

दुःखेष्वनुद्विग्नमनाः सुखेषु विगतस्पृहः ।
वीतरागभयक्रोधः स्थितधीर्मुनिरुच्यते ।।

duḥkheṣhv-anudvigna-manāḥ
sukheṣhu vigata-spṛihaḥ
vīta-rāga-bhaya-krodhaḥ
sthita-dhīr munir uchyate

That monk is called a man of steady wisdom when his mind is unperturbed in sorrow, he is free from longing for delights, and has gone beyond attachment, fear and anger.

☙ 57 ❧

यः सर्वत्रानभिस्नेहस्तत्तत्प्राप्य शुभाशुभम् ।
नाभिनन्दति न द्वेष्टि तस्य प्रज्ञा प्रतिष्ठिता ।।

yaḥ sarvatrānabhisnehas tat tat prāpya
śhubhāśhubham
nābhinandati na dveṣhṭi tasya
prajñā pratiṣhṭhitā

The wisdom of that person remains established who has not attachment for anything anywhere, who neither welcomes nor rejects anything whatever good or bad when he comes across it.

꧋ 58 ꧋

यदा संहरते चायं कूर्मोऽङ्गानीव सर्वशः ।
इन्द्रियाणीन्द्रियार्थेभ्यस्तस्य प्रज्ञा प्रतिष्ठिता ।।

yadā sanharate chāyaṁ
kūrmo ''ṅgānīva sarvaśhaḥ
indriyāṇīndriyārthebhyas tasya
prajñā pratiṣhṭhitā

And when this one fully withdraws the senses from the objects of the senses, as a tortoise wholly (withdraws) the limbs, then his wisdom remains established.

↻ 59 ↺

विषया विनिवर्तन्ते निराहारस्य देहिनः ।
रसवर्जं रसोऽप्यस्य परं दृष्ट्वा निवर्तते ॥

vişhayā vinivartante
nirāhārasya dehinaḥ
rasa-varjaṁ raso "pyasya
paraṁ dṛiṣhṭvā nivartate

The objects recede from an abstinent man, with the exception of the taste (for them). Even the taste of this person falls away after realization of the Absolute.

↻ 60 ↺

यततो ह्यपि कौन्तेय पुरुषस्य विपश्चितः ।
इन्द्रियाणि प्रमाथीनि हरन्ति प्रसभं मनः ॥

yatato hyapi kaunteya
puruṣhasya vipaśhchitaḥ
indriyāṇi pramāthīni
haranti prasabhaṁ manaḥ

For, O son of Kunti, the turbulent organs violently snatch away the mind of an intelligent person, even while he is striving diligently.

☙ 61 ❧

तानि सर्वाणि संयम्य युक्त आसीत मत्परः ।
वशे हि यस्येन्द्रियाणि तस्य प्रज्ञा प्रतिष्ठिता ॥

tāni sarvāṇi sanyamya
yukta āsīta mat-paraḥ
vaśhe hi yasyendriyāṇi
tasya prajñā pratiṣhṭhitā

Controlling all of them, one should remain concentrated on Me as the supreme. For, the wisdom of one whose organs are under control becomes steadfast.

☙ 62 ❧

ध्यायतो विषयान्पुंसः सङ्गस्तेषूपजायते ।
सङ्गात्सञ्जायते कामः कामात्क्रोधोऽभिजायते ॥

dhyāyato viṣhayān puṁsaḥ
saṅgas teṣhūpajāyate
saṅgāt sañjāyate kāmaḥ
kāmāt krodho "bhijāyate

In the case of a person who dwells on objects, there arises attachment for them. From attachment grows hankering, from hankering springs anger.

☙ 63 ❧

क्रोधाद्भवति सम्मोहः सम्मोहात्स्मृतिविभ्रमः ।
स्मृतिभ्रंशाद् बुद्धिनाशो बुद्धिनाशात्प्रणश्यति ।।

krodhād bhavati sammohaḥ
sammohāt smṛiti-vibhramaḥ
smṛiti-bhranśhād buddhi-nāśho
buddhi-nāśhāt praṇaśhyati

From anger follows delusion; from delusion, failure of memory; from failure of memory, the loss of understanding; from the loss of understanding, he perishes.

☙ 64 ❧

रागद्वेषवियुक्तैस्तु विषयानिन्द्रियैश्चरन् ।
आत्मवश्यैर्विधेयात्मा प्रसादमधिगच्छति ।।

rāga-dveṣha-viyuktais tu
viṣhayān indriyaiśh charan
ātma-vaśhyair-vidheyātmā
prasādam adhigachchhati

But by perceiving objects with the organs that are free from attraction and repulsion, and are under his own control, the self-controlled man attains serenity.

ଓଃ 65 ଌ

प्रसादे सर्वदुःखानां हानिरस्योपजायते ।
प्रसन्नचेतसो ह्याशु बुद्धिः पर्यवतिष्ठते ॥

prasāde sarva-duḥkhānāṁ hānir asyopajāyate
prasanna-chetaso hyāśhu buddhiḥ paryavatiṣhṭhate

When there is serenity, there follows eradication of all his sorrows, because the wisdom of one who has a serene mind soon becomes firmly established.

ଓଃ 66 ଌ

नास्ति बुद्धिरयुक्तस्य न चायुक्तस्य भावना ।
न चाभावयतः शान्तिरशान्तस्य कुतः सुखम् ॥

nāsti buddhir-ayuktasya na
chāyuktasya bhāvanā
na chābhāvayataḥ
śhāntir aśhāntasya kutaḥ sukham

For the unsteady there is no wisdom, and there is no meditation for the unsteady man. And for an unmeditative man there is no peace. How can there be happiness for one without peace?

☙ 67 ❧

इन्द्रियाणां हि चरतां यन्मनोऽनुविधीयते ।
तदस्य हरति प्रज्ञां वायुर्नावमिवाम्भसि ।।

indriyāṇāṁ hi charatāṁ
yan mano "nuvidhīyate
tadasya harati prajñāṁ
vāyur nāvam ivāmbhasi

For, the mind which follows in the wake of the wandering senses, that (mind) carries away his wisdom like the mind (diverting) a boat on the waters.

☙ 68 ❧

तस्माद्यस्य महाबाहो निगृहीतानि सर्वशः ।
इन्द्रियाणीन्द्रियार्थेभ्यस्तस्य प्रज्ञा प्रतिष्ठिता ।।

tasmād yasya mahā-bāho
nigṛihītāni sarvaśhaḥ
indriyāṇīndriyārthebhyas tasya
prajñā pratiṣhṭhitā

Therefore, O mighty-armed one, his wisdom becomes established whose organs in all their varieties are withdrawn from their objects.

ঙ 69 ৪ঌ

या निशा सर्वभूतानां तस्यां जागर्ति संयमी ।
यस्यां जाग्रति भूतानि सा निशा पश्यतो मुनेः ।।

yā niśhā sarva-bhūtānāṁ
tasyāṁ jāgarti sanyamī
yasyāṁ jāgrati bhūtāni sā
niśhā paśhyato muneḥ

The self-restrained man keeps awake during that which is night for all creatures. That during which creatures keep awake, it is night to the seeing sage.

ঙ 70 ৪ঌ

आपूर्यमाणमचलप्रतिष्ठं समुद्रमापः प्रविशन्ति यद्वत् ।
तद्वत्कामा यं प्रविशन्ति सर्वे स शान्तिमाप्नोति न कामकामी ।।

āpūryamāṇam achala-pratiṣhṭhaṁ
samudram āpaḥ praviśhanti yadvat
tadvat kāmā yaṁ praviśhanti sarve
sa śhāntim āpnoti na kāma-kāmī

That man attains peace into whom all desires enter in the same way as the waters flow into a sea that remains unchanged (even) when being filled up from all sides. Not so one who is desirous of objects.

ଓଃ 71 ৯୦

विहाय कामान्यः सर्वान्पुमांश्चरति निःस्पृहः ।
निर्ममो निरहङ्कारः स शान्तिमधिगच्छति ॥

vihāya kāmān yaḥ sarvān pumānśh charati niḥspṛihaḥ
nirmamo nirahankāraḥ sa śhāntim adhigachchhati

That man attains peace who, after rejecting all desires, moves about free from hankering, without the idea of ('me' and) 'mine', and devoid of pride.

ଓଃ 72 ৯୦

एषा ब्राह्मी स्थितिः पार्थ नैनां प्राप्य विमुह्यति ।
स्थित्वास्यामन्तकालेऽपि ब्रह्मनिर्वाणमृच्छति ॥

eṣhā brāhmī sthitiḥ pārtha naināṁ prāpya vimuhyati
sthitvāsyām anta-kāle "pi brahma-nirvāṇam ṛichchhati

O Partha, this is the state of being established in Brahman. One does not become deluded after attaining this. One attains identification with Brahman by being established in this state even in the closing years of one's life.

Chapter

03

Karma Yoga Importance of Karma in Life

1

अर्जुन उवाच ।
ज्यायसी चेत्कर्मणस्ते मता बुद्धिर्जनार्दन ।
तत्किं कर्मणि घोरे मां नियोजयसि केशव ।।

arjuna uvācha
jyāyasī chet karmaṇas te matā buddhir janārdana
tat kiṁ karmaṇi ghore māṁ niyojayasi keśhava

Arjuna said: O Janardana (Krishna), if it be Your opinion that wisdom is superior to action, why then, do you urge me to do horrible action, O Kesava?

2

व्यामिश्रेणेव वाक्येन बुद्धिं मोहयसीव मे ।
तदेकं वद निश्चित्य येन श्रेयोऽहमाप्नुयाम् ।।

vyāmiśhreṇeva vākyena
buddhiṁ mohayasīva me
tad ekaṁ vada niśhchitya
yena śhreyo "ham āpnuyām

You bewilder my understanding, as it were, by a seemingly conflicting statement! Tell me for certain one of these by which I may attain the highest Good.

☙ 3 ❧

श्रीभगवानुवाच ।
लोकेऽस्मिन्द्विविधा निष्ठा पुरा प्रोक्ता मयानघ ।
ज्ञानयोगेन साङ्ख्यानां कर्मयोगेन योगिनाम् ।।

śhrī bhagavān uvācha
loke"smin dvi-vidhā niṣhṭhā purā proktā mayānagha
jñāna-yogena sāṅkhyānāṁ karma-yogena yoginām

The Blessed Lord said: O unblemished one, two kinds of steadfastness in this world were spoken of by Me in the days of yore–through the Yoga of Knowledge for the men of realization; through the Yoga of Action for the yogis.

☙ 4 ❧

न कर्मणामनारम्भान्नैष्कर्म्यं पुरुषोऽश्नुते ।
न च संन्यसनादेव सिद्धिं समधिगच्छति ।।

na karmaṇām anārambhān naiṣhkarmyaṁ puruṣho "śhnute
na cha sannyasanād eva siddhiṁ samadhigachchhati

A person does not attain freedom from action by abstaining from action; nor does he attain fulfilment merely through renunciation.

☙ 5 ❧

न हि कश्चित्क्षणमपि जातु तिष्ठत्यकर्मकृत् ।
कार्यते ह्यवशः कर्म सर्वः प्रकृतिजैर्गुणैः ।।

na hi kaśhchit kṣhaṇam api
jātu tiṣhṭhatyakarma-kṛit
kāryate hyavaśhaḥ karma
sarvaḥ prakṛiti-jair guṇaiḥ

Because, no one ever remains even for a moment without doing work. For all are made to work under compulsion by the gunas born of Nature.

☙ 6 ❧

कर्मेन्द्रियाणि संयम्य य आस्ते मनसा स्मरन् ।
इन्द्रियार्थान्विमूढात्मा मिथ्याचारः स उच्यते ।।

karmendriyāṇi sanyamya ya
āste manasā smaran
indriyārthān vimūḍhātmā
mithyāchāraḥ sa uchyate

One, who after withdrawing the organs of action, sits mentally recollecting the objects of the senses, that one, of deluded mind, is called a hypocrite.

☙ 7 ❧

यस्त्विन्द्रियाणि मनसा नियम्यारभतेऽर्जुन ।
कर्मेन्द्रियैः कर्मयोगमसक्तः स विशिष्यते ।।

yas tvindriyāṇi manasā niyamyārabhate "rjuna
karmendriyaiḥ karma-yogam asaktaḥ sa viśhiṣhyate

But, O Arjuna, one who engages in Karma-yoga with the organs of action, controlling the organs with the mind and becoming unattached–that one excels.

☙ 8 ❧

नियतं कुरु कर्म त्वं कर्म ज्यायो ह्यकर्मणः ।
शरीरयात्रापि च ते न प्रसिद्ध्येदकर्मणः ।।

niyataṁ kuru karma tvaṁ
karma jyāyo hyakarmaṇaḥ
śharīra-yātrāpi cha te
na prasiddhyed akarmaṇaḥ

You perform the obligatory duties, for action is superior to inaction. And, through inaction, even the maintenance of your body will not be possible.

9

यज्ञार्थात्कर्मणोऽन्यत्र लोकोऽयं कर्मबन्धनः ।
तदर्थं कर्म कौन्तेय मुक्तसङ्गः समाचर ।।

yajñārthāt karmaṇo "nyatra
loko "yaṁ karma-bandhanaḥ
tad-arthaṁ karma kaunteya
mukta-saṅgaḥ samāchara

This man becomes bound by actions other than that action meant for God. Without being attached, O son of Kunti, you perform actions for Him.

10

सहयज्ञाः प्रजाः सृष्ट्वा पुरोवाच प्रजापतिः ।
अनेन प्रसविष्यध्वमेष वोऽस्त्विष्टकामधुक् ।।

saha-yajñāḥ prajāḥ sṛiṣhṭvā
purovācha prajāpatiḥ
anena prasaviṣhyadhvam eṣha
vo "stviṣhṭa-kāma-dhuk

In the days of yore, having created the beings together with the sacrifices, **Prajapati said:** 'By this you multiply. Let this be your yielder of coveted objects of desire.'

☙ 11 ❧

देवान्भावयतानेन ते देवा भावयन्तु वः ।
परस्परं भावयन्तः श्रेयः परमवाप्स्यथ ॥

devān bhāvayatānena te
devā bhāvayantu vaḥ
parasparaṁ bhāvayantaḥ
śhreyaḥ param avāpsyatha

'You nourish the gods with this. Let those gods nourish you. Nourishing one another, you shall attain the supreme Good.'

☙ 12 ❧

इष्टान्भोगान्हि वो देवा दास्यन्ते यज्ञभाविताः ।
तैर्दत्तानप्रदायैभ्यो यो भुङ्क्ते स्तेन एव सः ॥

iṣhṭān bhogān hi vo devā dāsyante yajña-bhāvitāḥ
tair dattān apradāyaibhyo yo bhuṅkte stena eva saḥ

'Being nourished by sacrifices, the gods will indeed give you the coveted enjoyments. He is certainly a thief who enjoys what have been given by them without offering (these) to them.'

ঙ 13 ঌ

यज्ञशिष्टाशिनः सन्तो मुच्यन्ते सर्वकिल्बिषैः ।
भुञ्जते ते त्वघं पापा ये पचन्त्यात्मकारणात् ।।

yajña-śhiṣhṭāśhinaḥ santo
muchyante sarva-kilbiṣhaiḥ
bhuñjate te tvaghaṁ pāpā
ye pachantyātma-kāraṇāt

By becoming partakers of the remembers of sacrifices, they become freed from all sins. But the unholy persons who cook for themselves, they incur sin.

ঙ 14 ঌ

अन्नाद्भवन्ति भूतानि पर्जन्यादन्नसम्भवः ।
यज्ञाद्भवति पर्जन्यो यज्ञः कर्मसमुद्भवः ।।

annād bhavanti bhūtāni
parjanyād anna-sambhavaḥ
yajñād bhavati parjanyo
yajñaḥ karma-samudbhavaḥ

From food are born the creatures; the origin of food is from rainfall; rainfall originates from sacrifice; sacrifice has action as its origin.

☙ 15 ❧

कर्म ब्रह्मोद्भवं विद्धि ब्रह्माक्षरसमुद्भवम् ।
तस्मात्सर्वगतं ब्रह्म नित्यं यज्ञे प्रतिष्ठितम् ।।

karma brahmodbhavaṁ viddhi
brahmākṣhara-samudbhavam
tasmāt sarva-gataṁ brahma
nityaṁ yajñe pratiṣhṭhitam

Know that actin has the Veda as its origin; the Vedas has the Immutable as its source. Hence, the all-pervading Veda is for ever based on sacrifice.

☙ 16 ❧

एवं प्रवर्तितं चक्रं नानुवर्तयतीह यः ।
अघायुरिन्द्रियारामो मोघं पार्थ स जीवति ।।

evaṁ pravartitaṁ chakraṁ nānuvartayatīha yaḥ
aghāyur indriyārāmo moghaṁ pārtha sa jīvati

O Partha, he lives in vain who does not follow here the wheel thus set in motion, whose life is sinful, and who indulges in the senses.

ଔ 17 ৯

यस्त्वात्मरतिरेव स्यादात्मतृप्तश्च मानवः ।
आत्मन्येव च सन्तुष्टस्तस्य कार्यं न विद्यते ।।

yas tvātma-ratir eva
syād ātma-tṛiptaśh cha mānavaḥ
ātmanyeva cha santuṣhṭas tasya
kāryaṁ na vidyate

But that man who rejoices only in the Self and is satisfied with the Self, and is contented only in the Self-for him there is no duty to perform.

ଔ 18 ৯

नैव तस्य कृतेनार्थो नाकृतेनेह कश्चन ।
न चास्य सर्वभूतेषु कश्चिदर्थव्यपाश्रयः ।।

naiva tasya kṛitenārtho
nākṛiteneha kaśhchana
na chāsya sarva-bhūteṣhu
kaśhchid artha-vyapāśhrayaḥ

For him there is no concern here at all with performing action; nor any (concern) with non-performance. Moreover, for him there is no dependence on any object to serve any purpose.

☙ 19 ❧

तस्मादसक्तः सततं कार्यं कर्म समाचर ।
असक्तो ह्याचरन्कर्म परमाप्नोति पूरुषः ।।

tasmād asaktaḥ satatam kāryam karma samāchara
asakto hyācharan karma param āpnoti pūruṣhaḥ

Therefore, remaining unattached, always perform the obligatory duty, for, by performing (one's) duty without attachment, a person attains the Highest.

☙ 20 ❧

कर्मणैव हि संसिद्धिमास्थिता जनकादयः ।
लोकसंग्रहमेवापि सम्पश्यन्कर्तुमर्हसि ।।

karmaṇaiva hi sansiddhim āsthitā janakādayaḥ
loka-saṅgraham evāpi sampaśhyan kartum arhasi

For Janaka and others strove to attain Liberation through action itself. You ought to perform (your duties) keeping also in view the prevention of mankind from going astray.

☙ 21 ❧

यद्यदाचरति श्रेष्ठस्तत्तदेवेतरो जनः ।
स यत्प्रमाणं कुरुते लोकस्तदनुवर्तते ।।

yad yad ācharati
śhreṣhṭhas tat tad evetaro janaḥ
sa yat pramāṇaṁ kurute
lokas tad anuvartate

Whatever a superior person does, another person does that very thing! Whatever he upholds as authority, an ordinary person follows that.

☙ 22 ❧

न मे पार्थास्ति कर्तव्यं त्रिषु लोकेषु किञ्चन ।
नानवाप्तमवाप्तव्यं वर्त एव च कर्मणि ।।

na me pārthāsti kartavyaṁ
triṣhu lokeṣhu kiñchana
nānavāptam avāptavyaṁ varta
eva cha karmaṇi

In all the three worlds, O Partha, there is no duty whatsoever for Me (to fulfil); nothing remains unachieved or to be achieved. (Still) I continue in action.

☙ 23 ❧

यदि ह्यहं न वर्तेयं जातु कर्मण्यतन्द्रितः ।
मम वर्त्मानुवर्तन्ते मनुष्याः पार्थ सर्वशः ।।

yadi hyahaṁ na varteyaṁ
jātu karmaṇyatandritaḥ
mama vartmānuvartante
manuṣhyāḥ pārtha sarvaśhaḥ

For, O Partha, if at any time I do not continue vigilantly in action, men will follow My path in every way.

☙ 24 ❧

उत्सीदेयुरिमे लोका न कुर्यां कर्म चेदहम् ।
सङ्करस्य च कर्ता स्यामुपहन्यामिमाः प्रजाः ।।

utsīdeyur ime lokā na
kuryāṁ karma ched aham
sankarasya cha kartā
syām upahanyām imāḥ prajāḥ

These worlds will be ruined if I do not perform action. And I shall become the agent of intermingling (of castes), and shall be destroying these beings.

ଓ 25 ୧୦

सक्ताः कर्मण्यविद्वांसो यथा कुर्वन्ति भारत ।
कुर्याद्विद्वांस्तथासक्तश्चिकीर्षुर्लोकसंग्रहम् ।।

saktāḥ karmaṇyavidvānso yathā kurvanti bhārata
kuryād vidvāns tathāsaktaśh chikīrṣhur loka-saṅgraham

O scion of the Bharata dynasty, as the unenlightened people act with attachment to work, so should the enlightened person act, without attachment, being desirous of the prevention of people from going astray.

ଓ 26 ୧୦

न बुद्धिभेदं जनयेदज्ञानां कर्मसङ्गिनाम् ।
जोषयेत्सर्वकर्माणि विद्वान्युक्तः समाचरन् ।।

na buddhi-bhedaṁ janayed ajñānāṁ
karma-saṅginām
joṣhayet sarva-karmāṇi
vidvān yuktaḥ samācharan

The enlightened man should not create disturbance in the beliefs of the ignorant, who are attached to work. Working, while himself remaining diligent, he should make them do all the duties.

☙ 27 ❧

प्रकृतेः क्रियमाणानि गुणैः कर्माणि सर्वशः ।
अहङ्कारविमूढात्मा कर्ताहमिति मन्यते ।।

prakṛiteḥ kriyamāṇāni guṇaiḥ karmāṇi sarvaśhaḥ
ahankāra-vimūḍhātmā kartāham iti manyate

While actions are being done in every way by the gunas (qualities) of Nature, one who is deluded by egoism thinks thus: 'I am the doer.'

☙ 28 ❧

तत्ववित्तु महाबाहो गुणकर्मविभागयोः ।
गुणा गुणेषु वर्तन्त इति मत्वा न सज्जते ।।

tattva-vit tu mahā-bāho guṇa-karma-vibhāgayoḥ
guṇā guṇeṣhu vartanta iti matvā na sajjate

But, O mighty-armed one, the one who is a knower of the facts about the varieties of the gunas and actions does not become attached, thinking thus: 'The organs rest (act) on the objects of the organs.'

☙ 29 ❧

प्रकृतेर्गुणसम्मूढाः सज्जन्ते गुणकर्मसु ।
तानकृत्स्नविदो मन्दान्कृत्स्नविन्न विचालयेत् ।।

prakṛiter guṇa-sammūḍhāḥ sajjante guṇa-karmasu
tān akṛitsna-vido mandān kṛitsna-vin na vichālayet

Those who are wholly deluded by the gunas of Nature become attached to the activities of the gunas. The knower of the All should not disturb those of dull intellect, who do not know the All.

☙ 30 ❧

मयि सर्वाणि कर्माणि संन्यस्याध्यात्मचेतसा ।
निराशीर्निर्ममो भूत्वा युध्यस्व विगतज्वरः ।।

mayi sarvāṇi karmāṇi
sannyasyādhyātma-chetasā
nirāśhīr nirmamo bhūtvā
yudhyasva vigata-jvaraḥ

Devoid of the fever of the soul, engage in battle by dedicating all actions to Me, with (your) mind intent on the Self, and becoming free from expectations and egoism.

☙ 31 ❧

ये मे मतमिदं नित्यमनुतिष्ठन्ति मानवाः ।
श्रद्धावन्तोऽनसूयन्तो मुच्यन्ते तेऽपि कर्मभिः ।।

ye me matam idaṁ
nityam anutiṣhṭhanti mānavāḥ
śhraddhāvanto "nasūyanto
muchyante te "pi karmabhiḥ

Those men who ever follow this teaching of Mine with faith and without cavil, they also become freed from actions.

☙ 32 ❧

ये त्वेतदभ्यसूयन्तो नानुतिष्ठन्ति मे मतम् ।
सर्वज्ञानविमूढांस्तान्विद्धि नष्टानचेतसः ।।

ye tvetad abhyasūyanto nānutiṣhṭhanti me matam
sarva-jñāna-vimūḍhāns tān viddhi naṣhṭān achetasaḥ

But those who, decaying [Finding fault where there is none] this, do not follow My teaching, know them –who are deluded about all knowledge [knowledge concerning the qualified and the un-qualified Brahman] and who are devoid of discrimination–to have gone to ruin.

☙ 33 ❧

सदृशं चेष्टते स्वस्याः प्रकृतेर्ज्ञानवानपि ।
प्रकृतिं यान्ति भूतानि निग्रहः किं करिष्यति ।।

sadṛiśhaṁ cheṣhṭate svasyāḥ prakṛiter jñānavān api
prakṛitiṁ yānti bhūtāni nigrahaḥ kiṁ kariṣhyati

Even a man of wisdom behaves according to his own nature. Beings follow (their) nature. What can restraint do?

☙ 34 ❧

इन्द्रियस्येन्द्रियस्यार्थे रागद्वेषौ व्यवस्थितौ ।
तयोर्न वशमागच्छेत्तौ ह्यस्य परिपन्थिनौ ।।

indriyasyendriyasyārthe
rāga-dveṣhau vyavasthitau
tayor na vaśham āgachchhet tau
hyasya paripanthinau

Attraction and repulsion are ordained with regard to the objects of all the organs. One should not come under the sway of these two, because they are his adversaries.

ᘓ 35 ᘐ

श्रेयान्स्वधर्मो विगुणः परधर्मात्स्वनुष्ठितात् ।
स्वधर्मे निधनं श्रेयः परधर्मो भयावहः ।।

śhreyān swa-dharmo viguṇaḥ
para-dharmāt sv-anuṣhṭhitāt
swa-dharme nidhanaṁ śhreyaḥ
para-dharmo bhayāvahaḥ

One's own duty [Customary or scripturally ordained observances of different castes and sects.], though defective, is superior to another's duty well-performed. Death is better while engaged in one's own duty; another's duty is fraught with fear.

ᘓ 36 ᘐ

अर्जुन उवाच ।
अथ केन प्रयुक्तोऽयं पापं चरति पूरुषः ।
अनिच्छन्नपि वार्ष्णेय बलादिव नियोजितः ।।

arjuna uvācha
atha kena prayukto "yaṁ pāpaṁ charati pūruṣhaḥ
anichchhann api vārṣhṇeya balād iva niyojitaḥ

Arjuna said: Now then, O scion of the Vrsni dynasty (Krishna), impelled by what does this man commit sin even against his wish, being constrained by force, as it were?

॥ 37 ॥

श्रीभगवानुवाच ।
काम एष क्रोध एष रजोगुणसमुद्भवः ।
महाशनो महापाप्मा विद्ध्येनमिह वैरिणम् ॥

śhrī bhagavān uvācha
kāma eṣha krodha eṣha rajo-guṇa-samudbhavaḥ
mahāśhano mahā-pāpmā viddhyenam iha vairiṇam

The Blessed Lord said: This desire, this anger, born of the guna of rajas, is a great devourer, a great sinner. Know this to be the enemy here.

॥ 38 ॥

धूमेनाव्रियते वह्निर्यथादर्शो मलेन च ।
यथोल्बेनावृतो गर्भस्तथा तेनेदमावृतम् ॥

dhūmenāvriyate vahnir yathādarśho malena cha
yatholbenāvṛito garbhas tathā tenedam āvṛitam

As fire is enveloped by smoke, as a mirror by dirt, and as a foetus remains enclosed in the womb, so in this shrouded by that.

☙ 39 ❧

आवृतं ज्ञानमेतेन ज्ञानिनो नित्यवैरिणा ।
कामरूपेण कौन्तेय दुष्पूरेणानलेन च ।।

āvṛitaṁ jñānam etena jñānino nitya-vairiṇā
kāma-rūpeṇa kaunteya duṣhpūreṇānalena cha

O son of Kunti, Knowledge is covered by this constant enemy of the wise in the form of desire, which is an insatiable fire.

☙ 40 ❧

इन्द्रियाणि मनो बुद्धिरस्याधिष्ठानमुच्यते ।
एतैर्विमोहयत्येष ज्ञानमावृत्य देहिनम् ।।

indriyāṇi mano buddhir asyādhiṣhṭhānam uchyate
etair vimohayatyeṣha jñānam āvṛitya dehinam

The organs, mind, and the intellect are said to be its abode. This one diversely deludes the embodied being by veiling Knowledge with the help of these.

॥ 41 ॥

तस्मात्त्वमिन्द्रियाण्यादौ नियम्य भरतर्षभ ।
पाप्मानं प्रजहि ह्येनं ज्ञानविज्ञाननाशनम् ॥

tasmāt tvam indriyāṇyādau
niyamya bharatarṣhabha
pāpmānaṁ prajahi hyenaṁ
jñāna-vijñāna-nāśhanam

Therefore, O scion of the Bharata dynasty, after first controlling the organs, renounce this one which is sinful and a destroyer of learning and wisdom.

॥ 42 ॥

इन्द्रियाणि पराण्याहुरिन्द्रियेभ्यः परं मनः ।
मनसस्तु परा बुद्धिर्यो बुद्धेः परतस्तु सः ॥

indriyāṇi parāṇyāhur indriyebhyaḥ paraṁ manaḥ
manasa tu parā buddhir yo buddheḥ paratas tu saḥ

They say that the organs are superior (to the gross body); the mind is superior to the organs; but the intellect is superior to the mind. However, the one who is superior to the intellect is He.

☙ 43 ❧

एवं बुद्धेः परं बुद्ध्वा संस्तभ्यात्मानमात्मना ।
जहि शत्रुं महाबाहो कामरूपं दुरासदम् ।।

evaṁ buddheḥ paraṁ buddhvā
sanstabhyātmānam ātmanā
jahi śhatruṁ mahā-bāho
kāma-rūpaṁ durāsadam

Understanding the Self thus [Understanding thus: that desires can be conquered through the knowledge of the Self.] as superior to the intellect, and completely establishing (the Self) is spiritual absorption with the (help of) the mind, O mighty-armed one, vanish the enemy in the form of desire, which is difficult to subdue.

Chapter 04

Jnana Karma Sanyasa Yoga
Knowledge and the Disciplines of Action

ᘓ 1 ᘐ

श्रीभगवानुवाच ।
इमं विवस्वते योगं प्रोक्तवानहमव्ययम् ।
विवस्वान्मनवे प्राह मनुरिक्ष्वाकवेऽब्रवीत् ।।

śhrī bhagavān uvācha
imaṁ vivasvate yogaṁ proktavān aham avyayam
vivasvān manave prāha manur ikṣhvākave "bravīt

The Blessed Lord said: I imparted this imperishable Yoga to Vivasvan(Sun-God), Vivasvan taught this to Manu, and Manu transmitted this to isavaku.

ᘓ 2 ᘐ

एवं परम्पराप्राप्तमिमं राजर्षयो विदुः ।
स कालेनेह महता योगो नष्टः परन्तप ।।

evaṁ paramparā-prāptam imaṁ rājarṣhayo viduḥ
sa kāleneha mahatā yogo naṣhṭaḥ parantapa

The king-sages knew this (yoga) which was received thus in regular succession. That Yoga, O destroyer of foes, in now lost owing to a long lapse of time.

॥ 3 ॥

स एवायं मया तेऽद्य योगः प्रोक्तः पुरातनः ।
भक्तोऽसि मे सखा चेति रहस्यं ह्येतदुत्तमम् ॥

sa evāyaṁ mayā te "dya yogaḥ proktaḥ purātanaḥ
bhakto "si me sakhā cheti rahasyaṁ hyetad uttamam

That ancient Yoga itself, which is this, has been taught to you by Me today, considering that you are My devotee and friend, For, this (Yoga) is a profound secret.

॥ 4 ॥

अर्जुन उवाच ।
अपरं भवतो जन्म परं जन्म विवस्वतः ।
कथमेतद्विजानीयां त्वमादौ प्रोक्तवानिति ॥

arjuna uvācha
aparaṁ bhavato janma paraṁ janma vivasvataḥ
katham etad vijānīyāṁ tvam ādau proktavān iti

Arjuna said: Your birth was later, (whereas) the birth of Vivasvan(Sun-God) was earlier. How am I to understand this that You instructed (him) in the beginning?

☙ 5 ❧

श्रीभगवानुवाच ।
बहूनि मे व्यतीतानि जन्मानि तव चार्जुन ।
तान्यहं वेद सर्वाणि न त्वं वेत्थ परन्तप ।।

śhrī bhagavān uvācha
bahūni me vyatītāni janmāni tava chārjuna
tānyahaṁ veda sarvāṇi na tvaṁ vettha parantapa

The Blessed Lord said: O Arjuna, many lives of Mine have passed, and so have yours. I know them all, (but) you know not, O scorcher of enemies!

☙ 6 ❧

अजोऽपि सन्नव्ययात्मा भूतानामीश्वरोऽपि सन् ।
प्रकृतिं स्वामधिष्ठाय सम्भवाम्यात्ममायया ।।

ajo "pi sannavyayātmā bhūtānām īśhvaro "pi san
prakṛitiṁ svām adhiṣhṭhāya sambhavāmyātma-
māyayā

Though I am birthless, undecaying by nature, and the Lord of beings, (still) by subjugating My Prakriti, I take birth by means of My own Maya.

૭ 7 ୪

यदा यदा हि धर्मस्य ग्लानिर्भवति भारत ।
अभ्युत्थानमधर्मस्य तदात्मानं सृजाम्यहम् ।।

yadā yadā hi dharmasya glānir bhavati bhārata
abhyutthānam adharmasya tadātmānaṁ sṛijāmyaham

O scion of the Bharata dynasty, whenever righteousness is on the decline, unrighteousness is in the ascendant, then I body Myself forth.

૭ 8 ୪

परित्राणाय साधूनां विनाशाय च दुष्कृताम् ।
धर्मसंस्थापनार्थाय सम्भवामि युगे युगे ।।

paritrāṇāya sādhūnāṁ vināśhāya cha duṣhkṛitām
dharma-sansthāpanārthāya sambhavāmi yuge yuge

For the protection of the pious, the destruction of the evil-doers, and establishing virtue, I manifest Myself in every age.

ଓ 9 ଡ଼

जन्म कर्म च मे दिव्यमेवं यो वेत्ति तत्त्वतः ।
त्यक्त्वा देहं पुनर्जन्म नैति मामेति सोऽर्जुन ।।

janma karma cha me
divyam evaṁ yo vetti tattvataḥ
tyaktvā dehaṁ punar janma
naiti mām eti so "rjuna

He who thus knows truly the divine birth and actions of Mine does not get re-birth after casting off the body. He attains Me, O Arjuna.

ଓ 10 ଡ଼

वीतरागभयक्रोधा मन्मया मामुपाश्रिताः ।
बहवो ज्ञानतपसा पूता मद्भावमागताः ।।

vīta-rāga-bhaya-krodhā
man-mayā mām upāśhritāḥ
bahavo jñāna-tapasā
pūtā mad-bhāvam āgatāḥ

Many who were devoid of attachment, fear and anger, who were absorbed in Me, who had taken refuge in Me, and were purified by the austerity of Knowledge, have attained My state.

ଓ 11 ଓ

ये यथा मां प्रपद्यन्ते तांस्तथैव भजाम्यहम् ।
मम वर्त्मानुवर्तन्ते मनुष्याः पार्थ सर्वशः ।।

ye yathā māṁ prapadyante
tāns tathaiva bhajāmyaham
mama vartmānuvartante
manuṣhyāḥ pārtha sarvaśhaḥ

According to the manner in which they approach Me, I favour them in that very manner. O son of Partha, human beings follow My path in every way.

ଓ 12 ଓ

काङ्क्षन्तः कर्मणां सिद्धिं यजन्त इह देवताः ।
क्षिप्रं हि मानुषे लोके सिद्धिर्भवति कर्मजा ।।

kāṅkṣhantaḥ karmaṇāṁ
siddhiṁ yajanta iha devatāḥ
kṣhipraṁ hi mānuṣhe loke
siddhir bhavati karmajā

Longing for the fruition of actions (of their rites and duties), they worship the gods here. For, in the human world, success from action comes quickly.

꧁ 13 ꧂

चातुर्वर्ण्यं मया सृष्टं गुणकर्मविभागशः ।
तस्य कर्तारमपि मां विद्ध्यकर्तारमव्ययम् ।।

chātur-varṇyaṁ mayā sṛiṣhṭaṁ
guṇa-karma-vibhāgaśhaḥ
tasya kartāram api māṁ
viddhyakartāram avyayam

The four castes have been created by Me through a classification of the gunas and duties. Even though I am the agent of that (act of classification), still know Me to be a non-agent and changeless.

꧁ 14 ꧂

न मां कर्माणि लिम्पन्ति न मे कर्मफले स्पृहा ।
इति मां योऽभिजानाति कर्मभिर्न स बध्यते ।।

na māṁ karmāṇi limpanti na
me karma-phale spṛihā
iti māṁ yo "bhijānāti k
armabhir na sa badhyate

Actions do not taint Me; for Me there is no hankering for the results of actions. One who knows Me thus, does not become bound by actions.

ᔑ 15 ᔕ

एवं ज्ञात्वा कृतं कर्म पूर्वैरपि मुमुक्षुभिः ।
कुरु कर्मैव तस्मात्त्वं पूर्वैः पूर्वतरं कृतम् ।।

evaṁ jñātvā kṛitaṁ karma
pūrvair api mumukṣhubhiḥ
kuru karmaiva tasmāttvaṁ
pūrvaiḥ pūrvataraṁ kṛitam

Having known thus, duties were performed even by the ancient seekers of Liberation. Therefore, you undertake action itself as was performed earlier by the ancient ones.

ᔑ 16 ᔕ

किं कर्म किमकर्मेति कवयोऽप्यत्र मोहिताः ।
तत्ते कर्म प्रवक्ष्यामि यज्ज्ञात्वा मोक्ष्यसेऽशुभात् ।।

kiṁ karma kim akarmeti
kavayo "pyatra mohitāḥ
tat te karma pravakṣhyāmi
yaj jñātvā mokṣhyase "śhubhāt

Even the intelligent are confounded as to what is action and what is inaction. I shall tell you of that action by knowing which you will become free from evil.

☙ 17 ❧

कर्मणो ह्यपि बोद्धव्यं बोद्धव्यं च विकर्मणः ।
अकर्मणश्च बोद्धव्यं गहना कर्मणो गतिः ।।

karmaṇo hyapi boddhavyaṁ
boddhavyaṁ cha vikarmaṇaḥ
akarmaṇaśh cha boddhavyaṁ
gahanā karmaṇo gatiḥ

For there is something to be known even about action, and something to be known about prohibited action; and something has to be known about inaction. The true nature of action is inscrutable.

☙ 18 ❧

कर्मण्यकर्म यः पश्येदकर्मणि च कर्म यः ।
स बुद्धिमान्मनुष्येषु स युक्तः कृत्स्नकर्मकृत् ।।

karmaṇyakarma yaḥ paśhyed akarmaṇi cha karma yaḥ
sa buddhimān manuṣhyeṣhu sa yuktaḥ kṛitsna-karma-kṛit

He who finds inaction in action, and action in inaction, he is the wise one [Possessed of the knowledge of Brahman] among men; he is engaged in yoga and is a performer of all actions!

☙ 19 ❧

यस्य सर्वे समारम्भाः कामसङ्कल्पवर्जिताः ।
ज्ञानाग्निदग्धकर्माणं तमाहुः पण्डितं बुधाः ।।

yasya sarve samārambhāḥ
kāma-saṅkalpa-varjitāḥ
jñānāgni-dagdha-karmāṇaṁ
tam āhuḥ paṇḍitaṁ budhāḥ

The wise call him learned whose actions are all devoid of desires and their thoughts, and whose actions have been burnt away by the fire of wisdom.

☙ 20 ❧

त्यक्त्वा कर्मफलासङ्गं नित्यतृप्तो निराश्रयः ।
कर्मण्यभिप्रवृत्तोऽपि नैव किञ्चित्करोति सः ।।

tyaktvā karma-phalāsaṅgaṁ
nitya-tṛipto nirāśhrayaḥ
karmaṇyabhipravṛitto "pi naiva
kiñchit karoti saḥ

Having given up attachment to the results of action, he who is ever-contented, dependent on nothing, he really does not do anything even though engaged in action.

☙ 21 ❧

निराशीर्यतचित्तात्मा त्यक्तसर्वपरिग्रहः ।
शारीरं केवलं कर्म कुर्वन्नाप्नोति किल्बिषम् ।।

nirāśhīr yata-chittātmā
tyakta-sarva-parigrahaḥ
śhārīraṁ kevalaṁ karma
kurvan nāpnoti kilbiṣham

One who is without solicitation, who has the mind and organs under control, (and) is totally without possessions, he incurs no sin by performing actions merely for the (maintenance of the) body.

☙ 22 ❧

यदृच्छालाभसन्तुष्टो द्वन्द्वातीतो विमत्सरः ।
समः सिद्धावसिद्धौ च कृत्वापि न निबध्यते ।।

yadṛichchhā-lābha-santuṣhṭo dvandvātīto vimatsaraḥ
samaḥ siddhāvasiddhau cha kṛitvāpi na nibadhyate

Remaining satisfied with what comes unasked for, having transcended the dualities, being free from spite, and equipoised under success and failure, he is not bound even by performing actions.

23

गतसङ्गस्य मुक्तस्य ज्ञानावस्थितचेतसः ।
यज्ञायाचरतः कर्म समग्रं प्रविलीयते ।।

gata-saṅgasya muktasya jñānāvasthita-chetasaḥ
yajñāyācharataḥ karma samagraṁ pravilīyate

Of the liberated person who has got rid of attachment, whose mind is fixed in Knowledge, actions undertaken for a sacrifice get totally destroyed.

24

ब्रह्मार्पणं ब्रह्म हविर्ब्रह्माग्नौ ब्रह्मणा हुतम् ।
ब्रह्मैव तेन गन्तव्यं ब्रह्मकर्मसमाधिना ।।

brahmārpaṇaṁ brahma havir
brahmāgnau brahmaṇā hutam
brahmaiva tena gantavyaṁ
brahma-karma-samādhinā

The ladle is Brahman, the oblations is Brahman, the offering is poured by Brahman in the fire of Brahman. Brahman alone is to be reached by him who has concentration on Brahman as the objective, to be known and attained.

꧁ 25 ꧂

दैवमेवापरे यज्ञं योगिनः पर्युपासते ।
ब्रह्माग्नावपरे यज्ञं यज्ञेनैवोपजुह्वति ।।

daivam evāpare yajñaṁ
yoginaḥ paryupāsate
brahmāgnāvapare yajñaṁ
yajñenaivopajuhvati

Other yogis undertake sacrifice to gods alone, Others offer the Self, as a sacrifice by the Self itself, in the fire of Brahman.

꧁ 26 ꧂

श्रोत्रादीनीन्द्रियाण्यन्ये संयमाग्निषु जुह्वति ।
शब्दादीन्विषयानन्य इन्द्रियाग्निषु जुह्वति ।।

śhrotrādīnīndriyāṇyanye
sanyamāgniṣhu juhvati
śhabdādīn viṣhayānanya
indriyāgniṣhu juhvati

Other offer as sacrifice their senses of hearing etc., into the fires of self-discipline. Other yogis, again, offer sound and other objects of perception into the fires of the senses.

27

सर्वाणीन्द्रियकर्माणि प्राणकर्माणि चापरे ।
आत्मसंयमयोगाग्नौ जुह्वति ज्ञानदीपिते ।।

sarvāṇīndriya-karmāṇi
prāṇa-karmāṇi chāpare
ātma-sanyama-yogāgnau
juhvati jñāna-dīpite

Others offer all the activities of the organs and the activities of the vital force into the fire of the yoga of self-control which has been lighted by Knowledge.

28

द्रव्ययज्ञास्तपोयज्ञा योगयज्ञास्तथापरे ।
स्वाध्यायज्ञानयज्ञाश्च यतयः संशितव्रताः ।।

dravya-yajñās tapo-yajñā
yoga-yajñās tathāpare
swādhyāya-jñāna-yajñāśh cha
yatayaḥ sanśhita-vratāḥ

Similarly, others are performers of sacrifices through wealth, through austerity, through yoga, and through study and knowledge; others are ascetics with severe vows.

൭ 29 ൰

अपाने जुह्वति प्राणं प्राणेऽपानं तथापरे ।
प्राणापानगती रुद्ध्वा प्राणायामपरायणाः ।।

൭ 30 ൰

अपरे नियताहाराः प्राणान्प्राणेषु जुह्वति ।
सर्वेऽप्येते यज्ञविदो यज्ञक्षपितकल्मषाः ।।

apāne juhvati prāṇaṁ
prāṇe "pānaṁ tathāpare
prāṇāpāna-gatī ruddhvā
prāṇāyāma-parāyaṇāḥ

apare niyatāhārāḥ
prāṇān prāṇeṣhu juhvati
sarve "pyete yajña-vido
yajña-kṣhapita-kalmaṣhāḥ

Constantly practising control of the vital forces by stopping the movements of the outgoing and the incoming breaths, some offer as a sacrifice the outgoing breath in the incoming breath; while still others, the incoming breath in the outgoing breath. Others, having their food regulated, offer the vital forces in the vital forces. All of them are knowers of the sacrifice and have their sins destroyed by sacrifice.

ও 31 ৯

यज्ञशिष्टामृतभुजो यान्ति ब्रह्म सनातनम् ।
नायं लोकोऽस्त्ययज्ञस्य कुतोऽन्यः कुरुसत्तम ।।

yajña-śhiṣhṭāmṛita-bhujo
yānti brahma sanātanam
nāyaṁ loko "styayajñasya
kuto "nyaḥ kuru-sattama

Those who partake of the nectar left over after a sacrifice, reach the eternal Brahman. This world ceases to exist for one who does not perform sacrifices. What to speak of the other (world), O best among the Kurus (Arjuna)!

ও 32 ৯

एवं बहुविधा यज्ञा वितता ब्रह्मणो मुखे ।
कर्मजान्विद्धि तान्सर्वानेवं ज्ञात्वा विमोक्ष्यसे ।।

evaṁ bahu-vidhā yajñā
vitatā brahmaṇo mukhe
karma-jān viddhi tān sarvān evaṁ
jñātvā vimokṣhyase

Thus, various kinds of sacrifices lie spread at the mouth of the Vedas. Know them all to be born of action. Knowing thus, you will become liberated.

☙ 33 ❧

श्रेयान्द्रव्यमयाद्यज्ञाज्ज्ञानयज्ञः परन्तप ।
सर्वं कर्माखिलं पार्थ ज्ञाने परिसमाप्यते ।।

śhreyān dravya-mayād yajñāj jñāna-yajñaḥ parantapa
sarvaṁ karmākhilaṁ pārtha jñāne parisamāpyate

O destroyer of enemies, Knowledge considered as a sacrifice is greater than sacrifices requiring materials. O son of Partha, all actions in their totality culminate in Knowledge.

☙ 34 ❧

तद्विद्धि प्रणिपातेन परिप्रश्नेन सेवया ।
उपदेक्ष्यन्ति ते ज्ञानं ज्ञानिनस्तत्त्वदर्शिनः ।।

tad viddhi praṇipātena paripraśhnena sevayā
upadekṣhyanti te jñānaṁ jñāninas tattva-darśhinaḥ

Know that through prostration, inquiry and service. The wise ones who have realized the Truth will impart the Knowledge to you.

☙ 35 ❧

यज्ज्ञात्वा न पुनर्मोहमेवं यास्यसि पाण्डव ।
येन भूतान्यशेषेण द्रक्ष्यस्यात्मन्यथो मयि ।।

yaj jñātvā na punar moham evaṁ yāsyasi pāṇḍava
yena bhūtānyaśheṣheṇa drakṣhyasyātmanyatho mayi

Knowing which, O Pandava (Arjuna), you will not come under delusion again in this way, and through which you will see all beings without exception in the Self and also in Me.

☙ 36 ❧

अपि चेदसि पापेभ्यः सर्वेभ्यः पापकृत्तमः ।
सर्वं ज्ञानप्लवेनैव वृजिनं सन्तरिष्यसि ।।

api ched asi pāpebhyaḥ sarvebhyaḥ pāpa-kṛit-tamaḥ
sarvaṁ jñāna-plavenaiva vṛijinaṁ santariṣhyasi

Even if you be the worst sinner among all sinners, still you will cross over all the wickedness with the raft of Knowledge alone.

॥ 37 ॥

यथैधांसि समिद्धोऽग्निर्भस्मसात्कुरुतेऽर्जुन ।
ज्ञानाग्निः सर्वकर्माणि भस्मसात्कुरुते तथा ॥

yathaidhānsi samiddho "gnir bhasma-sāt kurute "rjuna
jñānāgniḥ sarva-karmāṇi bhasma-sāt kurute tathā

O Arjuna, as a blazing fire reduces pieces of wood to ashes, similarly the fire of Knowledge reduces all actions to ashes.

॥ 38 ॥

न हि ज्ञानेन सदृशं पवित्रमिह विद्यते ।
तत्स्वयं योगसंसिद्धः कालेनात्मनि विन्दति ॥

na hi jñānena sadṛiśhaṁ pavitramiha vidyate
tatsvayaṁ yogasansiddhaḥ kālenātmani vindati

Indeed, there is nothing purifying here comparable to Knowledge. One who has become perfected after a (long) time through yoga, realizes That by himself in his own heart.

☙ 39 ❧

श्रद्धावान् लभते ज्ञानं तत्परः संयतेन्द्रियः ।
ज्ञानं लब्ध्वा परां शान्तिमचिरेणाधिगच्छति ।।

śhraddhāvān labhate jñānaṁ
tat-paraḥ sanyatendriyaḥ
jñānaṁ labdhvā parāṁ śhāntim
achireṇādhigachchhati

The man who has faith, is diligent and has control over the organs, attains Knowledge. Achieving Knowledge, one soon attains supreme Peace.

☙ 40 ❧

अज्ञश्चाश्रद्दधानश्च संशयात्मा विनश्यति ।
नायं लोकोऽस्ति न परो न सुखं संशयात्मनः ।।

ajñaśh chāśhraddadhānaśh cha
sanśhayātmā vinaśhyati
nāyaṁ loko "sti na paro na
sukhaṁ sanśhayātmanaḥ

One who is ignorant and faithless, and has a doubting mind perishes. Neither this world nor the next nor happiness exists for one who has a doubting mind.

☙ 41 ❧

योगसंन्यस्तकर्माणं ज्ञानसञ्छिन्नसंशयम् ।
आत्मवन्तं न कर्माणि निबध्नन्ति धनञ्जय ।।

yoga-sannyasta-karmāṇaṁ jñāna-sañchhinna-sanśhayam
ātmavantaṁ na karmāṇi nibadhnanti dhanañjaya

O Dhananjaya (Arjuna), actions do not bind one who has renounced actions through yoga, whose doubt has been fully dispelled by Knowledge, and who is not inadvertent.

☙ 42 ❧

तस्मादज्ञानसम्भूतं हृत्स्थं ज्ञानासिनात्मनः ।
छित्त्वैनं संशयं योगमातिष्ठोत्तिष्ठ भारत ।।

tasmād ajñāna-sambhūtaṁ
hṛit-sthaṁ jñānāsinātmanaḥ
chhittvainaṁ sanśhayaṁ
yogam ātiṣhṭhottiṣhṭha bhārata

Therefore, O scion of the Bharata dynasty, take recourse to yoga and rise up, cutting asunder with the sword of Knowledge this doubt of your own in the heart, arising from ignorance.

Chapter 05

Karma Sanyasa Yoga
Renunciation and Detachment

ᘓ 1 ᘐ

अर्जुन उवाच ।
संन्यासं कर्मणां कृष्ण पुनर्योगं च शंससि ।
यच्छ्रेय एतयोरेकं तन्मे ब्रूहि सुनिश्चितम् ॥

arjuna uvācha
sannyāsaṁ karmaṇāṁ kṛiṣhṇa punar yogaṁ cha śhansai
yach chhreya etayor ekaṁ tan me brūhi su-niśhchitam

Arjuna said: O Krishna, You praise renunciation of actions, and again, (Karma) yoga. Tell me for certain that one which is better between these two.

ᘓ 2 ᘐ

श्रीभगवानुवाच ।
संन्यासः कर्मयोगश्च निःश्रेयसकरावुभौ ।
तयोस्तु कर्मसंन्यासात्कर्मयोगो विशिष्यते ॥

śhrī bhagavān uvācha
sannyāsaḥ karma-yogaśh cha niḥśhreyasa-karāvubhau
tayos tu karma-sannyāsāt karma-yogo viśhiṣhyate

The Blessed Lord said: Both renunciation of actions and Karma-yoga lead to Liberation. Between the two, Karma-yoga, however, excels over renunciation of actions.

♋ 3 ♋

ज्ञेयः स नित्यसंन्यासी यो न द्वेष्टि न काङ्क्षति ।
निर्द्वन्द्वो हि महाबाहो सुखं बन्धात्प्रमुच्यते ॥

jñeyaḥ sa nitya-sannyāsī yo
na dveṣhṭi na kāṅkṣhati
nirdvandvo hi mahā-bāho
sukhaṁ bandhāt pramuchyate

He who does not hate and does not crave should be known as a man of constant renunciation.

♋ 4 ♋

साङ्ख्ययोगौ पृथग्बालाः प्रवदन्ति न पण्डिताः ।
एकमप्यास्थितः सम्यगुभयोर्विन्दते फलम् ॥

sānkhya-yogau pṛithag bālāḥ
pravadanti na paṇḍitāḥ
ekamapyāsthitaḥ
samyag ubhayor vindate phalam

The fools, not the learned ones, speak of Sankhya (the path of Knowledge) and (Karma) yoga as different. Anyone who properly resorts to even one (of them) gets the result of both.

☙ 5 ❧

यत्साङ्ख्यैः प्राप्यते स्थानं तद्योगैरपि गम्यते ।
एकं साङ्ख्यं च योगं च यः पश्यति स पश्यति ।।

yat sānkhyaiḥ prāpyate sthānaṁ
tad yogair api gamyate
ekaṁ sānkhyaṁ cha yogaṁ cha yaḥ
paśhyati sa paśhyati

The State [Sthana (State) is used in the derivative sense of 'the place in which one remains established, and from which one does not become relegated']. That is reached by the Sankhyas, that is reached by the yogis as well. He sees who sees Sankhya and yoga as one.

☙ 6 ❧

संन्यासस्तु महाबाहो दुःखमाप्तुमयोगतः ।
योगयुक्तो मुनिर्ब्रह्म नचिरेणाधिगच्छति ।।

sannyāsa tu mahā-bāho duḥkham āptum ayogataḥ
yoga-yukto munir brahma na chireṇādhigachchhati

But, O mighty-armed one, renunciation is hard to attain without (Karma) yoga. The meditative man equipped with yoga attains Brahman without delay.

7

योगयुक्तो विशुद्धात्मा विजितात्मा जितेन्द्रियः ।
सर्वभूतात्मभूतात्मा कुर्वन्नपि न लिप्यते ॥

yoga-yukto viśhuddhātmā vijitātmā jitendriyaḥ
sarva-bhūtātma-bhūtātmā kurvann api na lipyate

Endowed with yoga, pure in mind, controlled in body, a conqueror of the organs, the Self of the selves of all beings–he does not become tainted even while performing actions.

8

नैव किञ्चित्करोमीति युक्तो मन्येत तत्ववित् ।
पश्यञ्शृण्वन्स्पृशञ्जिघ्रन्नश्नन्गच्छन्स्वपञ्श्वसन् ॥

9

प्रलपन्विसृजन्गृह्णन्नुन्मिषन्निमिषन्नपि ।
इन्द्रियाणीन्द्रियार्थेषु वर्तन्त इति धारयन् ॥

naiva kiñchit karomīti yukto manyeta tattva-vit
paśhyañ śhṛiṇvan spṛiśhañjighrann aśhnangachchhan svapañśhvasan

pralapan visṛijan gṛihṇann unmiṣhan nimiṣhann api
indriyāṇīndriyārtheṣhu vartanta iti dhārayan

Remaining absorbed in the Self, the knower of Reality should think, 'I certainly do not do anything', even while seeing, hearing, touching, smelling, eating, moving, sleeping, breathing, speaking, releasing, holding, opening and closing the eyes–remembering that the organs function in relation to the objects of the organs.

ᏈᏐ 10 ᏈᏐ

ब्रह्मण्याधाय कर्माणि सङ्गं त्यक्त्वा करोति यः ।
लिप्यते न स पापेन पद्मपत्रमिवाम्भसा ।।

brahmaṇyādhāya karmāṇi saṅgaṁ
tyaktvā karoti yaḥ
lipyate na sa pāpena p
adma-patram ivāmbhasā

One who acts by dedicating actions to Brahman and by renouncing attachment, he does not become polluted by sin, just as a lotus leaf is not by water.

ଓ 11 ଓ

कायेन मनसा बुद्ध्या केवलैरिन्द्रियैरपि ।
योगिनः कर्म कुर्वन्ति सङ्गं त्यक्त्वात्मशुद्धये ॥

kāyena manasā buddhyā kevalair indriyair api
yoginaḥ karma kurvanti saṅgaṁ tyaktvātma-
śhuddhaye

By giving up attachment, the yogis undertake work merely through the body, mind, intellect and even the organs, for the purification of themselves.

ଓ 12 ଓ

युक्तः कर्मफलं त्यक्त्वा शान्तिमाप्नोति नैष्ठिकीम् ।
अयुक्तः कामकारेण फले सक्तो निबध्यते ॥

yuktaḥ karma-phalaṁ tyaktvā
śhāntim āpnoti naiṣhṭhikīm
ayuktaḥ kāma-kāreṇa phale
sakto nibadhyate

Giving up the result of work by becoming resolute in faith, one attains Peace arising from steadfastness. One who is lacking in resolute faith, being attached to the result under the impulsion of desire, becomes bound.

૭ 13 ૪૦

सर्वकर्माणि मनसा संन्यस्यास्ते सुखं वशी ।
नवद्वारे पुरे देही नैव कुर्वन्न कारयन् ॥

sarva-karmāṇi manasā
sannyasyāste sukhaṁ vaśhī
nava-dvāre pure dehī naiva
kurvan na kārayan

The embodied man of self-control, having given up all actions mentally, continues happily in the town of nine gates, without doing or causing (others) to do anything at all.

૭ 14 ૪૦

न कर्तृत्वं न कर्माणि लोकस्य सृजति प्रभुः ।
न कर्मफलसंयोगं स्वभावस्तु प्रवर्तते ॥

na kartṛitvaṁ na karmāṇi
lokasya sṛijati prabhuḥ
na karma-phala-saṅyogaṁ
svabhāvas tu pravartate

The Self does not create agentship or any objects (of desire) for anyone; nor association with the results of actions. But it is Nature that acts.

ര 15 ೩

नादत्ते कस्यचित्पापं न चैव सुकृतं विभुः ।
अज्ञानेनावृतं ज्ञानं तेन मुह्यन्ति जन्तवः ॥

nādatte kasyachit pāpaṁ na
chaiva sukṛitaṁ vibhuḥ
ajñānenāvṛitaṁ jñānaṁ
tena muhyanti jantavaḥ

The Omnipresent neither accepts anybody's sin nor even virtue. Knowledge remains covered by ignorance. Hence, the creatures become deluded.

ര 16 ೩

ज्ञानेन तु तदज्ञानं येषां नाशितमात्मनः ।
तेषामादित्यवज्ज्ञानं प्रकाशयति तत्परम् ॥

jñānena tu tad ajñānaṁ
yeṣhāṁ nāśhitam ātmanaḥ
teṣhām āditya-vaj jñānaṁ
prakāśhayati tat param

But in the case of those of whom that ignorance of theirs becomes destroyed by the knowledge (of the Self), their Knowledge, like the sun, reveals that supreme Reality.

☙ 17 ❧

तद्बुद्धयस्तदात्मानस्तन्निष्ठास्तत्परायणाः ।
गच्छन्त्यपुनरावृत्तिं ज्ञाननिर्धूतकल्मषाः ।।

tad-buddhayas tad-ātmānas
tan-niṣhṭhās tat-parāyaṇāḥ
gachchhantyapunar-āvṛittiṁ
jñāna-nirdhūta-kalmaṣhāḥ

Those who have their intellect absorbed in That, whose Self is That, who are steadfast in That, who have That as their supreme Goal–they attain the state of non-returning, their dirt having been removed by Knowledge.

☙ 18 ❧

विद्याविनयसम्पन्ने ब्राह्मणे गवि हस्तिनि ।
शुनि चैव श्वपाके च पण्डिताः समदर्शिनः ।।

vidyā-vinaya-sampanne brāhmaṇe gavi hastini
śhuni chaiva śhva-pāke cha paṇḍitāḥ sama-darśhinaḥ

The learned ones look with equanimity on a Brahmana endowed with learning and humility, a cow, an elephant and even a dog as well as an eater of dog's meat.

☙ 19 ❧

इहैव तैर्जितः सर्गो येषां साम्ये स्थितं मनः ।
निर्दोषं हि समं ब्रह्म तस्माद् ब्रह्मणि ते स्थिताः ।।

ihaiva tair jitaḥ sargo yeṣhāṁ
sāmye sthitaṁ manaḥ
nirdoṣhaṁ hi samaṁ brahma
tasmād brahmaṇi te sthitāḥ

Even in this world they conquer their earth–life whose minds, fixed on the Supreme, remain always balanced; for the Supreme has neither blemish nor bias.

☙ 20 ❧

न प्रहृष्येत्प्रियं प्राप्य नोद्विजेत्प्राप्य चाप्रियम् ।
स्थिरबुद्धिरसम्मूढो ब्रह्मविद् ब्रह्मणि स्थितः ।।

na prahṛiṣhyet priyaṁ prāpya
nodvijet prāpya chāpriyam
sthira-buddhir asammūḍho
brahma-vid brahmaṇi sthitaḥ

A knower of Brahman, who is established in Brahman, should have his intellect steady and should not be deluded. He should not get delighted by getting what is desirable, nor become dejected by getting what is undesirable.

☙ 21 ❧

बाह्यस्पर्शेष्वसक्तात्मा विन्दत्यात्मनि यत्सुखम् ।
स ब्रह्मयोगयुक्तात्मा सुखमक्षयमश्नुते ।।

bāhya-sparśheṣhvasaktātmā
vindatyātmani yat sukham
sa brahma-yoga-yuktātmā
sukham akṣhayam aśhnute

With his heart unattached to external objects, he gets the bliss that is in the Self. With his heart absorbed in meditation on Brahman, he acquires undecaying Bliss.

☙ 22 ❧

ये हि संस्पर्शजा भोगा दुःखयोनय एव ते ।
आद्यन्तवन्तः कौन्तेय न तेषु रमते बुधः ।।

ye hi sansparśha-jā bhogā
duḥkha-yonaya eva te
ādyantavantaḥ kaunteya na
teṣhu ramate budhaḥ

Since enjoyments that result from contact (with objects) are verily the sources of sorrow and have a beginning and an end, (therefore) O son of Kunti, the wise one does not delight in them.

ଔ 23 ଔ

शक्नोतीहैव यः सोढुं प्राक्शरीरविमोक्षणात् ।
कामक्रोधोद्भवं वेगं स युक्तः स सुखी नरः ।।

śhaknotīhaiva yaḥ soḍhuṁ
prāk śharīra-vimokṣhaṇāt
kāma-krodhodbhavaṁ vegaṁ sa
yuktaḥ sa sukhī naraḥ

One who can withstand here itself, before departing from the body, the impulse arising from desire and anger, that man is a yogi; he is happy.

ଔ 24 ଔ

योऽन्तःसुखोऽन्तरारामस्तथान्तर्ज्योतिरेव यः ।
स योगी ब्रह्मनिर्वाणं ब्रह्मभूतोऽधिगच्छति ।।

yo 'ntaḥ-sukho 'ntar-ārāmas tathāntar-jyotir eva yaḥ
sa yogī brahma-nirvāṇaṁ
brahma-bhūto 'dhigachchhati

One who is happy within, whose pleasure is within, and who has his light only within, that yogi, having become Brahman, attains absorption in Brahman.

ও 25 ৩

लभन्ते ब्रह्मनिर्वाणमृषयः क्षीणकल्मषाः ।
छिन्नद्वैधा यतात्मानः सर्वभूतहिते रताः ।।

labhante brahma-nirvāṇam ṛiṣhayaḥ
kṣhīṇa-kalmaṣhāḥ
chhinna-dvaidhā yatātmānaḥ
sarva-bhūta-hite ratāḥ

The seers whose sins have been attenuated, who are freed from doubt, whose organs are under control, who are engaged in doing good to all beings, attain absorption in Brahman.

ও 26 ৩

कामक्रोधवियुक्तानां यतीनां यतचेतसाम् ।
अभितो ब्रह्मनिर्वाणं वर्तते विदितात्मनाम् ।।

kāma-krodha-viyuktānāṁ
yatīnāṁ yata-chetasām
abhito brahma-nirvāṇaṁ
vartate viditātmanām

To the monks who have control over their internal organ, who are free from desire and anger, who have known the Self, there is absorption in Brahman either way.

27

स्पर्शान्कृत्वा बहिर्बाह्यांश्चक्षुश्चैवान्तरे भ्रुवोः ।
प्राणापानौ समौ कृत्वा नासाभ्यन्तरचारिणौ ।।

28

यतेन्द्रियमनोबुद्धिर्मुनिर्मोक्षपरायणः ।
विगतेच्छाभयक्रोधो यः सदा मुक्त एव सः ।।

sparśhān kṛitvā
bahir bāhyānśh chakṣhuśh chaivāntare bhruvoḥ
prāṇāpānau samau kṛitvā
nāsābhyantara-chāriṇau

yatendriya-mano-buddhir munir mokṣha-parāyaṇaḥ
vigatechchhā-bhaya-krodho yaḥ sadā mukta eva saḥ

Keeping the external objects outside, the eyes at the juncture of the eyebrows, and making equal the outgoing and incoming breaths that move through the nostrils, the contemplative who has control over his organs, mind and intellect should be fully intent on Liberation and free from desire, fear and anger. He who is ever is verily free.

☙ 29 ❧

भोक्तारं यज्ञतपसां सर्वलोकमहेश्वरम् ।
सुहृदं सर्वभूतानां ज्ञात्वा मां शान्तिमृच्छति ।।

bhoktāraṁ yajña-tapasāṁ
sarva-loka-maheśhvaram
suhṛidaṁ sarva-bhūtānāṁ
jñātvā māṁ śhāntim ṛichchhati

One attains Peace by knowing Me who, as the great Lord of all the worlds, am the enjoyer of sacrifices and austerities, (and) who am the friend of all creatures.

Chapter

06

Dhyana Yoga
Yoga of Meditation

ଓ 1 ଓ

श्रीभगवानुवाच ।
अनाश्रितः कर्मफलं कार्यं कर्म करोति यः ।
स संन्यासी च योगी च न निरग्निर्न चाक्रियः ।।

śhrī bhagavān uvācha
anāśhritaḥ karma-phalaṁ kāryaṁ karma karoti yaḥ
sa sannyāsī cha yogī cha na niragnir na chākriyaḥ

The Blessed Lord said: He who performs an action which is his duty, without depending on the result of action, he is a monk and a yogi; (but) not (so in) he who does not keep a fire and is action-less.

ଓ 2 ଓ

यं संन्यासमिति प्राहुर्योगं तं विद्धि पाण्डव ।
न ह्यसंन्यस्तसङ्कल्पो योगी भवति कश्चन ।।

yaṁ sannyāsam iti prāhur yogaṁ taṁ viddhi pāṇḍava
na hyasannyasta-saṅkalpo yogī bhavati kaśhchana

That which they call monasticism, know that to be Sannyasa Yoga, O Pandava, For, nobody who has not given up expectations can be a yogi.

≈ 3 ≈

आरुरुक्षोर्मुनेर्योगं कर्म कारणमुच्यते ।
योगारूढस्य तस्यैव शमः कारणमुच्यते ।।

ārurukṣhor muner yogaṁ karma kāraṇam uchyate
yogārūḍhasya tasyaiva śhamaḥ kāraṇam uchyate

For the sage who wishes to ascend to (Dhyana) yoga, action is said to be the means. For that person, when he has ascended to (Dhyana)yoga, inaction alone is said to be the means.

≈ 4 ≈

यदा हि नेन्द्रियार्थेषु न कर्मस्वनुषज्जते ।
सर्वसङ्कल्पसंन्यासी योगारूढस्तदोच्यते ।।

yadā hi nendriyārtheṣhu na karmasv-anuṣhajjate
sarva-saṅkalpa-sannyāsī yogārūḍhas tadochyate

When a man who has given up thought about everything does not get attached to sense objects or actions, he is then said to be established in Yoga.

☙ 5 ❧

उद्धरेदात्मनात्मानं नात्मानमवसादयेत् ।
आत्मैव ह्यात्मनो बन्धुरात्मैव रिपुरात्मनः ।।

uddhared ātmanātmānaṁ nātmānam avasādayet
ātmaiva hyātmano bandhur ātmaiva ripur ātmanaḥ

One should save oneself by oneself; one should not lower oneself. For oneself is verily one's own friend; oneself is verily one's own enemy.

☙ 6 ❧

बन्धुरात्मात्मनस्तस्य येनात्मैवात्मना जितः ।
अनात्मनस्तु शत्रुत्वे वर्तेतात्मैव शत्रुवत् ।।

bandhur ātmātmanas tasya yenātmaivātmanā jitaḥ
anātmanas tu śhatrutve vartetātmaiva śhatru-vat

Of him, by whom has been conquered his very self by the self, his self is the friend of his self. But, for one who has not conquered his self, his self itself acts inimically like an enemy.

☙ 7 ❧

जितात्मनः प्रशान्तस्य परमात्मा समाहितः ।
शीतोष्णसुखदुःखेषु तथा मानापमानयोः ।।

jitātmanaḥ praśhāntasya paramātmā samāhitaḥ
śhītoṣhṇa-sukha-duḥkheṣhu tathā mānāpamānayoḥ

The supreme Self of one who has control over the aggregate of his body and organs, and who is tranquil, becomes manifest, even in the middle of cold and heat, happiness and sorrow, as also honour and dishonour.

☙ 8 ❧

ज्ञानविज्ञानतृप्तात्मा कूटस्थो विजितेन्द्रियः ।
युक्त इत्युच्यते योगी समलोष्टाश्मकाञ्चनः ।।

jñāna-vijñāna-tṛiptātmā kūṭa-stho vijitendriyaḥ
yukta ityuchyate yogī sama-loṣhṭāśhma-kāñchanaḥ

One whose mind is satisfied with knowledge and realization, who is unmoved, who has his organs under control, is said to be Self-absorbed. The yogi treats equally a lump of earth, a stone and gold.

☙ 9 ❧

सुहृन्मित्रार्युदासीनमध्यस्थद्वेष्यबन्धुषु ।
साधुष्वपि च पापेषु समबुद्धिर्विशिष्यते ॥

suhṛin-mitrāryudāsīna-madhyastha-dveṣhya-bandhuṣhu
sādhuṣhvapi cha pāpeṣhu sama-buddhir viśhiṣhyate

He excels who has sameness of view with regard to a benefactor, a friend, a foe, a neutral, an arbiter, the hateful, a relative, good people and even sinners.

☙ 10 ❧

योगी युञ्जीत सततमात्मानं रहसि स्थितः ।
एकाकी यतचित्तात्मा निराशीरपरिग्रहः ॥

yogī yuñjīta satatam ātmānaṁ rahasi sthitaḥ
ekākī yata-chittātmā nirāśhīr aparigrahaḥ

A yogi should constantly concentrate his mind by staying in a solitary place, alone, with mind and body controlled, free from expectations, (and) free from acquisition.

☙ 11 ❧

शुचै देशे प्रतिष्ठाप्य स्थिरमासनमात्मनः ।
नात्युच्छ्रितं नातिनीचं चैलाजिनकुशोत्तरम् ।।

śhuchau deśhe pratiṣhṭhāpya sthiram āsanam
ātmanaḥ
nātyuchchhritaṁ nāti-nīchaṁ chailājina-kuśhottaram

Having firmly established in a clean place his seat, neither too high nor too low, and made of cloth, skin and kusa-grass, placed successively one below the other;

☙ 12 ❧

तत्रैकाग्रं मनः कृत्वा यतचित्तेन्द्रियक्रियः ।
उपविश्यासने युञ्ज्याद्योगमात्मविशुद्धये ।।

tatraikāgraṁ manaḥ kṛitvā yata-chittendriya-kriyaḥ
upaviśhyāsane yuñjyād yogam ātma-viśhuddhaye

(and) sitting on that seat, he should concentrate his mind for the purification of the internal organ, making the mind one-pointed and keeping the actions of the mind and senses under control.

॥ 13 ॥

सम्ं कायशिरोग्रीवं धारयन्नचलं स्थिरः ।
सम्प्रेक्ष्य नासिकाग्रं स्वं दिशश्चानवलोकयन् ॥

samaṁ kāya-śhiro-grīvaṁ
dhārayann achalaṁ sthiraḥ
samprekṣhya nāsikāgraṁ
svaṁ diśhaśh chānavalokayan

Holding the body, head and neck erect and still, being steady, looking at the tip of his own nose and not looking around.

॥ 14 ॥

प्रशान्तात्मा विगतभीर्ब्रह्मचारिव्रते स्थितः ।
मनः संयम्य मच्चित्तो युक्त आसीत मत्परः ॥

praśhāntātmā
vigata-bhīr brahmachāri-vrate sthitaḥ
manaḥ sanyamya mach-chitto
yukta āsīta mat-paraḥ

He should remain seated with a placid mind, free from fear, firm in the vow of a celibate, and with the mind fixed on Me by controlling it through concentration, having Me as the supreme Goal.

௸ 15 ௷

युञ्जन्नेवं सदात्मानं योगी नियतमानसः ।
शान्तिं निर्वाणपरमां मत्संस्थामधिगच्छति ।।

yuñjann evaṁ sadātmānaṁ
yogī niyata-mānasaḥ
śhantiṁ nirvāṇa-paramāṁ
mat-sansthām adhigachchhati

Concentrating the mind thus for ever, the yogi of controlled mind achieves the Peace which culminates in Liberation and which abides in Me.

௸ 16 ௷

नात्यश्नतस्तु योगोऽस्ति न चैकान्तमनश्नतः ।
न चाति स्वप्नशीलस्य जाग्रतो नैव चार्जुन ।।

nātyaśhnatastu yogo "sti na
chaikāntam anaśhnataḥ
na chāti-svapna-śhīlasya
jāgrato naiva chārjuna

But, O Arjuna, Yoga is not for one who eats too much, nor for one who does not eat at all; neither for one who habitually sleeps too long, nor surely for one who keeps awake.

☙ 17 ❧

युक्ताहारविहारस्य युक्तचेष्टस्य कर्मसु ।
युक्तस्वप्नावबोधस्य योगो भवति दुःखहा ॥

yuktāhāra-vihārasya yukta-cheṣhṭasya karmasu
yukta-svapnāvabodhasya yogo bhavati duḥkha-hā

Yoga becomes a destroyer of sorrow of one whose eating and movements are regulated, whose effort in works is moderate, and whose sleep and wakefulness are temperate.

☙ 18 ❧

यदा विनियतं चित्तमात्मन्येवावतिष्ठते ।
निःस्पृहः सर्वकामेभ्यो युक्त इत्युच्यते तदा ॥

yadā viniyataṁ chittam ātmanyevāvatiṣhṭhate
niḥspṛihaḥ sarva-kāmebhyo yukta ityuchyate tadā

A man who has become free from hankering for all desirable objects is then said to be Self-absorbed when the controlled mind rests in the Self alone.

ण 19 ॐ

यथा दीपो निवातस्थो नेङ्गते सोपमा स्मृता ।
योगिनो यतचित्तस्य युञ्जतो योगमात्मनः ।।

yathā dīpo nivāta-stho neṅgate sopamā smṛitā
yogino yata-chittasya yuñjato yogam ātmanaḥ

As a lamp kept in a windless place does not flicker, such is the simile thought of for the yogi whose mind is under control, and who is engaged in concentration on the Self.

ण 20 ॐ

यत्रोपरमते चित्तं निरुद्धं योगसेवया ।
यत्र चैवात्मनात्मानं पश्यन्नात्मनि तुष्यति ।।

yatroparamate chittaṁ niruddhaṁ yoga-sevayā
yatra chaivātmanātmānaṁ paśhyann ātmani tuṣhyati

At the time when the mind restrained through the practice of Yoga gets withdrawn, and just when by seeing the Self by the self-one remains contented in the Self alone.

☙ 21 ❧

सुखमात्यन्तिकं यत्तद्बुद्धिग्राह्यमतीन्द्रियम् ।
वेत्ति यत्र न चैवायं स्थितश्चलति तत्वतः ।।

sukham ātyantikaṁ
yat tad buddhi-grāhyam atīndriyam
vetti yatra na chaivāyaṁ
sthitaśh chalati tattvataḥ

When one experiences that absolute Bliss which can be intuited by the intellect and which is beyond the senses, and being established (thus) this person surely does not swerve from Reality.

☙ 22 ❧

यं लब्ध्वा चापरं लाभं मन्यते नाधिकं ततः ।
यस्मिन्स्थितो न दुःखेन गुरुणापि विचाल्यते ।।

yaṁ labdhvā chāparaṁ lābhaṁ
manyate nādhikaṁ tataḥ
yasmin sthito na duḥkhena
guruṇāpi vichālyate

Obtaining which one does not think of any other acquisition to be superior to that, and being established in which one is not perturbed even by great sorrow.

☙ 23 ❧

तं विद्याद् दुःखसंयोगवियोगं योगसञ्ज्ञितम् ।
स निश्चयेन योक्तव्यो योगोऽनिर्विण्णचेतसा ॥

tam̐ vidyād duḥkha-sanyoga-viyogam̐
yogasañjñitam
sa niśhchayena yoktavyo
yogo "nirviṇṇa-chetasā

One should know that severance of contact with sorrow to be what is called Yoga. That Yoga has to be practised with perseverance and with an undepressed heart.

☙ 24 ❧

सङ्कल्पप्रभवान्कामांस्त्यक्त्वा सर्वानशेषतः ।
मनसैवेन्द्रियग्रामं विनियम्य समन्ततः ॥

sañkalpa-prabhavān kāmāns tyaktvā
sarvān aśheṣhataḥ
manasaivendriya-grāmam̐
viniyamya samantataḥ

Bytotallyeschewingalldesireswhicharisefromthoughts, and restraining with the mind itself all the organs from every side.

☙ 25 ❧

शनैः शनैरुपरमेद्बुद्ध्या धृतिगृहीतया ।
आत्मसंस्थं मनः कृत्वा न किञ्चिदपि चिन्तयेत् ॥

śhanaiḥ śhanair uparamed buddhyā
dhṛiti-gṛihītayā
ātma-sansthaṁ manaḥ kṛitvā na
kiñchid api chintayet

One should gradually withdraw with the intellect endowed with steadiness. Making the mind fixed in the Self, one should not think of anything whatsoever.

☙ 26 ❧

यतो यतो निश्चरति मनश्चञ्चलमस्थिरम् ।
ततस्ततो नियम्यैतदात्मन्येव वशं नयेत् ॥

yato yato niśhcharati
manaśh chañchalam asthiram
tatas tato niyamyaitad ātmanyeva
vaśhaṁ nayet

(The yogi) should bring (this mind) under the subjugation of the Self Itself, by restraining it from all those causes whatever due to which the restless, unsteady mind wanders away.

☙ 27 ❧

प्रशान्तमनसं ह्येनं योगिनं सुखमुत्तमम् ।
उपैति शान्तरजसं ब्रह्मभूतमकल्मषम् ।।

praśhānta-manasaṁ hyenaṁ
yoginaṁ sukham uttamam
upaiti śhānta-rajasaṁ
brahma-bhūtam akalmaṣham

Supreme Bliss comes to this yogi alone whose mind has become perfectly tranquil, whose (quality of) rajas has been eliminated, who has become identified with Brahman, and is taintless.

☙ 28 ❧

युञ्जन्नेवं सदात्मानं योगी विगतकल्मषः ।
सुखेन ब्रह्मसंस्पर्शमत्यन्तं सुखमश्नुते ।।

yuñjann evaṁ sadātmānaṁ
yogī vigata-kalmaṣhaḥ
sukhena brahma-sansparśham atyantaṁ
sukham aśhnute

By concentrating his mind constantly thus, the taintless yogi easily attains the absolute Bliss of contact with Brahman.

ও 29 ৯ও

सर्वभूतस्थमात्मानं सर्वभूतानि चात्मनि ।
ईक्षते योगयुक्तात्मा सर्वत्र समदर्शनः ।।

sarva-bhūta-stham ātmānaṁ
sarva-bhūtāni chātmani
īkṣhate yoga-yuktātmā
sarvatra sama-darśhanaḥ

One who has his mind Self-absorbed through Yoga, and who has the vision of sameness everywhere, see this Self existing in everything, and everything in his Self.

ও 30 ৯ও

यो मां पश्यति सर्वत्र सर्वं च मयि पश्यति ।
तस्याहं न प्रणश्यामि स च मे न प्रणश्यति ।।

yo māṁ paśhyati sarvatra
sarvaṁ cha mayi paśhyati
tasyāhaṁ na praṇaśhyāmi sa cha
me na praṇaśhyati

One who sees Me in everything, and sees all things in Me, he is never out of My sight, nor am I ever out of his sight.

☙ 31 ❧

सर्वभूतस्थितं यो मां भजत्येकत्वमास्थितः ।
सर्वथा वर्तमानोऽपि स योगी मयि वर्तते ।।

sarva-bhūta-sthitaṁ yo māṁ
bhajatyekatvam āsthitaḥ
sarvathā vartamāno "pi sa
yogī mayi vartate

That yogi who, being established in unity, adores Me as existing in all things, he exists in Me–in whatever condition he may be.

☙ 32 ❧

आत्मौपम्येन सर्वत्र समं पश्यति योऽर्जुन ।
सुखं वा यदि वा दुःखं स योगी परमो मतः ।।

ātmaupamyena sarvatra samaṁ
paśhyati yo "rjuna
sukhaṁ vā yadi vā duḥkhaṁ
sa yogī paramo mataḥ

O Arjuna, that yogi is considered the best who judges what is happiness and sorrow in all beings by the same standard as he would apply to himself.

☙ 33 ❧

अर्जुन उवाच ।
योऽयं योगस्त्वया प्रोक्तः साम्येन मधुसूदन ।
एतस्याहं न पश्यामि चञ्चलत्वात्स्थितिं स्थिराम् ॥

arjuna uvācha
yo "yaṁ yogas tvayā proktaḥ sāmyena madhusūdana
etasyāhaṁ na paśhyāmi chañchalatvāt sthitiṁ sthirām

Arjuna said: O Madhusudana (Krishna), this Yoga that has been spoken of by You as sameness, I do not see its steady continuance, owing to the restlessness (of the mind).

☙ 34 ❧

चञ्चलं हि मनः कृष्ण प्रमाथि बलवद्दृढम् ।
तस्याहं निग्रहं मन्ये वायोरिव सुदुष्करम् ॥

chañchalaṁ hi manaḥ kṛiṣhṇa
pramāthi balavad dṛiḍham
tasyāhaṁ nigrahaṁ manye
vāyor iva su-duṣhkaram

For, O Krishna, the mind is unsteady, turbulent, strong and obstinate. I consider its control to be as greatly difficult as of the wind.

ॐ 35 ॐ

श्रीभगवानुवाच ।
असंशयं महाबाहो मनो दुर्निग्रहं चलम् ।
अभ्यासेन तु कौन्तेय वैराग्येण च गृह्यते ।।

śhrī bhagavān uvācha
asanśhayaṁ mahā-bāho mano durnigrahaṁ chalam
abhyāsena tu kaunteya vairāgyeṇa cha gṛihyate

The Blessed Lord said: O mighty-armed one, undoubtedly the mind is intractable and restless. But, O son of Kunti, it is brought under control through practice and detachment.

ॐ 36 ॐ

असंयतात्मना योगो दुष्प्राप इति मे मतिः ।
वश्यात्मना तु यतता शक्योऽवाप्तुमुपायतः ।।

asaṅyatātmanā yogo duṣhprāpa iti me matiḥ
vaśhyātmanā tu yatatā śhakyo "vāptum upāyataḥ

My conviction is that Yoga is difficult to be attained by one of uncontrolled mind. But it is possible to be attained through the (above) means by one who strives and has a controlled mind.

☙ 37 ❧

अर्जुन उवाच ।
अयतिः श्रद्धयोपेतो योगाच्चलितमानसः ।
अप्राप्य योगसंसिद्धिं कां गतिं कृष्ण गच्छति ।।

arjuna uvācha
ayatiḥ śhraddhayopeto yogāch chalita-mānasaḥ
aprāpya yoga-sansiddhiṁ kāṅ gatiṁ kṛiṣhṇa gachchhati

Arjuna said: O Krishna, failing to achieve perfection in Yoga, what goal does one attain, who, though possessed of faith, is not diligent and whose mind becomes deflected from Yoga?

☙ 38 ❧

कच्चिन्नोभयविभ्रष्टश्छिन्नाभ्रमिव नश्यति ।
अप्रतिष्ठो महाबाहो विमूढो ब्रह्मणः पथि ।।

kachchinnobhaya-vibhraṣhṭaśhchhinnābhramiva naśhyati
apratiṣhṭho mahā-bāho vimūḍho brahmaṇaḥ pathi

O mighty-armed one, fallen from both, without support, deluded on the path to Brahman, does he not get ruined like a scattered cloud?

☙ 39 ❧

एतन्मे संशयं कृष्ण छेत्तुमर्हस्यशेषतः ।
त्वदन्यः संशयस्यास्य छेत्ता न ह्युपपद्यते ॥

etan me sanśhayaṁ kṛiṣhṇa c
hhettum arhasyaśheṣhataḥ
tvad-anyaḥ sanśhayasyāsya
chhettā na hyupapadyate

O Krishna, You should totally eradicate this doubt of mine. For, none other than Yourself can be the dispeller of this doubt!

☙ 40 ❧

श्रीभगवानुवाच ।
पार्थ नैवेह नामुत्र विनाशस्तस्य विद्यते ।
न हि कल्याणकृत्कश्चिद्दुर्गतिं तात गच्छति ॥

śhrī bhagavān uvācha
pārtha naiveha nāmutra vināśhas tasya vidyate
na hi kalyāṇa-kṛit kaśhchid durgatiṁ tāta gachchhati

The Blessed Lord said: O Partha, there is certainly no ruin for him here or hereafter. For, no one engaged in good meets with a deplorable end, My son!

ᐡ 41 ᐡ

प्राप्य पुण्यकृतां लोकानुषित्वा शाश्वतीः समाः ।
शुचीनां श्रीमतां गेहे योगभ्रष्टोऽभिजायते ।।

prāpya puṇya-kṛitāṁ
lokān uṣhitvā śhāśhvatīḥ samāḥ
śhuchīnāṁ śhrīmatāṁ gehe
yoga-bhraṣhṭo"bhijāyate

Attaining the worlds of the righteous, and residing there for eternal years, the man fallen from Yoga is born in the house of the pious and the prosperous.

ᐡ 42 ᐡ

अथवा योगिनामेव कुले भवति धीमताम् ।
एतद्धि दुर्लभतरं लोके जन्म यदीदृशम् ।।

atha vā yoginām eva
kule bhavati dhīmatām
etad dhi durlabhataraṁ
loke janma yad īdṛiśham

Or he is born in the family of wise yogis only. Such a birth as is of this kind is surely more difficult to get in the world.

❧ 43 ❧

तत्र तं बुद्धिसंयोगं लभते पौर्वदेहिकम् ।
यतते च ततो भूयः संसिद्धौ कुरुनन्दन ।।

tatra taṁ buddhi-sanyogaṁ
labhate paurva-dehikam
yatate cha tato bhūyaḥ
sansiddhau kuru-nandana

There he becomes endowed with that wisdom acquired in the previous body. and he strives more than before for perfection, O scion of the Kuru dynasty.

❧ 44 ❧

पूर्वाभ्यासेन तेनैव ह्रियते ह्यवशोऽपि सः ।
जिज्ञासुरपि योगस्य शब्दब्रह्मातिवर्तते ।।

pūrvābhyāsena tenaiva
hriyate hyavaśho "pi saḥ
jijñāsur api yogasya
śhabda-brahmātivartate

For, by that very past practice, he is carried forward even in spite of himself! Even a seeker of Yoga transcends the result of the performance of Vedic rituals!

♈ 45 ♈

प्रयत्नाद्यतमानस्तु योगी संशुद्धकिल्बिषः ।
अनेकजन्मसंसिद्धस्ततो याति परां गतिम् ।।

prayatnād yatamānas tu
yogī sanśhuddha-kilbiṣhaḥ
aneka-janma-sansiddhas
tato yāti paraṁ gatim

However, the yogi, applying himself assiduously, becoming purified from sin and attaining perfection through many births, thereby achieves the highest Goal.

♈ 46 ♈

तपस्विभ्योऽधिकोयोगी ज्ञानिभ्योऽपिमतोऽधिकः ।
कर्मिभ्यश्चाधिकोयोगी तस्माद्योगीभवार्जुन ।।

tapasvibhyo "dhiko yogī
jñānibhyo "pi mato "dhikaḥ
karmibhyaśh chādhiko yogī
tasmād yogī bhavārjuna

A yogi is higher than men of austerity; he is considered higher even than men of knowledge. The yogi is also higher than men of action. Therefore, O Arjuna, you become a yogi.

☙ 47 ❧

योगिनामपि सर्वेषां मद्गतेनान्तरात्मना ।
श्रद्धावान्भजते यो मां स मे युक्ततमो मतः ।।

yoginām api sarveṣhāṁ
mad-gatenāntar-ātmanā
śhraddhāvān bhajate yo māṁ sa me
yuktatamo mataḥ

Even among all the yogis, he who adores Me with his mind fixed on Me and with faith, he is considered by Me to be the best of the yogis.

Chapter

07

Gyan Vigyana Yoga
Supreme Truth, Knowledge and Enlightenment

ॐ 1 ॐ

श्रीभगवानुवाच ।
मय्यासक्तमनाः पार्थ योगं युञ्जन्मदाश्रयः ।
असंशयं समग्रं मां यथा ज्ञास्यसि तच्छृणु ॥

śhrī bhagavān uvācha
mayyāsakta-manāḥ pārtha
yogaṁ yuñjan mad-āśhrayaḥ
asanśhayaṁ samagraṁ māṁ yathā
jñāsyasi tach chhṛiṇu

The Blessed Lord said: O Partha, hear how you, having the mind fixed on Me, practising the Yoga of Meditation and taking refuge in Me, will know Me with certainty and in fullness.

ॐ 2 ॐ

ज्ञानं तेऽहं सविज्ञानमिदं वक्ष्याम्यशेषतः ।
यज्ज्ञात्वा नेह भूयोऽन्यज्ज्ञातव्यमवशिष्यते ॥

jñānaṁ te "haṁ sa-vijñānam idaṁ
vakṣhyāmyaśheṣhataḥ
yaj jñātvā neha
bhūyo "nyaj jñātavyam-avaśhiṣhyate

I shall tell you in detail of this Knowledge which is combined with realization, after experiencing which there remains nothing else here to be known again.

☙ 3 ❧

मनुष्याणां सहस्रेषु कश्चिद्यतति सिद्धये ।
यततामपि सिद्धानां कश्चिन्मां वेत्ति तत्वतः ।।

manuṣhyāṇāṁ sahasreṣhu kaśhchid yatati siddhaye
yatatām api siddhānāṁ kaśhchin māṁ vetti tattvataḥ

Among thousands of men a rare one endeavours for perfection. Even of the perfected ones who are diligent, one perchance knows Me in truth.

☙ 4 ❧

भूमिरापोऽनलो वायुः खं मनो बुद्धिरेव च ।
अहङ्कार इतीयं मे भिन्ना प्रकृतिरष्टधा ।।

bhūmir-āpo "nalo vāyuḥ khaṁ mano buddhir eva cha
ahankāra itīyaṁ me bhinnā prakṛitir aṣhṭadhā

This Prakrti of Mine is divided eight-fold thus: earth, water, fire, air, space, mind, intellect and also egoism.

ℭ 5 ℘

अपरेयमितस्त्वन्यां प्रकृतिं विद्धि मे पराम् ।
जीवभूतां महाबाहो ययेदं धार्यते जगत् ।।

apareyam itas tvanyāṁ
prakṛitiṁ viddhi me parām
jīva-bhūtāṁ mahā-bāho
yayedaṁ dhāryate jagat

O mighty-armed one, this is the inferior (Prakrti). Know the other Prakrti of Mine which, however, is higher than this, which has taken the form of individual souls, and by which this world is upheld.

ℭ 6 ℘

एतद्योनीनि भूतानि सर्वाणीत्युपधारय ।
अहं कृत्स्नस्य जगतः प्रभवः प्रलयस्तथा ।।

etad-yonīni bhūtāni
sarvāṇītyupadhāraya
ahaṁ kṛitsnasya jagataḥ
prabhavaḥ pralayas tathā

Understand thus that all things (sentient and insentient) have these as their source. I am the origin as also the end of the whole Universe.

↺ 7 ↻

मत्तः परतरं नान्यत्किञ्चिदस्ति धनञ्जय ।
मयि सर्वमिदं प्रोतं सूत्रे मणिगणा इव ।।

mattaḥ parataraṁ
nānyat kiñchid asti dhanañjaya
mayi sarvam idaṁ protaṁ
sūtre maṇi-gaṇā iva .

O Dhananjaya, there is nothing else whatsoever higher than Myself. All this is strung on Me like pearls on a string.

↺ 8 ↻

रसोऽहमप्सु कौन्तेय प्रभास्मि शशिसूर्ययोः ।
प्रणवः सर्ववेदेषु शब्दः खे पौरुषं नृषु ।।

raso "ham apsu kaunteya
prabhāsmi śhaśhi-sūryayoḥ
praṇavaḥ sarva-vedeṣhu śhabdaḥ
khe pauruṣhaṁ nṛiṣhu

O son of Kunti, I am the taste of water, I am the effulgence of the moon and the sun; (the letter) Om in all the Vedas, the sound in space, and manhood in men.

☙ 9 ❧

पुण्यो गन्धः पृथिव्यां च तेजश्चास्मि विभावसौ ।
जीवनं सर्वभूतेषु तपश्चास्मि तपस्विषु ।।

puṇyo gandhaḥ pṛithivyāṁ cha
tejaś chāsmi vibhāvasau
jīvanaṁ sarva-bhūteṣhu
tapaś chāsmi tapasviṣhu

I am also the sweet fragrance in the earth; I am the brilliance in the fire, and the life in all beings; and I am the austerity of the ascetics.

☙ 10 ❧

बीजं मां सर्वभूतानां विद्धि पार्थ सनातनम् ।
बुद्धिर्बुद्धिमतामस्मि तेजस्तेजस्विनामहम् ।।

bījaṁ māṁ sarva-bhūtānāṁ viddhi
pārtha sanātanam
buddhir buddhimatām asmi tejas
tejasvinām aham

O Partha, know Me to be the eternal Seed of all beings. I am the intellect of the intelligent; I am the courage of the courageous.

☙ 11 ❧

बलं बलवतां चाहं कामरागविवर्जितम् ।
धर्माविरुद्धो भूतेषु कामोऽस्मि भरतर्षभ ।।

balaṁ balavatāṁ chāhaṁ
kāma-rāga-vivarjitam
dharmāviruddho bhūteṣhu
kāmo "smi bharatarṣhabha

And of the strong I am the strength which is devoid of passion and attachment. Among creatures I am desire which is not contrary to righteousness, O scion of the Bharata dynasty.

☙ 12 ❧

ये चैव सात्विका भावा राजसास्तामसाश्च ये ।
मत्त एवेति तान्विद्धि न त्वहं तेषु ते मयि ।।

ye chaiva sāttvikā bhāvā rājasās tāmasāśh cha ye
matta eveti tān viddhi na tvahaṁ teṣhu te mayi

Those things that indeed are made of (the quality of) sattva, and those things that are made of (the quality of) rajas and tamas, know them to have sprung from Me alone. However, I am not in them; they are in Me!

☙ 13 ❧

त्रिभिर्गुणमयैर्भावैरेभिः सर्वमिदं जगत् ।
मोहितं नाभिजानाति मामेभ्यः परमव्ययम् ।।

tribhir guṇa-mayair bhāvair ebhiḥ
sarvam idaṁ jagat
mohitaṁ nābhijānāti
māmebhyaḥ param avyayam

All this world, deluded as it is by these three things made of the gunas (qualities), does not know Me who am transcendental to these and undecaying.

☙ 14 ❧

दैवी ह्येषा गुणमयी मम माया दुरत्यया ।
मामेव ये प्रपद्यन्ते मायामेतां तरन्ति ते ।।

daivī hyeṣhā guṇa-mayī
mama māyā duratyayā
mām eva ye prapadyante
māyām etāṁ taranti te

Since this divine Maya of Mine which is constituted by the gunas is difficult to cross over, (therefore) those who take refuge in Me alone cross over this Maya.

☙ 15 ❧

न मां दुष्कृतिनो मूढाः प्रपद्यन्ते नराधमाः ।
माययापहृतज्ञाना आसुरं भावमाश्रिताः ।।

na māṁ duṣhkṛitino mūḍhāḥ
prapadyante narādhamāḥ
māyayāpahṛita-jñānā āsuraṁ
bhāvam āśhritāḥ

The foolish evildoers, who are the most depraved among men, who are deprived of (their) wisdom by Maya, and who resort to demoniacal ways, do not take refuge in Me.

☙ 16 ❧

चतुर्विधा भजन्ते मां जनाः सुकृतिनोऽर्जुन ।
आर्तो जिज्ञासुरर्थार्थी ज्ञानी च भरतर्षभ ।।

chatur-vidhā bhajante māṁ janāḥ sukṛitino "rjuna
ārto jijñāsur arthārthī jñānī cha bharatarṣhabha

O Arjuna, foremost of the Bharata dynasty, four classes of people of virtuous deeds adore Me: the afflicted, the seeker of Knowledge, the seeker of wealth and the man of Knowledge.

☙ 17 ❧

तेषां ज्ञानी नित्ययुक्त एकभक्तिर्विशिष्यते ।
प्रियो हि ज्ञानिनोऽत्यर्थमहं स च मम प्रियः ।।

teṣhāṁ jñānī nitya-yukta
eka-bhaktir viśhiṣhyate
priyo hi jñānino "tyartham ahaṁ
sa cha mama priyaḥ

Of them, the man of Knowledge, endowed with constant steadfastness and one-pointed devotion, excels. For I am very much dear to the man of Knowledge, and he too is dear to Me.

☙ 18 ❧

उदाराः सर्व एवैते ज्ञानी त्वात्मैव मे मतम् ।
आस्थितः स हि युक्तात्मा मामेवानुत्तमां गतिम् ।।

udārāḥ sarva evaite jñānī tvātmaiva me matam
āsthitaḥ sa hi yuktātmā mām evānuttamāṁ gatim

All of these, indeed, are noble, but the man of Knowledge is the very Self. (This is) My opinion. For, with a steadfast mind, he is set on the path leading to Me alone who am the super-excellent Goal.

☙ 19 ❧

बहूनां जन्मनामन्ते ज्ञानवान्मां प्रपद्यते ।
वासुदेवः सर्वमिति स महात्मा सुदुर्लभः ।।

bahūnāṁ janmanām ante
jñānavān māṁ prapadyate
vāsudevaḥ sarvam iti sa
mahātmā su-durlabhaḥ

At the end of many births the man of Knowledge attains Me, (realizing) that Vasudeva is all. Such a high-souled one is very rare.

☙ 20 ❧

कामैस्तैस्तैर्हृतज्ञानाः प्रपद्यन्तेऽन्यदेवताः ।
तं तं नियममास्थाय प्रकृत्या नियताः स्वया ।।

kāmais tais tair hṛita-jñānāḥ
prapadyante "nya-devatāḥ
taṁ taṁ niyamam āsthāya
prakṛityā niyatāḥ svayā

People, deprived of their wisdom by desires for various objects and guided by their own nature, resort to other deities following the relevant methods.

ଓ 21 ଌ

यो यो यां यां तनुं भक्तः श्रद्धयार्चितुमिच्छति ।
तस्य तस्याचलां श्रद्धां तामेव विदधाम्यहम् ।।

yo yo yāṁ yāṁ tanuṁ bhaktaḥ
śhraddhayārchitum ichchhati
tasya tasyāchalāṁ śhraddhāṁ
tām eva vidadhāmyaham

Whichever form (of a deity) any devotee wants to worship with faith, that very firm faith of his I strengthen.

ଓ 22 ଌ

स तया श्रद्धया युक्तस्तस्याराधनमीहते ।
लभते च ततः कामान्मयैव विहितान्हि तान् ।।

sa tayā śhraddhayā
yuktas tasyārādhanam īhate
labhate cha tataḥ kāmānmayaiva
vihitānhi tān

Being imbued with that faith, that person engages in worshipping that form, and he gets those very desired results therefrom as they are dispensed by Me alone.

23

अन्तवत्तु फलं तेषां तद्भवत्यल्पमेधसाम् ।
देवान्देवयजो यान्ति मद्भक्ता यान्ति मामपि ।।

antavat tu phalaṁ teṣhāṁ
tad bhavatyalpa-medhasām
devān deva-yajo yānti
mad-bhaktā yānti mām api

That result of theirs who are of poor intellect is indeed limited. The worshippers of gods go to the gods. My devotees go to Me alone.

24

अव्यक्तं व्यक्तिमापन्नं मन्यन्ते मामबुद्धयः ।
परं भावमजानन्तो ममाव्ययमनुत्तमम् ।।

avyaktaṁ vyaktim āpannaṁ
manyante mām abuddhayaḥ
paraṁ bhāvam ajānanto
mamāvyayam anuttamam

The unintelligent, unaware of My supreme state which is immutable and unsurpassable, think of Me as the unmanifest that has become manifest.

ଔ 25 ରु

नाहं प्रकाशः सर्वस्य योगमायासमावृतः ।
मूढोऽयं नाभिजानाति लोको मामजमव्ययम् ।।

nāhaṁ prakāśhaḥ sarvasya
yoga-māyā-samāvṛitaḥ
mūḍho "yaṁ nābhijānāti
loko mām ajam avyayam

Being enveloped by yoga-maya, I do not become manifest to all. This deluded world does not know Me who am birthless and undecaying.

ଔ 26 ରु

वेदाहं समतीतानि वर्तमानानि चार्जुन ।
भविष्याणि च भूतानि मां तु वेद न कश्चन ।।

vedāhaṁ samatītāni
vartamānāni chārjuna
bhaviṣhyāṇi cha bhūtāni māṁ
tu veda na kaśhchana

O Arjuna, I know the past and the present as also the future beings; but no one knows Me!

꧁ 27 ꧂

इच्छाद्वेषसमुत्थेन द्वन्द्वमोहेन भारत ।
सर्वभूतानि सम्मोहं सर्गे यान्ति परन्तप ।।

ichchhā-dveṣha-samutthena dvandva-mohena bhārata
sarva-bhūtāni sammohaṁ sarge yānti parantapa

O scion of the Bharata dynasty, O destroyer of foes, due to the delusion of duality arising from likes and dislikes, all creatures become bewildered at the time of their birth.

꧁ 28 ꧂

येषां त्वन्तगतं पापं जनानां पुण्यकर्मणाम् ।
ते द्वन्द्वमोहनिर्मुक्ता भजन्ते मां दृढव्रताः ।।

yeṣhāṁ tvanta-gataṁ pāpaṁ
janānāṁ puṇya-karmaṇām
te dvandva-moha-nirmuktā bhajante
māṁ dṛiḍha-vratāḥ

On the other hand, those persons who are of virtuous deeds, whose sin has come to an end, they, being free from the delusion of duality and firm in their convictions, adore Me.

☙ 29 ❧

जरामरणमोक्षाय मामाश्रित्य यतन्ति ये ।
ते ब्रह्म तद्विदुः कृत्स्नमध्यात्मं कर्म चाखिलम् ।।

jarā-maraṇa-mokṣhāya
mām āśhritya yatanti ye
te brahma tadviduḥ kṛitsnam
adhyātmaṁ karma chākhilam

Those who strive by resorting to Me for becoming free from old age and death, they know that Brahman, everything about the individual Self, and all about actions.

☙ 30 ❧

साधिभूताधिदैवं मां साधियज्ञं च ये विदुः ।
प्रयाणकालेऽपि च मां ते विदुर्युक्तचेतसः ।।

sādhibhūtādhidaivaṁ māṁ sādhiyajñaṁ cha ye viduḥ
prayāṇa-kāle "pi cha māṁ te vidur yukta-chetasaḥ

Those who know me as existing in the physical and the divine planes, and also in the context of the sacrifice, they of concentrated minds know Me even at the time of death.

Chapter 08

Akshara Brahma Yoga
Attaining the Eternal God

☙ 1 ❧

अर्जुन उवाच ।
किं तद्ब्रह्म किमध्यात्मं किं कर्म पुरुषोत्तम ।
अधिभूतं च किं प्रोक्तमधिदैवं किमुच्यते ।।

arjuna uvācha
kiṁ tad brahma kim adhyātmaṁ
kiṁ karma puruṣhottama
adhibhūtaṁ cha kiṁ
proktam adhidaivaṁ kim uchyate

Arjuna said: O supreme person, what is that Brahman? What is that which exists in the individual plane? What is action? And what is that which is said to exist in the physical plane? What is that which is said to be existing in the divine plane?

☙ 2 ❧

अधियज्ञः कथं कोऽत्र देहेऽस्मिन्मधुसूदन ।
प्रयाणकाले च कथं ज्ञेयोऽसि नियतात्मभिः ।।

adhiyajñaḥ kathaṁ ko "tra
dehe "smin madhusūdana
prayāṇa-kāle cha kathaṁ
jñeyo "si niyatātmabhiḥ

O Madhusudana, how, and who, is the entity existing in the sacrifice here in this body? And at the time of death, how are You to be known by people of concentrated minds?

ଓ 3 ୨୦

श्रीभगवानुवाच ।
अक्षरं ब्रह्म परमं स्वभावोऽध्यात्ममुच्यते ।
भूतभावोद्भवकरो विसर्गः कर्मसञ्ज्ञितः ।।

śhrī bhagavān uvācha
akṣharaṁ brahma paramaṁ
svabhāvo "dhyātmam uchyate
bhūta-bhāvodbhava-karo
visargaḥ karma-sanjñitaḥ

The Blessed Lord said: The Immutable is the supreme Brahman; self-hood is said to be the entity present in the individual plane. By action is meant the offerings which bring about the origin of the existence of things.

☙ 4 ❧

अधिभूतं क्षरो भावः पुरुषश्चाधिदैवतम् ।
अधियज्ञोऽहमेवात्र देहे देहभृतां वर ।।

adhibhūtaṁ kṣharo bhāvaḥ
puruṣhaśh chādhidaivatam
adhiyajño "ham evātra dehe
deha-bhṛitāṁ vara

That which exists in the physical plane is the mutable entity, and what exists in the divine plane is the Person. O best among the embodied beings, I Myself am the entity that exists in the sacrifice in this body.

☙ 5 ❧

अन्तकाले च मामेव स्मरन्मुक्त्वा कलेवरम् ।
यः प्रयाति स मद्भावं याति नास्त्यत्र संशयः ।।

anta-kāle cha mām eva
smaran muktvā kalevaram
yaḥ prayāti sa mad-bhāvaṁ
yāti nāstyatra sanśhayaḥ

And at the time of death, anyone who departs by giving up the body while thinking of Me alone, he attains My state. There is no doubt about this.

☙ 6 ❧

यं यं वापि स्मरन्भावं त्यजत्यन्ते कलेवरम् ।
तं तमेवैति कौन्तेय सदा तद्भावभावितः ।।

yaṁ yaṁ vāpi smaran bhāvaṁ
tyajatyante kalevaram
taṁ tam evaiti kaunteya sadā
tad-bhāva-bhāvitaḥ

O son of Kunti, thinking of any entity whichever it may be one gives up the body at the end, he attains that very one, having been always engrossed in its thought.

☙ 7 ❧

तस्मात्सर्वेषु कालेषु मामनुस्मर युध्य च ।
मय्यर्पितमनोबुद्धिर्मामेवैष्यस्यसंशयम् ।।

tasmāt sarveṣhu kāleṣhu
mām anusmara yudhya cha
mayyarpita-mano-buddhir mām
evaiṣhyasyasanśhayam

Therefore, think of Me at all times and fight. There is no doubt that by dedicating your mind and intellect to Me, you will attain Me alone.

☙ 8 ❧

अभ्यासयोगयुक्तेन चेतसा नान्यगामिना ।
परमं पुरुषं दिव्यं याति पार्थानुचिन्तयन् ।।

abhyāsa-yoga-yuktena chetasā nānya-gāminā
paramaṁ puruṣhaṁ divyaṁ yāti pārthānuchintayan

O son of Partha, by meditating with a mind which is engaged in the yoga of practice and which does not stray away to anything else, one reaches the supreme Person existing in the effulgent region.

☙ 9 ❧

कविं पुराणमनुशासितार मणोरणीयांसमनुस्मरेद्यः ।
सर्वस्य धातारमचिन्त्यरूप मादित्यवर्णं तमसः परस्तात् ।।

kaviṁ purāṇam anuśhāsitāram
aṇor aṇīyānsam anusmared yaḥ
sarvasya dhātāram achintya-rūpam
āditya-varṇaṁ tamasaḥ parastāt

He who meditates on the Omniscient, the Ancient, the Ruler, subtler than the subtle, the Ordainer of everything, of inconceivable form, effulgent like the sun, and beyond darkness (he attains the supreme Person).

☙ 10 ❧

प्रयाणकाले मनसाचलेन भक्त्या युक्तो योगबलेन चैव ।
भ्रुवोर्मध्ये प्राणमावेश्य सम्यक् स तं परं पुरुषमुपैति दिव्यम् ।।

prayāṇa-kāle manasāchalena
bhaktyā yukto yoga-balena chaiva
bhruvor madhye prāṇam āveśhya samyak
sa taṁ paraṁ puruṣham upaiti divyam

At the time of death, having fully fixed the Prana (vita force) between the eyebrows with an unswerving mind, and being imbued with devotion as also the strength of concentration, he reaches that resplendent supreme person.

☙ 11 ❧

यदक्षरं वेदविदो वदन्ति विशन्ति यद्यतयो वीतरागाः ।
यदिच्छन्तो ब्रह्मचर्यं चरन्ति तत्ते पदं संग्रहेण प्रवक्ष्ये ।।

yad akṣharaṁ veda-vido vadanti
viśhanti yad yatayo vīta-rāgāḥ
yad ichchhanto brahmacharyaṁ charanti
tat te padaṁ saṅgraheṇa pravakṣhye

I shall speak to you briefly of that immutable Goal which the knowers of the Vedas declare, into which enter the diligent ones free from attachment, and aspiring for which people practise celibacy.

12

सर्वद्वाराणि संयम्य मनो हृदि निरुध्य च ।
मूर्ध्न्याधायात्मनः प्राणमास्थितो योगधारणाम् ।।

sarva-dvārāṇi sanyamya mano hṛidi nirudhya cha
mūrdhnyādhāyātmanaḥ prāṇam āsthito yoga-dhāraṇām

Having controlled all the passages, having confined the mind in the heart, and having fixed his own vital force in the head, (and then) continuing in the firmness in yoga.

13

ओमित्येकाक्षरं ब्रह्म व्याहरन्मामनुस्मरन् ।
यः प्रयाति त्यजन्देहं स याति परमां गतिम् ।।

oṁ ityekākṣharaṁ brahma vyāharan mām anusmaran
yaḥ prayāti tyajan dehaṁ sa yāti paramāṁ gatim

He who departs by leaving the body while uttering the single syllable, viz Om, which is Brahman, and thinking of Me, he attains the supreme Goal.

ଓ 14 ଃ

अनन्यचेताः सततं यो मां स्मरति नित्यशः ।
तस्याहं सुलभः पार्थ नित्ययुक्तस्य योगिनः ।।

ananya-chetāḥ satataṁ yo
māṁ smarati nityaśhaḥ
tasyāhaṁ sulabhaḥ pārtha
nitya-yuktasya yoginaḥ

O son of Partha, to that yogi of constant concentration and single-minded attention, who remembers Me uninterruptedly and for long, I am easy of attainment.

ଓ 15 ଃ

मामुपेत्य पुनर्जन्म दुःखालयमशाश्वतम् ।
नाप्नुवन्ति महात्मानः संसिद्धिं परमां गताः ।।

mām upetya punar janma
duḥkhālayam aśhāśhvatam
nāpnuvanti mahātmānaḥ
sansiddhiṁ paramāṁ gatāḥ

As a result of reaching Me, the exalted ones who have attained the highest perfection do not get rebirth which is an abode of sorrows and which is impermanent.

☙ 16 ❧

आब्रह्मभुवनाल्लोकाः पुनरावर्तिनोऽर्जुन ।
मामुपेत्य तु कौन्तेय पुनर्जन्म न विद्यते ।।

ā-brahma-bhuvanāl lokāḥ
punar āvartino "rjuna
mām upetya tu kaunteya
punar janma na vidyate

O Arjuna, all the worlds together with the world of Brahma are subject to return. But, O son of Kunti, there is no rebirth after reaching Me.

☙ 17 ❧

सहस्रयुगपर्यन्तमहर्यद्ब्रह्मणो विदुः ।
रात्रिं युगसहस्रान्तां तेऽहोरात्रविदो जनाः ।।

sahasra-yuga-paryantam
ahar yad brahmaṇo viduḥ
rātriṁ yuga-sahasrāntāṁ
te "ho-rātra-vido janāḥ

Those people who are knowers of what day and night are, know the day of Brahma which ends in a thousand yugas and His night which ends in a thousand yugas.

◊ 18 ◊

अव्यक्ताद्व्यक्तयः सर्वाः प्रभवन्त्यहरागमे ।
रात्र्यागमे प्रलीयन्ते तत्रैवाव्यक्तसञ्ज्ञके ।।

avyaktād vyaktayaḥ sarvāḥ
prabhavantyahar-āgame
rātryāgame pralīyante
tatraivāvyakta-sanjñake

With the coming of day all manifested things emerge from the Unmanifest and when night comes they merge in that itself which is called the Unmanifested.

◊ 19 ◊

भूतग्रामः स एवायं भूत्वा भूत्वा प्रलीयते ।
रात्र्यागमेऽवशः पार्थ प्रभवत्यहरागमे ।।

bhūta-grāmaḥ sa evāyaṁ
bhūtvā bhūtvā pralīyate
rātryāgame "vaśhaḥ
pārtha prabhavatyahar-āgame

O son of Partha, after being born again and again, that very multitude of beings disappears in spite of itself at the approach of night. It comes to life at the approach of day.

ॐ 20 ॐ

परस्तस्मात्तु भावोऽन्योऽव्यक्तोऽव्यक्तात्सनातनः ।
यः स सर्वेषु भूतेषु नश्यत्सु न विनश्यति ॥

paras tasmāt tu bhāvo "nyo
"vyakto "vyaktāt sanātanaḥ
yaḥ sa sarveṣhu bhūteṣhu
naśhyatsu na vinaśhyati

But distinct from that Unmanifested is the other eternal unmainfest Reality, who does not get destroyed when all beings get destroyed.

ॐ 21 ॐ

अव्यक्तोऽक्षर इत्युक्तस्तमाहुः परमां गतिम् ।
यं प्राप्य न निवर्तन्ते तद्धाम परमं मम ॥

avyakto "kṣhara ityuktas
tam āhuḥ paramāṁ gatim
yaṁ prāpya na nivartante
tad dhāma paramaṁ mama

He who has been mentioned as the Unmanifested, the Immutable, they call Him the supreme Goal. That is the supreme abode of Mine, reaching which they do not return.

☙ 22 ❧

पुरुषः स परः पार्थ भक्त्या लभ्यस्त्वनन्यया ।
यस्यान्तःस्थानि भूतानि येन सर्वमिदं ततम् ।।

puruṣhaḥ sa paraḥ pārtha
bhaktyā labhyas tvananyayā
yasyāntaḥ-sthāni bhūtāni
yena sarvam idaṁ tatam

O son of Partha, that supreme Person–in whom are included (all) the beings and by whom all this is pervaded–is, indeed, reached through one-pointed devotion.

☙ 23 ❧

यत्र काले त्वनावृत्तिमावृत्तिं चैव योगिनः ।
प्रयाता यान्ति तं कालं वक्ष्यामि भरतर्षभ ।।

yatra kāle tvanāvṛittim āvṛittiṁ
chaiva yoginaḥ
prayātā yānti taṁ kālaṁ
vakṣhyāmi bharatarṣhabha

O best of the Bharata dynasty, I shall now speak of that time by departing at which the yogis attain the State of Non-return, and also (of the time by departing at which they attain) the State of Return.

☙ 24 ❧

अग्निर्ज्योतिरहः शुक्लः षण्मासा उत्तरायणम् ।
तत्र प्रयाता गच्छन्ति ब्रह्म ब्रह्मविदो जनाः ॥

agnir jyotir ahaḥ śhuklaḥ
ṣhaṇ-māsā uttarāyaṇam
tatra prayātā gachchhanti brahma
brahma-vido janāḥ

Fire, light, daytime, the bright fortnight, the six months of the Northern solstice by following this Path, persons who are knowers of Brahman attain Brahman when they die.

☙ 25 ❧

धूमो रात्रिस्तथा कृष्णः षण्मासा दक्षिणायनम् ।
तत्र चान्द्रमसं ज्योतिर्योगी प्राप्य निवर्तते ॥

dhūmo rātris tathā kṛiṣhṇaḥ
ṣhaṇ-māsā dakṣhiṇāyanam
tatra chāndramasaṁ jyotir yogī
prāpya nivartate

Smoke, night, as also the dark fortnight and the six months of the Southern solstice following this Path the yogi having reached the lunar light, returns.

☙ 26 ❧

शुक्लकृष्णे गती ह्येते जगतः शाश्वते मते ।
एकया यात्यनावृत्तिमन्ययावर्तते पुनः ।।

śhukla-kṛiṣhṇe gatī hyete
jagataḥ śhāśhvate mate
ekayā yātyanāvṛittim
anyayāvartate punaḥ

These two courses of the world, which are white and black, are verily considered eternal. By the one a man goes to the State of Non-return; by the other he returns again.

☙ 27 ❧

नैते सृती पार्थ जानन्योगी मुह्यति कश्चन ।
तस्मात्सर्वेषु कालेषु योगयुक्तो भवार्जुन ।।

naite sṛitī pārtha jānan yogī muhyati kaśhchana
tasmāt sarveṣhu kāleṣhu yoga-yukto bhavārjuna

O son of Partha, no yogi [One steadfast in meditation] whosoever has known these two courses becomes deluded. Therefore, O Arjuna, be you steadfast in yoga at all times.

❧ 28 ☙

वेदेषु यज्ञेषु तपःसु चैव दानेषु यत्पुण्यफलं प्रदिष्टम् ।
अत्येति तत्सर्वमिदं विदित्वा योगी परं स्थानमुपैति चाद्यम् ।।

vedeṣhu yajñeṣhu tapaḥsu chaiva
dāneṣhu yat puṇya-phalaṁ pradiṣhṭam
atyeti tat sarvam idaṁ viditvā
yogī paraṁ sthānam upaiti chādyam

Having known this, the yogi transcends all those results of righteous deeds that are declared with regard to the Vedas, sacrifices, austerities and also charities, and he reaches the primordial supreme State.

Chapter 09

Raja Vidya Yoga
Yoga through Bhakti and Science

ଓ 1 ଓ

श्रीभगवानुवाच ।
इदं तु ते गुह्यतमं प्रवक्ष्याम्यनसूयवे ।
ज्ञानं विज्ञानसहितं यज्ज्ञात्वा मोक्ष्यसेऽशुभात् ॥

śhrī bhagavān uvācha
idaṁ tu te guhyatamaṁ
pravakṣhyāmyanasūyave
jñānaṁ vijñāna-sahitaṁ yaj jñātvā
mokṣhyase "śhubhāt

The Blessed Lord said: However, to you who are not given to cavilling I shall speak of this highest secret itself, which is Knowledge [Jnana may mean Brahman that is Consciousness, or its knowledge gathered from the Vedas (paroksa-jnana); Vijnana is direct experience (aparoksa-jnana)] combined with experience, by realizing which you shall be free from evil.

ᏹ 2 ᏸ

राजविद्या राजगुह्यं पवित्रमिदमुत्तमम् ।
प्रत्यक्षावगमं धर्म्यं सुसुखं कर्तुमव्ययम् ।।

rāja-vidyā rāja-guhyaṁ
pavitram idam uttamam
pratyakṣhāvagamaṁ dharmyaṁ
su-sukhaṁ kartum avyayam

This is the Sovereign Knowledge, the Sovereign Profundity, the best sanctifier; directly realizable, righteous, very easy to practise and imperishable.

ᏹ 3 ᏸ

अश्रद्दधानाः पुरुषा धर्मस्यास्य परन्तप ।
अप्राप्य मां निवर्तन्ते मृत्युसंसारवर्त्मनि ।।

aśhraddadhānāḥ puruṣhā
dharmasyāsya parantapa
aprāpya māṁ nivartante
mṛityu-samsāra-vartmani

O destroyer of foes, persons who are regardless of this Dharma (knowledge of the Self) certainly go round and round, without reaching Me, along the path of transmigration which is fraught with death.

ꕥ 4 ꕥ

मया ततमिदं सर्वं जगदव्यक्तमूर्तिना ।
मत्स्थानि सर्वभूतानि न चाहं तेष्ववस्थितः ।।

mayā tatam idaṁ sarvaṁ
jagad avyakta-mūrtinā
mat-sthāni sarva-bhūtāni na
chāhaṁ teṣhvavasthitaḥ

This whole world is pervaded by Me in My unmanifest form. All beings exist in Me, but I am not contained in them!

ꕥ 5 ꕥ

न च मत्स्थानि भूतानि पश्य मे योगमैश्वरम् ।
भूतभृन्न च भूतस्थो ममात्मा भूतभावनः ।।

na cha mat-sthāni bhūtāni
paśhya me yogam aiśhwaram
bhūta-bhṛin na cha bhūta-stho
mamātmā bhūta-bhāvanaḥ

Nor do the beings dwell in Me. Behold My Divine Yoga! I am the sustainer and originator of beings, but My Self is not contained in the beings.

ᘓ 6 ᘐ

यथाकाशस्थितो नित्यं वायुः सर्वत्रगो महान् ।
तथा सर्वाणि भूतानि मत्स्थानीत्युपधारय ।।

yathākāśha-sthito nityaṁ vāyuḥ sarvatra-go mahān
tathā sarvāṇi bhūtāni mat-sthānītyupadhāraya

Understand thus that just as the voluminous wind moving everywhere is ever present in space, similarly all beings abide in Me.

ᘓ 7 ᘐ

सर्वभूतानि कौन्तेय प्रकृतिं यान्ति मामिकाम् ।
कल्पक्षये पुनस्तानि कल्पादौ विसृजाम्यहम् ।।

sarva-bhūtāni kaunteya
prakṛitiṁ yānti māmikām
kalpa-kṣhaye punas tāni
kalpādau visṛijāmyaham

O son of Kunti, all the beings go back at the end of a cycle to My Prakrti. I project them forth again at the beginning of a cycle.

☙ 8 ❧

प्रकृतिं स्वामवष्टभ्य विसृजामि पुनः पुनः ।
भूतग्राममिमं कृत्स्नमवशं प्रकृतेर्वशात् ।।

prakṛitiṁ svām avaṣhṭabhya
visṛijāmi punaḥ punaḥ
bhūta-grāmam imaṁ
kṛitsnam avaśhaṁ prakṛiter vaśhāt

Keeping My own Prakrti under control, I project forth again and again the whole of this multitude of beings which are powerless owing to the influence of (their own) nature.

☙ 9 ❧

न च मां तानि कर्माणि निबध्नन्ति धनञ्जय ।
उदासीनवदासीनमसक्तं तेषु कर्मसु ।।

na cha māṁ tāni karmāṇi
nibadhnanti dhanañjaya
udāsīna-vad āsīnam asaktaṁ
teṣhu karmasu

O Dhananjaya (Arjuna), nor do those actions bind Me, remaining (as I do) like one unconcerned with, and unattached to, those actions.

☙ 10 ❧

मयाध्यक्षेण प्रकृतिः सूयते सचराचरम् ।
हेतुनानेन कौन्तेय जगद्विपरिवर्तते ।।

mayādhyakṣheṇa prakṛitiḥ
sūyate sa-charācharam
hetunānena kaunteya
jagad viparivartate

Under Me as the supervisor, the Prakrti produces (the world) of the moving and the non-moving things. Owing to this reason, O son of Kunti, the world revolves.

☙ 11 ❧

अवजानन्ति मां मूढा मानुषीं तनुमाश्रितम् ।
परं भावमजानन्तो मम भूतमहेश्वरम् ।।

avajānanti māṁ mūḍhā
mānuṣhīṁ tanum āśhritam
paraṁ bhāvam ajānanto mama
bhūta-maheśhvaram

Not knowing My supreme nature as the Lord of all beings, foolish people disregard Me who have taken a human body.

☙ 12 ❧

मोघाशा मोघकर्माणो मोघज्ञाना विचेतसः ।
राक्षसीमासुरीं चैव प्रकृतिं मोहिनीं श्रिताः ।।

moghāśhā mogha-karmāṇo
mogha-jñānā vichetasaḥ
rākṣhasīm āsurīṁ chaiva
prakṛitiṁ mohinīṁ śhritāḥ

Of vain hopes, of vain actions, of vain knowledge, and senseless, they become verily possessed of the deceptive disposition of fiends and demons.

☙ 13 ❧

महात्मानस्तु मां पार्थ दैवीं प्रकृतिमाश्रिताः ।
भजन्त्यनन्यमनसो ज्ञात्वा भूतादिमव्ययम् ।।

mahātmānas tu māṁ pārtha
daivīṁ prakṛitim āśhritāḥ
bhajantyananya-manaso
jñātvā bhūtādim avyayam

O son of Partha, the noble ones, being possessed of divine nature, surely adore Me with single-mindedness, knowing Me as the immutable source of all objects.

☙ 14 ❧

सततं कीर्तयन्तो मां यतन्तश्च दृढव्रताः ।
नमस्यन्तश्च मां भक्त्या नित्ययुक्ता उपासते ।।

satataṁ kīrtayanto māṁ
yatantaśh cha dṛiḍha-vratāḥ
namasyantaśh cha māṁ bhaktyā
nitya-yuktā upāsate

Always glorifying Me and striving, the men of firm vows worship Me by paying obeisance to Me and being ever endowed with devotion.

☙ 15 ❧

ज्ञानयज्ञेन चाप्यन्ये यजन्तो मामुपासते ।
एकत्वेन पृथक्त्वेन बहुधा विश्वतोमुखम् ।।

jñāna-yajñena chāpyanye yajanto mām upāsate
ekatvena pṛithaktvena bahudhā viśhvato-mukham

Others verily worship Me by adoring exclusively through the sacrifice of the knowledge of oneness; (others worship Me) multifariously, and (others) as the multiform existing variously.

☙ 16 ❧

अहं क्रतुरहं यज्ञः स्वधाहमहमौषधम् ।
मन्त्रोऽहमहमेवाज्यमहमग्निरहं हुतम् ॥

ahaṁ kratur ahaṁ yajñaḥ
svadhāham aham auṣhadham
mantro "ham aham evājyam
aham agnir ahaṁ hutam

I am the kratu, I am the yajna, I am the svadha, I am the ausadha, I am the mantra, I Myself am the ajay, I am the fire, and I am the act of offering.

☙ 17 ❧

पिताहमस्य जगतो माता धाता पितामहः ।
वेद्यं पवित्रमोङ्कार ऋक्साम यजुरेव च ॥

pitāham asya jagato
mātā dhātā pitāmahaḥ
vedyaṁ pavitram oṁkāra
ṛik sāma yajur eva cha

Of this world I am the father, mother, ordainer, (and the), grand-father; I am the knowable, the sanctifier, the syllable Om as also Rk, Sama and Yajus.

☙ 18 ❧

गतिर्भर्ता प्रभुः साक्षी निवासः शरणं सुहृत् ।
प्रभवः प्रलयः स्थानं निधानं बीजमव्ययम् ।।

gatir bhartā prabhuḥ sākṣhī
nivāsaḥ śharaṇaṁ suhṛit
prabhavaḥ pralayaḥ sthānaṁ
nidhānaṁ bījam avyayam

(I am) the fruit of actions, the nourisher, the Lord, witness, abode, refuge, friend, origin, end, foundation, store and the imperishable seed.

☙ 19 ❧

तपाम्यहमहं वर्षं निगृह्णाम्युत्सृजामि च ।
अमृतं चैव मृत्युश्च सदसच्चाहमर्जुन ।।

tapāmyaham ahaṁ varṣhaṁ
nigṛihṇāmyutsṛijāmi cha
amṛitaṁ chaiva mṛityuśh cha
sad asach chāham arjuna

O Arjuna, I give heat, I withhold and pour down rain. I am verily the nectar, and also death existence and nonexistence.

20

त्रैविद्या मां सोमपाः पूतपापा यज्ञैरिष्ट्वा स्वर्गतिं प्रार्थयन्ते ।
ते पुण्यमासाद्य सुरेन्द्रलोक मश्नन्ति दिव्यान्दिवि देवभोगान् ।।

trai-vidyā māṁ soma-pāḥ pūta-pāpā
yajñair iṣhṭvā svar-gatiṁ prārthayante
te puṇyam āsādya surendra-lokam
aśhnanti divyān divi deva-bhogān

Those who are versed in the Vedas, who are drinkers of Soma and are purified of sin, pray for the heavenly goal by worshipping Me through sacrifices. Having reached the place (world) of the king of gods, which is the result of righteousness, they enjoy in heaven th divine pleasure of gods.

☙ 21 ❧

ते तं भुक्त्वा स्वर्गलोकं विशालं क्षीणे पुण्ये मर्त्यलोकं विशन्ति ।
एवं त्रयीधर्ममनुप्रपन्ना गतागतं कामकामा लभन्ते ।।

te taṁ bhuktvā swarga-lokaṁ viśhālaṁ
kṣhīṇe puṇye martya-lokaṁ viśhanti
evaṁ trayī-dharmam anuprapannā
gatāgataṁ kāma-kāmā labhante

Those who follow the rites and duties prescribed in the three Vedas, and are desirous of pleasures; attain the state of going and returning.

☙ 22 ❧

अनन्याश्चिन्तयन्तो मां ये जनाः पर्युपासते ।
तेषां नित्याभियुक्तानां योगक्षेमं वहाम्यहम् ।।

ananyāśh chintayanto māṁ ye janāḥ paryupāsate
teṣhāṁ nityābhiyuktānāṁ yoga-kṣhemaṁ vahāmyaham

Those persons who, becoming non-different from Me and meditative, worship Me everywhere, for them, who are ever attached (to Me), I arrange for securing what they lack and preserving what they have.

☙ 23 ❧

येऽप्यन्यदेवता भक्ता यजन्ते श्रद्धयान्विताः ।
तेऽपि मामेव कौन्तेय यजन्त्यविधिपूर्वकम् ।।

ye "pyanya-devatā-bhaktā
yajante śhraddhayānvitāḥ
te "pi mām eva kaunteya
yajantyavidhi-pūrvakam

Even those who, being devoted to other deities and endowed with faith, worship (them), they also, O son of Kunti, worship Me alone (though) following the wrong method.

☙ 24 ❧

अहं हि सर्वयज्ञानां भोक्ता च प्रभुरेव च ।
न तु मामभिजानन्ति तत्वेनातश्च्यवन्ति ते ।।

ahaṁ hi sarva-yajñānāṁ
bhoktā cha prabhureva cha
na tu mām abhijānanti
tattvenātaśh chyavanti te

I indeed am the enjoyer as also the Lord of all sacrifices; but they do not know Me in reality. Therefore, they fall.

꧁ 25 ꧂

यान्ति देवव्रता देवान्पितॄ न्यान्ति पितृव्रताः ।
भूतानि यान्ति भूतेज्या यान्ति मद्याजिनोऽपि माम् ।।

yānti deva-vratā devān
pitṝn yānti pitṛi-vratāḥ
bhūtāni yānti bhūtejyā
yānti mad-yājino "pi mām

Votaries of the gods reach the gods; the votaries of the manes go to the manes; the worshippers of the Beings reach the Beings; and those who worship Me reach Me.

꧁ 26 ꧂

पत्रं पुष्पं फलं तोयं यो मे भक्त्या प्रयच्छति ।
तदहं भक्त्युपहृतमश्नामि प्रयतात्मनः ।।

patraṁ pușhpaṁ phalaṁ toyaṁ yo
me bhaktyā prayachchhati
tadahaṁ bhaktyupahṛitam aśhnāmi
prayatātmanaḥ

Whoever offers Me with devotion-a leaf, a flower, a fruit, or water, I accept that (gift) of the pure-hearted man which has been devotionally presented.

☙ 27 ❧

यत्करोषि यदश्नासि यज्जुहोषि ददासि यत् ।
यत्तपस्यसि कौन्तेय तत्कुरुष्व मदर्पणम् ।।

yat karoṣhi yad aśhnāsi yaj juhoṣhi dadāsi yat
yat tapasyasi kaunteya tat kuruṣhva mad-arpaṇam

O son of Kunti, whatever you do, whatever you eat, whatever you offer as a sacrifice, whatever you give and whatever austerities you undertake, (all) that you offer to Me.

☙ 28 ❧

शुभाशुभफलैरेवं मोक्ष्यसे कर्मबन्धनैः ।
संन्यासयोगयुक्तात्मा विमुक्तो मामुपैष्यसि ।।

śhubhāśhubha-phalair evaṁ
mokṣhyase karma-bandhanaiḥ
sannyāsa-yoga-yuktātmā
vimukto mām upaiṣhyasi

Thus, you will become free from bondage in the form of actions which are productive of good and bad results. Having your mind imbued with the yoga of renunciation and becoming free, you will attain Me.

29

समोऽहं सर्वभूतेषु न मे द्वेष्योऽस्ति न प्रियः ।
ये भजन्ति तु मां भक्त्या मयि ते तेषु चाप्यहम् ।।

samo "haṁ sarva-bhūteṣhu na me
dveṣhyo "sti na priyaḥ
ye bhajanti tu māṁ bhaktyā
mayi te teṣhu chāpyaham

I am impartial towards all beings; to Me there is none detestable or none dear. But those who worship Me with devotion, they exist in Me, and I too exist in them.

30

अपि चेत्सुदुराचारो भजते मामनन्यभाक् ।
साधुरेव स मन्तव्यः सम्यग्व्यवसितो हि सः ।।

api chet su-durāchāro bhajate
mām ananya-bhāk
sādhur eva sa mantavyaḥ
samyag vyavasito hi saḥ

Even if a man of very bad conduct worships Me with one-pointed devotion, he is to be considered verily good; for he has resolved rightly.

☙ 31 ❧

क्षिप्रं भवति धर्मात्मा शश्वच्छान्तिं निगच्छति ।
कौन्तेय प्रतिजानीहि न मे भक्तः प्रणश्यति ।।

kṣhipraṁ bhavati dharmātmā
śhaśhvach-chhāntiṁ nigachchhati
kaunteya pratijānīhi na
me bhaktaḥ praṇaśhyati

He soon becomes possessed of a virtuous mind; he attains everlasting peace. Do you proclaim boldly, O son of Kunti, that My devotee does not get ruined.

☙ 32 ❧

मां हि पार्थ व्यपाश्रित्य येऽपि स्युः पापयोनयः ।
स्त्रियो वैश्यास्तथा शूद्रास्तेऽपि यान्ति परां गतिम् ।।

māṁ hi pārtha vyapāśhritya
ye "pi syuḥ pāpa-yonayaḥ
striyo vaiśhyās tathā
śhūdrās te "pi yānti parāṁ gatim

For, O son of Partha, even those who are born of sin-women, Vaisyas, as also Sudras, even they reach the highest Goal by taking shelter under Me.

33

किं पुनर्ब्राह्मणाः पुण्या भक्ता राजर्षयस्तथा ।
अनित्यमसुखं लोकमिमं प्राप्य भजस्व माम् ।।

kiṁ punar brāhmaṇāḥ puṇyā bhaktā rājarṣhayas tathā
anityam asukhaṁ lokam imaṁ prāpya bhajasva mām

What to speak of the holy Brahmanas as also of devout king-sages! Having come to this ephemeral and miserable world, do you worship Me.

34

मन्मना भव मद्भक्तो मद्याजी मां नमस्कुरु ।
मामेवैष्यसि युक्त्वैवमात्मानं मत्परायणः ।।

man-manā bhava mad-bhakto
mad-yājī māṁ namaskuru
mām evaiṣhyasi
yuktvaivam ātmānaṁ mat-parāyaṇaḥ

Having your mind fixed on Me, be devoted to Me, sacrifice to Me, and bow down to Me. By concentrating your mind and accepting Me as the supreme Goal, you shall surely attain Me who am thus the Self.

Chapter 10

Vibhooti Yoga Yoga through Appreciating the Infinite Opulences of God

ଓ 1 ଛ

श्रीभगवानुवाच ।
भूय एव महाबाहो शृणु मे परमं वचः ।
यत्तेऽहं प्रीयमाणाय वक्ष्यामि हितकाम्यया ।।

śhrī bhagavān uvācha
bhūya eva mahā-bāho śhṛiṇu me paramaṁ vachaḥ
yatte "haṁ prīyamāṇāya vakṣhyāmi hita-kāmyayā

The Blessed Lord said: O mighty-armed one, listen over again to My supreme utterance, which I, wishing your welfare, shall speak to you who take delight (in it).

ଓ 2 ଛ

न मे विदुः सुरगणाः प्रभवं न महर्षयः ।
अहमादिर्हि देवानां महर्षीणां च सर्वशः ।।

na me viduḥ sura-gaṇāḥ
prabhavaṁ na maharṣhayaḥ
aham ādir hi devānāṁ
maharṣhīṇāṁ cha sarvaśhaḥ

Neither the gods nor the great sages know My majesty. For, in all respects, I am the source of the gods and the great sages.

৩ 3 ৯

यो मामजमनादिं च वेत्ति लोकमहेश्वरम् ।
असम्मूढः स मर्त्येषु सर्वपापैः प्रमुच्यते ।।

yo māmajam anādiṁ cha
vetti loka-maheśhvaram
asammūḍhaḥ sa martyeṣhu
sarva-pāpaiḥ pramuchyate

He who knows Me–the birth-less, the beginning-less, and the great Lord of the worlds, he, the undeluded one among mortals, becomes freed from all sins.

৩ 4 ৯

बुद्धिर्ज्ञानमसम्मोहः क्षमा सत्यं दमः शमः ।
सुखं दुःखं भवोऽभावो भयं चाभयमेव च ।।

৩ 5 ৯

अहिंसा समता तुष्टिस्तपो दानं यशोऽयशः ।
भवन्ति भावा भूतानां मत्त एव पृथग्विधाः ।।

buddhir jñānam asammohaḥ kṣhamā
satyaṁ damaḥ śhamaḥ
sukhaṁ duḥkhaṁ bhavo "bhāvo
bhayaṁ chābhayameva cha

ahimsaa samataa tushtistapo
daanam yasho'yashah
bhavanti bhaavaa bhootaanaam
matta eva prithagvidhaah

Intelligence, wisdom, non-delusion, forgiveness, truth, control of the external organs, control of the internal organs, happiness, sorrow, birth, death and fear as also fearlessness, non-injury, equanimity, satisfaction, austerity, charity, fame, infamy (these) different dispositions of beings spring from Me alone.

6

महर्षयः सप्त पूर्वे चत्वारो मनवस्तथा ।
मद्भावा मानसा जाता येषां लोक इमाः प्रजाः ।।

maharṣhayaḥ sapta pūrve
chatvāro manavas tathā
mad-bhāvā mānasā jātā
yeṣhāṁ loka imāḥ prajāḥ

The seven great sages as also the four Manus of ancient days, of whom are these creatures in the world, had their thoughts fixed on Me, and they were born from My mind.

☙ 7 ❧

एतां विभूतिं योगं च मम यो वेत्ति तत्वतः ।
सोऽविकम्पेन योगेन युज्यते नात्र संशयः ।।

etāṁ vibhūtiṁ yogaṁ cha
mama yo vetti tattvataḥ
so "vikampena yogena
yujyate nātra sanśhayaḥ

One who knows truly this majesty and yoga of Mine, he becomes imbued with unwavering Yoga. There is no doubt about this.

☙ 8 ❧

अहं सर्वस्य प्रभवो मत्तः सर्वं प्रवर्तते ।
इति मत्वा भजन्ते मां बुधा भावसमन्विताः ।।

ahaṁ sarvasya prabhavo mattaḥ
sarvaṁ pravartate
iti matvā bhajante māṁ
budhā bhāva-samanvitāḥ

I am the origin of all; everything moves on owing to Me. Realizing thus, the wise ones, filled with fervour, adore Me.

ও 9 ৩

मच्चित्ता मद्गतप्राणा बोधयन्तः परस्परम् ।
कथयन्तश्च मां नित्यं तुष्यन्ति च रमन्ति च ।।

mach-chittā mad-gata-prāṇā
bodhayantaḥ parasparam
kathayantaśh cha māṁ nityaṁ
tuṣhyanti cha ramanti cha

With minds fixed on Me, with lives dedicated to Me, enlightening each other, and always speaking of Me, they derive satisfaction and rejoice.

ও 10 ৩

तेषां सततयुक्तानां भजतां प्रीतिपूर्वकम् ।
ददामि बुद्धियोगं तं येन मामुपयान्ति ते ।।

teṣhāṁ satata-yuktānāṁ
bhajatāṁ prīti-pūrvakam
dadāmi buddhi-yogaṁ taṁ
yena mām upayānti te

To them who are ever devoted and worship Me with love, I grant that possession of wisdom by which they reach Me.

ଓ 11 ଷ

तेषामेवानुकम्पार्थमहमज्ञानजं तमः ।
नाशयाम्यात्मभावस्थो ज्ञानदीपेन भास्वता ।।

teṣhām evānukampārtham
aham ajñāna-jaṁ tamaḥ
nāśhayāmyātma-bhāva-stho
jñāna-dīpena bhāsvatā

Out of compassion for them alone, I, residing in their hearts, destroy the darkness born of ignorance with the luminous lamp of Knowledge.

ଓ 12 ଷ

अर्जुन उवाच ।
परं ब्रह्म परं धाम पवित्रं परमं भवान् ।
पुरुषं शाश्वतं दिव्यमादिदेवमजं विभुम् ।।

arjuna uvācha
paraṁ brahma paraṁ dhāma
pavitraṁ paramaṁ bhavān
puruṣhaṁ śhāśhvataṁ
divyam ādi-devam ajaṁ vibhum

Arjuna said: You are the supreme Brahman, the supreme Light, the supreme Sanctifier.

ᏦᏕ 13 ᏦᏕ

आहुस्त्वामृषयः सर्वे देवर्षिर्नारदस्तथा ।
असितो देवलो व्यासः स्वयं चैव ब्रवीषि मे ।।

āhus tvām ṛiṣhayaḥ sarve
devarṣhir nāradas tathā
asito devalo vyāsaḥ
svayaṁ chaiva bravīṣhi me

All the sages as also the divine sage Narada, Asita, Devala and Vyasa call You the eternal divine Person, the Primal God, the Birth-less, the Omnipresent; and You Yourself verily tell me (so).

14

सर्वमेतदृतं मन्ये यन्मां वदसि केशव ।
न हि ते भगवन्व्यक्तिं विदुर्देवा न दानवाः ।।

sarvam etad ṛitaṁ manye
yan māṁ vadasi keśhava
na hi te bhagavan vyaktiṁ
vidur devā na dānavāḥ

O Kesava, I accept to be true all this which You tell me. Certainly, O Lord, neither the gods nor the demons comprehend Your glory.

ఆ 15 ఐ

स्वयमेवात्मनात्मानं वेत्थ त्वं पुरुषोत्तम ।
भूतभावन भूतेश देवदेव जगत्पते ।।

swayam evātmanātmānaṁ
vettha tvaṁ puruṣhottama
bhūta-bhāvana bhūteśha
deva-deva jagat-pate

O supreme Person, the Creator of beings, the Lord of beings, God of gods, the Lord of the worlds, You Yourself alone know Yourself by Yourself.

ఆ 16 ఐ

वक्तुमर्हस्यशेषेण दिव्या ह्यात्मविभूतयः ।
याभिर्विभूतिभिर्लोकानिमांस्त्वं व्याप्य तिष्ठसि ।।

vaktum arhasyaśheṣheṇa
divyā hyātma-vibhūtayaḥ
yābhir vibhūtibhir lokān imāṁs tvaṁ
vyāpya tiṣhṭhasi

Be pleased to speak in full of Your own manifestations which are indeed divine, through which manifestations You exist pervading these worlds.

ଓଃ 17 ଃଠ

कथं विद्यामहं योगिंस्त्वां सदा परिचिन्तयन् ।
केषु केषु च भावेषु चिन्त्योऽसि भगवन्मया ॥

kathaṁ vidyām ahaṁ yogins tvāṁ
sadā parichintayan
keṣhu keṣhu cha bhāveṣhu
chintyo "si bhagavan mayā

O Yogi, how shall I know You by remaining ever-engaged in meditation? And through what objects, O Lord, are You to be meditated on by me?

ଓଃ 18 ଃଠ

विस्तरेणात्मनो योगं विभूतिं च जनार्दन ।
भूयः कथय तृप्तिर्हि शृण्वतो नास्ति मेऽमृतम् ॥

vistareṇātmano yogaṁ
vibhūtiṁ cha janārdana
bhūyaḥ kathaya tṛiptir hi
śhṛiṇvato nāsti me "mṛitam

O Janardana, narrate to me again our own yoga and (divine) manifestations elaborately. For, while hearing (Your) nectar-like (words), there is no satiety in me.

ꕥ 19 ꕥ

श्रीभगवानुवाच ।
हन्त ते कथयिष्यामि दिव्या ह्यात्मविभूतयः ।
प्राधान्यतः कुरुश्रेष्ठ नास्त्यन्तो विस्तरस्य मे ।।

śhrī bhagavān uvācha
hanta te kathayiṣhyāmi
divyā hyātma-vibhūtayaḥ
prādhānyataḥ kuru-śhreṣhṭha
nāstyanto vistarasya me

The Blessed Lord said: O best of the Kurus, now, according to their importance, I shall describe to you My own glories, which are indeed divine. There is no end to my manifestations.

ꕥ 20 ꕥ

अहमात्मा गुडाकेश सर्वभूताशयस्थितः ।
अहमादिश्च मध्यं च भूतानामन्त एव च ।।

aham ātmā guḍākeśha sarva-bhūtāśhaya-sthitaḥ
aham ādiśh cha madhyaṁ cha bhūtānām anta eva cha

O Gudakesa, I am the Self residing in the hearts of all beings, and I am the beginning and the middle as also the end of (all) beings.

ও 21 ৩

आदित्यानामहं विष्णुर्ज्योतिषां रविरंशुमान् ।
मरीचिर्मरुतामस्मि नक्षत्राणामहं शशी ।।

ādityānām ahaṁ
viṣhṇur jyotiṣhāṁ ravir anśhumān
marīchir marutām asmi
nakṣhatrāṇām ahaṁ śhaśhī

Among the Adityas I am Visnu; among the luminaries, the radiant sun; among the (forty-nine) Maruts] I am Marici; among the stars I am the moon.

ও 22 ৩

वेदानां सामवेदोऽस्मि देवानामस्मि वासवः ।
इन्द्रियाणां मनश्चास्मि भूतानामस्मि चेतना ।।

vedānāṁ sāma-vedo "smi
devānām asmi vāsavaḥ
indriyāṇāṁ manaśh chāsmi
bhūtānām asmi chetanā

Among the Vedas I am Sama-veda; among the gods I am Indra. Among the organs I am the mind, and I am the intelligence in creatures.

23

रुद्राणां शङ्करश्चास्मि वित्तेशो यक्षरक्षसाम् ।
वसूनां पावकश्चास्मि मेरुः शिखरिणामहम् ।।

rudrāṇāṁ śhaṅkaraśh chāsmi
vitteśho yakṣha-rakṣhasām
vasūnāṁ pāvakaśh chāsmi
meruḥ śhikhariṇām aham

Among the Rudras I am Sankara, and among the Yaksa and goblins I am Kubera . Among the Vasus I am Fire, and among the mountains I am Meru.

24

पुरोधसां च मुख्यं मां विद्धि पार्थ बृहस्पतिम् ।
सेनानीनामहं स्कन्दः सरसामस्मि सागरः ।।

purodhasāṁ cha mukhyaṁ māṁ
viddhi pārtha bṛihaspatim
senānīnām ahaṁ skandaḥ
sarasām asmi sāgaraḥ

O son of Partha, know me to be Brhaspati, the foremost among the priests of kings. Among commanders of armies I am Skanda; among large expanses of water I am the sea.

ଓ 25 ଓ

महर्षीणां भृगुरहं गिरामस्म्येकमक्षरम् ।
यज्ञानां जपयज्ञोऽस्मि स्थावराणां हिमालयः ।।

maharṣhīṇāṁ bhṛigur ahaṁ
girām asmyekam akṣharam
yajñānāṁ japa-yajño "smi
sthāvarāṇāṁ himālayaḥ

Among the great sages I am Bhrgu; of words, I am the single syllable (Om). Among rituals I am the ritual of Japa, of the immovable, the Himalaya.

ଓ 26 ଓ

अश्वत्थः सर्ववृक्षाणां देवर्षीणां च नारदः ।
गन्धर्वाणां चित्ररथः सिद्धानां कपिलो मुनिः ।।

aśhvatthaḥ sarva-vṛikṣhāṇāṁ
devarṣhīṇāṁ cha nāradaḥ
gandharvāṇāṁ chitrarathaḥ
siddhānāṁ kapilo muniḥ

Among all trees (I am) the Asvatha (peepul), and Narada among the divine sages. Among the gandharvas (I am) Citraratha; among the perfected ones, the sage Kapila.

27

उच्चैःश्रवसमश्वानां विद्धि माममृतोद्भवम् ।
ऐरावतं गजेन्द्राणां नराणां च नराधिपम् ।।

uchchaiḥśhravasam aśhvānāṁ
viddhi mām amṛitodbhavam
airāvataṁ gajendrāṇāṁ
narāṇāṁ cha narādhipam

Among horses, know Me to be Uccaihsravas, born of nectar; Airavata among the lordly elephants; and among men, the Kind of men.

28

आयुधानामहं वज्रं धेनूनामस्मि कामधुक् ।
प्रजनश्चास्मि कन्दर्पः सर्पाणामस्मि वासुकिः ।।

āyudhānām ahaṁ vajraṁ
dhenūnām asmi kāmadhuk
prajanaśh chāsmi kandarpaḥ
sarpāṇām asmi vāsukiḥ

Among weapons I am the thunderbolt; among cows I am Kamadhenu. I am Kandarpa, the Progenitor, and among serpents I am Vasuki

☙ 29 ❧

अनन्तश्चास्मि नागानां वरुणो यादसामहम् ।
पितॄणामर्यमा चास्मि यमः संयमतामहम् ॥

anantaśh chāsmi nāgānāṁ
varuṇo yādasām aham
pitṝiṇām aryamā chāsmi
yamaḥ sanyamatām aham

Among snakes I am Ananta, and Varuna among gods of the waters. Among the manes I am Aryama, and among the maintainers of law and order I am Yama.

☙ 30 ❧

प्रह्लादश्चास्मि दैत्यानां कालः कलयतामहम् ।
मृगाणां च मृगेन्द्रोऽहं वैनतेयश्च पक्षिणाम् ॥

prahlādaśh chāsmi daityānāṁ
kālaḥ kalayatām aham
mṛigāṇāṁ cha mṛigendro "haṁ
vainateyaśh cha pakṣhiṇām

Among demons I am Prahlada, and I am Time among reckoners of time. And among animals I am the lion, and among birds I am Garuda.

☙ 31 ❧

पवनः पवतामस्मि रामः शस्त्रभृतामहम् ।
झषाणां मकरश्चास्मि स्रोतसामस्मि जाह्नवी ।।

pavanaḥ pavatām asmi rāmaḥ
śhastra-bhṛitām aham
jhaṣhāṇāṁ makaraśh chāsmi
srotasām asmi jāhnavī

Of the purifiers I am air; among the wielders of weapons I am Rama. Among fishes, too, I am the shark; I am Ganga among rivers.

☙ 32 ❧

सर्गाणामादिरन्तश्च मध्यं चैवाहमर्जुन ।
अध्यात्मविद्या विद्यानां वादः प्रवदतामहम् ।।

sargāṇām ādir antaśh cha
madhyaṁ chaivāham arjuna
adhyātma-vidyā vidyānāṁ
vādaḥ pravadatām aham

O Arjuna, of creations I am the beginning and the end as also the middle, I am the knowledge of the Self among knowledge; of those who date I am Vada.

ᘓ 33 ᘐ

अक्षराणामकारोऽस्मि द्वन्द्वः सामासिकस्य च ।
अहमेवाक्षयः कालो धाताहं विश्वतोमुखः ।।

akṣharāṇām a-kāro "smi dvandvaḥ sāmāsikasya cha
aham evākṣhayaḥ kālo dhātāhaṁ viśhvato-mukhaḥ

Of the letters I am the letter a, and of the group of compound words I am (the compound called) Dvandva. I Myself am the infinite time; I am the Dispenser with faces everywhere.

ᘓ 34 ᘐ

मृत्युः सर्वहरश्चाहमुद्भवश्च भविष्यताम् ।
कीर्तिः श्रीर्वाक्च नारीणां स्मृतिर्मेधा धृतिः क्षमा ।।

mṛityuḥ sarva-haraśh chāham
udbhavaśh cha bhaviṣhyatām
kīrtiḥ śhrīr vāk cha nārīṇāṁ
smṛitir medhā dhṛitiḥ kṣhamā

And I am Death, the destroyer of all; and the prosperity of those destined to be prosperous. Of the feminine (I am) fame, beauty, speech, memory, intelligence, fortitude and forbearance.

35

बृहत्साम तथा साम्नां गायत्री छन्दसामहम् ।
मासानां मार्गशीर्षोऽहमृतूनां कुसुमाकरः ।।

bṛihat-sāma tathā sāmnāṁ
gāyatrī chhandasām aham
māsānāṁ mārga-śhīrṣho "ham
ṛitūnāṁ kusumākaraḥ

I am also the Brihat-sama of the Sama (mantras); of the metres, Gayatri. Of the months, I am Marga-sirsa, and of the seasons, spring.

36

द्यूतं छलयतामस्मि तेजस्तेजस्विनामहम् ।
जयोऽस्मि व्यवसायोऽस्मि सत्त्वं सत्त्ववतामहम् ।।

dyūtaṁ chhalayatām asmi
tejas tejasvinām aham
jayo "smi vyavasāyo "smi
sattvaṁ sattvavatām aham

Of the fraudulent I am the gambling; I am the irresistible command of the mighty. I am excellence, I am effort, I am the sattva quality of those possessed of sattva.

૯ 37 ৯

वृष्णीनां वासुदेवोऽस्मि पाण्डवानां धनञ्जयः ।
मुनीनामप्यहं व्यासः कवीनामुशना कविः ।।

vṛiṣhṇīnāṁ vāsudevo "smi
pāṇḍavānāṁ dhanañjayaḥ
munīnām apyahaṁ vyāsaḥ
kavīnām uśhanā kaviḥ

Of the vrsnis I am Vasudeva; of the Pandavas, Dhananjaya (Arjuna). And of the wise, I am Vyasa; of the omniscient, the omniscient Usanas.

૯ 38 ৯

दण्डो दमयतामस्मि नीतिरस्मि जिगीषताम् ।
मौनं चैवास्मि गुह्यानां ज्ञानं ज्ञानवतामहम् ।।

daṇḍo damayatām asmi
nītir asmi jigīṣhatām
maunaṁ chaivāsmi guhyānāṁ
jñānaṁ jñānavatām aham

Of the punishers I am the rod; I am the righteous policy of those who desire to conquer. And of things secret, I am verily silence; I am knowledge of the men of knowledge.

☙ 39 ❧

यच्चापि सर्वभूतानां बीजं तदहमर्जुन ।
न तदस्ति विना यत्स्यान्मया भूतं चराचरम् ।।

yach chāpi sarva-bhūtānāṁ
bījaṁ tad aham arjuna
na tad asti vinā yat syān mayā
bhūtaṁ charācharam

Moreover, O Arjuna, whatsoever is the seed of all beings that I am. There is no thing moving or non-moving which can exist without Me.

☙ 40 ❧

नान्तोऽस्ति मम दिव्यानां विभूतीनां परन्तप ।
एष तूद्देशतः प्रोक्तो विभूतेर्विस्तरो मया ।।

nānto "sti mama divyānāṁ
vibhūtīnāṁ parantapa
eṣha tūddeśhataḥ prokto
vibhūter vistaro mayā

O destroyer of enemies, there is no limit to My divine manifestations. This description of (My) manifestations, however, has been stated by Me by way of illustration.

ଓ 41 ନ

यद्यद्विभूतिमत्सत्वं श्रीमदूर्जितमेव वा ।
तत्तदेवावगच्छ त्वं मम तेजोंऽशसम्भवम् ।।

yad yad vibhūtimat sattvaṁ
śhrīmad ūrjitam eva vā
tat tad evāvagachchha tvaṁ mama
tejo "nśha-sambhavam

Whatever object [All living beings] is verily endowed with majesty, possessed of prosperity, or is energetic, you know for certain each of them as having a part of My power as its source.

ଓ 42 ନ

अथवा बहुनैतेन किं ज्ञातेन तवार्जुन ।
विष्टभ्याहमिदं कृत्स्नमेकांशेन स्थितो जगत् ।।

atha vā bahunaitena kiṁ jñātena tavārjuna
viṣhṭabhyāham idaṁ kṛitsnam ekānśhena sthito jagat

Or, on the other hand, what is the need of your knowing this extensively, O Arjuna? I remain sustaining this whole creation in a special way with a part (of Myself).

Chapter 11

Vishwaroopa Darshana Yoga
Revealing Universal Cosmic Form

ᘓ 1 ᘐ

अर्जुन उवाच ।
मदनुग्रहाय परमं गुह्यमध्यात्मसञ्ज्ञितम् ।
यत्त्वयोक्तं वचस्तेन मोहोऽयं विगतो मम ।।

arjuna uvācha
mad-anugrahāya paramaṁ
guhyam adhyātma-sanjñitam
yat tvayoktaṁ vachas tena
moho "yaṁ vigato mama

Arjuna said: This delusion of mine has departed as a result of that speech which is most secret and known as pertaining to the Self, and which was uttered by You for my benefit.

ᘓ 2 ᘐ

भवाप्ययौ हि भूतानां श्रुतौ विस्तरशो मया ।
त्वत्तः कमलपत्राक्ष माहात्म्यमपि चाव्ययम् ।।

bhavāpyayau hi bhūtānāṁ śhrutau vistaraśho mayā
tvattaḥ kamala-patrākṣha māhātmyam api chāvyayam

O you with eyes like lotus leaves, the origin and dissolution of beings have been heard by me in detail from You. And (Your) undecaying glory, too, (has been heard).

☙ 3 ❧

एवमेतद्यथात्थ त्वमात्मानं परमेश्वर ।
द्रष्टुमिच्छामि ते रूपमैश्वरं पुरुषोत्तम ।।

evam etad yathāttha
tvam ātmānaṁ parameśhvara
draṣhṭum ichchhāmi te
rūpam aiśhwaraṁ puruṣhottama

O supreme Lord, so it is, as You speak about Yourself. O supreme Person, I wish to see the divine form of Yours.

☙ 4 ❧

मन्यसे यदि तच्छक्यं मया द्रष्टुमिति प्रभो ।
योगेश्वर ततो मे त्वं दर्शयात्मानमव्ययम् ।।

manyase yadi tach chhakyaṁ
mayā draṣhṭum iti prabho
yogeśhvara tato me tvaṁ
darśhayātmānam avyayam

O Lord, if You think that it is possible to be seen by me, then, O Lord of Yoga, You show me Your eternal Self.

ᗡ 5 ᗡ

श्रीभगवानुवाच ।
पश्य मे पार्थ रूपाणि शतशोऽथ सहस्रशः ।
नानाविधानि दिव्यानि नानावर्णाकृतीनि च ।।

śhrī-bhagavān uvācha
paśhya me pārtha rūpāṇi
śhataśho "tha sahasraśhaḥ
nānā-vidhāni divyāni
nānā-varṇākṛitīni cha

The Blessed Lord said: O son of Partha, behold My forms in (their) hundreds and in thousands, of different kinds, celestial, and of various colours and shapes.

ᗡ 6 ᗡ

पश्यादित्यान्वसून् रुद्रानश्विनौ मरुतस्तथा ।
बहून्यदृष्टपूर्वाणि पश्याश्चर्याणि भारत ।।

paśhyādityān vasūn rudrān aśhvinau marutas tathā
bahūny adṛiṣhṭa-pūrvāṇi paśhyāśhcharyāṇi bhārata

See the Adiyas, the Vasus, the Rudras, the two Asvins and the Maruts. O scion of the Bharata dynasty, behold also the many wonders not seen before.

☙ 7 ❧

इहैकस्थं जगत्कृत्स्नं पश्याद्य सचराचरम् ।
मम देहे गुडाकेश यच्चान्यद्द्रष्टुमिच्छसि ।।

ihaika-sthaṁ jagat kṛitsnaṁ
paśhyādya sa-charācharam
mama dehe guḍākeśha
yach chānyad draṣhṭum ichchhasi

See now, O Gudakesa (Arjuna), the entire Universe together with the moving and the non-moving, concentrated at the same place here in My body, as also whatever else you would like to see.

☙ 8 ❧

न तु मां शक्यसे द्रष्टुमनेनैव स्वचक्षुषा ।
दिव्यं ददामि ते चक्षुः पश्य मे योगमैश्वरम् ।।

na tu māṁ śhakyase
draṣhṭum anenaiva sva-chakṣhuṣhā
divyaṁ dadāmi te chakṣhuḥ
paśhya me yogam aiśhwaram

But you are not able to see Me merely with this eye of yours. I grant you the supernatural eye; behold My Divine Yoga.

☙ 9 ❧

सञ्जय उवाच ।
एवमुक्त्वा ततो राजन्महायोगेश्वरो हरिः ।
दर्शयामास पार्थाय परमं पमैश्वरम् ।।

sañjaya uvācha
evam uktvā tato
rājan mahā-yogeśhvaro hariḥ
darśhayām āsa pārthāya
paramaṁ rūpam aiśhwaram

Sanjaya said: O King, having spoken thus, thereafter, Hari [Hari: destroyer of ignorance along with its consciences.] (Krishna) the great Master of Yoga, showed to the son of Partha the supreme divine form:

☙ 10 ❧

अनेकवक्त्रनयनमनेकाद्भुतदर्शनम् ।
अनेकदिव्याभरणं दिव्यानेकोद्यतायुधम् ।।

aneka-vaktra-nayanam anekādbhuta-darśhanam
aneka-divyābharaṇaṁ divyānekodyatāyudham

Having many faces and eyes, possessing many wonderful sights, adorned with numerous celestial ornaments, holding many uplifted heavenly weapons.

☙ 11 ❧

दिव्यमाल्याम्बरधरं दिव्यगन्धानुलेपनम् ।
सर्वाश्चर्यमयं देवमनन्तं विश्वतोमुखम् ॥

divya-mālyāmbara-dharaṁ
divya-gandhānulepanam
sarvāśhcharya-mayaṁ devam anantaṁ
viśhvato-mukham

Wearing heavenly garlands and apparel, anointed with heavenly scents, abounding in all kinds of wonder, resplendent, infinite, and with faces everywhere.

☙ 12 ❧

दिवि सूर्यसहस्रस्य भवेद्युगपदुत्थिता ।
यदि भाः सदृशी सा स्याद्भासस्तस्य महात्मनः ॥

divi sūrya-sahasrasya
bhaved yugapad utthitā
yadi bhāḥ sadṛiśhī sā
syād bhāsa tasya mahātmanaḥ

Should the effulgence of a thousand suns blaze forth simultaneously in the sky, that might be similar to the radiance of that exalted One.

☙ 13 ❧

तत्रैकस्थं जगत्कृत्स्नं प्रविभक्तमनेकधा ।
अपश्यद्देवदेवस्य शरीरे पाण्डवस्तदा ।।

tatraika-sthaṁ jagat kṛitsnaṁ
ravibhaktam anekadhā
apaśhyad deva-devasya
śharīre pāṇḍavas tadā

At that time, Pandava saw there, in the body of the God of gods, the whole diversely differentiated Universe united in the one (Cosmic form).

☙ 14 ❧

ततः स विस्मयाविष्टो हृष्टरोमा धनञ्जयः ।
प्रणम्य शिरसा देवं कृताञ्जलिरभाषत ।।

tataḥ sa vismayāviṣhṭo
hṛiṣhṭa-romā dhanañjayaḥ
praṇamya śhirasā devaṁ
kṛitāñjalir abhāṣhata

Then, filled with wonder, with hairs standing on end, he, Dhananjaya, (Arjuna), bowing down with his head to the Lord, said with folded hands:

☙ 15 ❧

अर्जुन उवाच ।
पश्यामि देवांस्तव देव देहे सर्वांस्तथा भूतविशेषसङ्घान् ।
ब्रह्माणमीशं कमलासनस्थ. मृषींश्च सर्वानुरगांश्च दिव्यान् ॥

arjuna uvācha
paśhyāmi devāns tava deva dehe
sarvāns tathā bhūta-viśheṣha-saṅghān
brahmāṇam īśhaṁ kamalāsana-stham
ṛiṣhīnśh cha sarvān uragānśh cha divyān

Arjuna said: O God, I see in Your body all the gods as also hosts of (various) classes of beings; Brahma the ruler, sitting on a lotus seat, and all the heavenly sages and serpents.

☙ 16 ❧

अनेकबाहूदरवक्त्रनेत्रं पश्यामि त्वां सर्वतोऽनन्तरूपम् ।
नान्तं न मध्यं न पुनस्तवादिं पश्यामि विश्वेश्वर विश्वरूप ॥

aneka-bāhūdara-vaktra-netraṁ
paśhyāmi tvāṁ sarvato "nanta-rūpam
nāntaṁ na madhyaṁ na punas tavādiṁ
paśhyāmi viśhveśhvara viśhva-rūpa

I see You as possessed of numerous arms, bellies, mouths and eyes; as having infinite forms all around. O Lord of the Universe, O Cosmic Person, I see not Your limit nor the middle, nor again the beginning!

ଓ 17 ଓ

किरीटिनं गदिनं चक्रिणं । तेजोराशिं सर्वतो दीप्तिमन्तम् ।
पश्यामि त्वां दुर्निरीक्ष्यं समन्ताद् दीप्तानलार्कद्युतिमप्रमेयम् ।।

kirīṭinaṁ gadinaṁ chakriṇaṁ cha
tejo-rāśhiṁ sarvato dīptimantam
paśhyāmi tvāṁ durnirīkṣhyaṁ samantād
dīptānalārka-dyutim aprameyam

I see You as wearing a crown, wielding a mace, and holding a disc; a mass of brilliance glowing all around, difficult to look at from all sides, possessed of the radiance of the blazing fire and sun, and immeasurable.

🙞 18 🙜

त्वमक्षरं परमं वेदितव्यं त्वमस्य विश्वस्य परं निधानम् ।
त्वमव्ययः शाश्वतधर्मगोप्ता सनातनस्त्वं पुरुषो मतो मे ।।

tvam akṣharaṁ paramaṁ veditavyaṁ
tvam asya viśhvasya paraṁ nidhānam
tvam avyayaḥ śhāśhvata-dharma-goptā
sanātanas tvaṁ puruṣho mato me

You are the Immutable, the supreme One to be known; You are the most perfect repository of this Universe. You are the Imperishable, the Protector of the ever-existing religion; You are the eternal Person. This is my belief.

🙞 19 🙜

अनादिमध्यान्तमनन्तवीर्य. मनन्तबाहुं शशिसूर्यनेत्रम् ।
पश्यामि त्वां दीप्तहुताशवक्त्रं. स्वतेजसा विश्वमिदं तपन्तम् ।।

anādi-madhyāntam ananta-vīryam
ananta-bāhuṁ śhaśhi-sūrya-netram
paśhyāmi tvāṁ dīpta-hutāśha-vaktraṁ
sva-tejasā viśhvam idaṁ tapantam

I see You as without beginning, middle and end, possessed of infinite valour, having innumerable arms, having the sun and the moon as eyes, having a mouth like a blazing fire, and heating up this Universe by Your own brilliance.

20

द्यावापृथिव्योरिदमन्तरं हि व्याप्तं त्वयैकेन दिशश्च सर्वाः ।
दृष्ट्वाद्भुतं रूपमुग्रं तवेदं लोकत्रयं प्रव्यथितं महात्मन् ॥

dyāv ā-pṛithivyor idam antaraṁ hi
vyāptaṁ tvayaikena diśhaśh cha sarvāḥ
dṛiṣhṭvādbhutaṁ rūpam ugraṁ tavedaṁ
loka-trayaṁ pravyathitaṁ mahātman

Indeed, this intermediate space between heaven and earth as also all the directions are pervaded by You alone. O exalted One, the three worlds are struck with fear by seeing this strange, fearful form of Yours.

21

अमी हि त्वां सुरसङ्घा विशन्ति केचिद्भीताः प्राञ्जलयो गृणन्ति ।
स्वस्तीत्युक्त्वा महर्षिसिद्धसङ्घाः स्तुवन्ति त्वां स्तुतिभिः पुष्कलाभिः ॥

amī hi tvāṁ sura-saṅghā viśhanti
kechid bhītāḥ prāñjalayo gṛiṇanti
svastīty uktvā maharṣhi-siddha-saṅghāḥ
stuvanti tvāṁ stutibhiḥ puṣhkalābhiḥ

Those very groups of gods enter into You; struck with fear, some extol (You) with joined palms. Groups of great sages and perfected beings praise You with elaborate hymns, saying 'May it be well!'

☙ 22 ❧

रुद्रादित्या वसवो ये च साध्या विश्वेऽश्विनौ मरुतश्चैष्मपाश्च ।
गन्धर्वयक्षासुरसिद्धसङ्घा वीक्षन्ते त्वां विस्मिताश्चैव सर्वे ।।

rudrādityā vasavo ye cha sādhyā
viśhve "śhvinau marutaśh choṣhmapāśh cha
gandharva-yakṣhāsura-siddha-saṅghā
vīkṣhante tvāṁ vismitāśh chaiva sarve

Those who are the Rudras, the Adityas, the Vasus and the Sadhyas , the Visve (devas), the two Asvins, the Maruts and the Usmapas, and hosts of Gandharvas, Yaksa, demons and Siddhas–all of those very one's gaze at You, being indeed struck with wonder.

☙ 23 ❧

रूपं महत्ते बहुवक्त्रनेत्रं महाबाहो बहुबाहूरुपादम् ।
बहूदरं बहुदंष्ट्राकरालं दृष्ट्वा लोकाः प्रव्यथितास्तथाहम् ।।

rūpaṁ mahat te bahu-vaktra-netraṁ
mahā-bāho bahu-bāhūru-pādam
bahūdaraṁ bahu-danṣhṭrā-karālaṁ
dṛiṣhṭvā lokāḥ pravyathitās tathāham

O mighty-armed One, seeing Your immense form with many mouths and eyes, having numerous arms, thighs and feet, with many bellies, and fearful with many teeth, the creatures are struck with terror, and so am I.

☙ 24 ❧

नभःस्पृशं दीप्तमनेकवर्णं व्यात्ताननं दीप्तविशालनेत्रम् ।
दृष्ट्वा हि त्वां प्रव्यथितान्तरात्मा धृतिं न विन्दामि शमं च विष्णो ।।

nabhaḥ-spṛiśhaṁ dīptam aneka-varṇaṁ
vyāttānanaṁ dīpta-viśhāla-netram
dṛiṣhṭvā hi tvāṁ pravyathitāntar-ātmā
dhṛitiṁ na vindāmi śhamaṁ cha viṣhṇo

O Visnu, verily, seeing Your form touching heaven, blazing, with many colours, open-mouthed, with fiery large eyes, I, becoming terrified in my mind, do not find steadiness and peace.

ଓ 25 ଔ

दंष्ट्राकरालानि च ते मुखानि दृष्ट्वैव कालानलसन्निभानि ।
दिशो न जाने न लभे च शर्म प्रसीद देवेश जगन्निवास ॥

danṣhṭrā-karālāni cha te mukhāni
dṛiṣhṭvaiva kālānala-sannibhāni
diśho na jāne na labhe cha śharma
prasīda deveśha jagan-nivāsa

Having merely seen Your mouths made terrible with (their) teeth and resembling the fire of Dissolution, I have lost the sense of direction and find no comfort. Be gracious, O Lord of gods, O Abode of the Universe.

᪥ 26 ᪥

अमी च त्वां धृतराष्ट्रस्य पुत्राः सर्वे सहैवावनिपालसङ्घैः ।
भीष्मो द्रोणः सूतपुत्रस्तथासौ सहास्मदीयैरपि योधमुख्यैः ॥

᪥ 27 ᪥

वक्त्राणि ते त्वरमाणा विशन्ति दंष्ट्राकरालानि भयानकानि ।
केचिद्विलग्ना दशनान्तरेषु सन्दृश्यन्ते चूर्णितैरुत्तमाङ्गैः ॥

amī cha tvāṁ dhṛitarāśhtrasya putrāḥ
sarve sahaivāvani-pāla-saṅghaiḥ
bhīṣhmo droṇaḥ sūta-putras tathāsau
sahāsmadīyair api yodha-mukhyaiḥ

vaktrāṇi te tvaramāṇā viśhanti
danṣhṭrā-karālāni bhayānakāni
kechid vilagnā daśhanāntareṣhu
sandṛiśhyante chūrṇitair uttamāṅgaiḥ

And into You (enter) all those sons of Dhritarashtra along with multitudes of the rulers of the earth; (also) Bhisma, äona and that son of a Suta (Karna), together with even our prominent warriors. They rapidly enter into Your terrible mouths with cruel teeth! Some are seen sticking in the gaps between the teeth, with their heads crushed!

☙ 28 ❧

यथा नदीनां बहवोऽम्बुवेगाः समुद्रमेवाभिमुखा द्रवन्ति ।
तथा तवामी नरलोकवीरा विशन्ति वक्त्राण्यभिविज्वलन्ति ।।

yathā nadīnāṁ bahavo "mbu-vegāḥ
samudram evābhimukhā dravanti
tathā tavāmī nara-loka-vīrā
viśhanti vaktrāṇy abhivijvalanti

As the numerous currents of the waters of rivers rush towards the sea alone so also do those heroes of the human world enter into Your blazing mouths.

☙ 29 ❧

यथा प्रदीप्तं ज्वलनं पतङ्गा विशन्ति नाशाय समृद्धवेगाः ।
तथैव नाशाय विशन्ति लोका. स्तवापि वक्त्राणि समृद्धवेगाः ।।

yathā pradīptaṁ jvalanaṁ pataṅgā
viśhanti nāśhāya samṛiddha-vegāḥ
tathaiva nāśhāya viśhanti lokās
tavāpi vaktrāṇi samṛiddha-vegāḥ

As moths enter with increased haste into a glowing fire for destruction, in that very way do the creatures enter into Your mouths too, with increased hurry for destruction.

☙ 30 ❧

लेलिह्यसे ग्रसमानः समन्ता. ल्लोकान्समग्रान्वदनैर्ज्वलद्भिः ।
तेजोभिरापूर्य जगत्समग्रं भासस्तवोग्राः प्रतपन्ति विष्णो ।।

lelihyase grasamānaḥ samantāl
lokān samagrān vadanair jvaladbhiḥ
tejobhir āpūrya jagat samagraṁ
bhāsa tavogrāḥ pratapanti viṣhṇo

You lick Your lips while devouring all the creatures from every side with flaming mouths which are completely filling the entire world with heat.

☙ 31 ❧

आख्याहि मे को भवानुग्ररूपो नमोऽस्तु ते देववर प्रसीद ।
विज्ञातुमिच्छामि भवन्तमाद्यं न हि प्रजानामि तव प्रवृत्तिम् ।।

ākhyāhi me ko bhavān ugra-rūpo
namo "stu te deva-vara prasīda
vijñātum ichchhāmi bhavantam ādyaṁ
na hi prajānāmi tava pravṛittim

Tell me who You are, fierce in form. Salutation be to you, O supreme God; be gracious. I desire to fully know You who are the Prima One. For I do not understand Your actions!

☙ 32 ❧

श्रीभगवानुवाच ।
कालोऽस्मि लोकक्षयकृत्प्रवृद्धो लोकान्समाहर्तुमिह प्रवृत्तः ।
ऋतेऽपि त्वां न भविष्यन्ति सर्वे येऽवस्थिताः प्रत्यनीकेषु योधाः ।।

śhrī-bhagavān uvācha
kālo "smi loka-kṣhaya-kṛit pravṛiddho
lokān samāhartum iha pravṛittaḥ
ṛite "pi tvāṁ na bhaviṣhyanti sarve
ye "vasthitāḥ pratyanīkeṣhu yodhāḥ

The Blessed Lord said: I am the world-destroying Time, grown in stature and now engaged in annihilating the creatures. Even without you, all the warriors who are arrayed in the confronting armies will cease to exist!

☙ 33 ❧

तस्मात्वमुत्तिष्ठ यशो लभस्व जित्वा शत्रून्भुङ्क्ष्व राज्यं समृद्धम् ।
मयैवैते निहताः पूर्वमेव निमित्तमात्रं भव सव्यसाचिन् ।।

tasmāt tvam uttiṣhṭha yaśho labhasva
jitvā śhatrūn bhuṅkṣhva rājyaṁ samṛiddham
mayaivaite nihatāḥ pūrvam eva
nimitta-mātraṁ bhava savya-sāchin

Therefore you rise up, (and) gain fame; and defeating the enemies, enjoy a prosperous kingdom. These have been killed verily by Me even earlier; be you merely an instrument, O Savyasacin (Arjuna).

॥ 34 ॥

द्रोणं च भीष्मं च जयद्रथं च कर्णं तथान्यानपि योधवीरान् ।
मया हतांस्त्वं जहि मा व्यथिष्ठा युध्यस्व जेतासि रणे सपत्नान् ॥

droṇaṁ cha bhīṣhmaṁ cha jayadrathaṁ cha
karṇaṁ tathānyān api yodha-vīrān
mayā hatāṁs tvaṁ jahi mā vyathiṣhṭhā
yudhyasva jetāsi raṇe sapatnān

You destroy äona and Bhisma, and Jayadratha and Karna as also the other heroic warriors who have been killed by Me. Do not be afraid. Fight! You shall conquer the enemies in battle.

॥ 35 ॥

सञ्जय उवाच ।
एतच्छ्रुत्वा वचनं केशवस्य कृताञ्जलिर्वेपमानः किरीटी ।
नमस्कृत्वा भूय एवाह कृष्णं सगद्गदं भीतभीतः प्रणम्य ॥

sañjaya uvācha
etach chhrutvā vachanaṁ keśhavasya
kṛitāñjalir vepamānaḥ kirīṭī
namaskṛitvā bhūya evāha kṛiṣhṇaṁ
sa-gadgadaṁ bhīta-bhītaḥ praṇamya

Sanjaya said: Hearing this utterance of Kesava, Kiriti (Arjuna), with joined palms and trembling, prostrating himself, said again to Krishna with a faltering voice, bowing down overcome by fits of fear:

36

अर्जुन उवाच ।
स्थाने हृषीकेश तव प्रकीर्त्या जगत्प्रहृष्यत्यनुरज्यते च ।
रक्षांसि भीतानि दिशो द्रवन्ति सर्वे नमस्यन्ति च सिद्धसङ्घाः ।।

arjuna uvācha
sthāne hṛiṣhīkeśha tava prakīrtyā
jagat prahṛiṣhyaty anurajyate cha
rakṣhānsi bhītāni diśho dravanti
sarve namasyanti cha siddha-saṅghāḥ

Arjuna said: It is proper, O Hrsikesa, that the world becomes delighted and attracted by Your praise; that the Raksas, stricken with fear, run in all directions; and that all the groups of the Siddhas bow down (to You).

☙ 37 ❧

कस्माच्च ते न नमेरन्महात्मन् गरीयसे ब्रह्मणोऽप्यादिकर्त्रे ।
अनन्त देवेश जगन्निवास त्वमक्षरं सदसतत्परं यत् ।।

kasmāch cha te na nameran mahātman
garīyase brahmaṇo "py ādi-kartre
ananta deveśha jagan-nivāsa
tvam akṣharaṁ sad-asat tat paraṁ yat

And why should they not bow down to You, O exalted. One, who are greater (than all) and who are the first Creator even of Brahma! O infinite One, supreme God, Abode of the Universe, You are the Immutable, being and non-being, (and) that which is Transcendental.

☙ 38 ❧

त्वमादिदेवः पुरुषः पुराण. स्त्वमस्य विश्वस्य परं निधानम् ।
वेत्तासि वेद्यं च परं च धाम त्वया ततं विश्वमनन्तरूप ।।

tvam ādi-devaḥ puruṣhaḥ purāṇas
tvam asya viśhvasya paraṁ nidhānam
vettāsi vedyaṁ cha paraṁ cha dhāma
tvayā tataṁ viśhvam ananta-rūpa

You are the primal Deity, the ancient Person; You are the supreme Resort of this world. You are the knower as also the object of knowledge, and the supreme Abode. O You of infinite forms, the Universe is pervaded by You!

ଓ 39 ଽ

वायुर्यमोऽग्निर्वरुणः शशाङ्कः प्रजापतिस्त्वं प्रपितामहश्च ।
नमो नमस्तेऽस्तु सहस्रकृत्वः पुनश्च भूयोऽपि नमो नमस्ते ॥

vāyur yamo "gnir varuṇaḥ śhaśhāṅkaḥ
prajāpatis tvaṁ prapitāmahaśh cha
namo namas te "stu sahasra-kṛitvaḥ
punaśh cha bhūyo "pi namo namas te

You are Air, Death, Fire, the god of the waters, the moon, the Lord of the creatures, and the Greater-grandfather. Salutations! Salutation be to You a thousand times; salutation to You again and again! Salutation!

ଓ 40 ଽ

नमः पुरस्तादथ पृष्ठतस्ते नमोऽस्तु ते सर्वत एव सर्व ।
अनन्तवीर्यामितविक्रमस्त्वं सर्वं समाप्नोषि ततोऽसि सर्वः ॥

namaḥ purastād atha pṛiṣhṭhatas te
namo "stu te sarvata eva sarva
ananta-vīryāmita-vikramas tvaṁ
sarvaṁ samāpnoṣhi tato "si sarvaḥ

Salutation to You in the East and behind. Salutation be to You on all sides indeed, O All! You are possessed of infinite strength and infinite heroism. You pervade everything; hence You are all!

ॐ 41 ॐ

सखेति मत्वा प्रसभं यदुक्तं हे कृष्ण हे यादव हे सखेति ।
अजानता महिमानं तवेदं मया प्रमादात्प्रणयेन वापि ।।

sakheti matvā prasabhaṁ yad uktaṁ
he kṛiṣhṇa he yādava he sakheti
ajānatā mahimānaṁ tavedaṁ
mayā pramādāt praṇayena vāpi

Without knowing this greatness of Yours, whatever was said by me (to You) rashly, through inadvertence or even out of intimacy, thinking (You to be) a friend, addressing (You) as 'O Krsna,' 'O Yadava,' 'O friend,' etc.

ॐ 42 ॐ

यच्चावहासार्थमसत्कृतोऽसि विहारशय्यासनभोजनेषु ।
एकोऽथवाप्यच्युत तत्समक्षं तत्क्षामये त्वामहमप्रमेयम् ।।

yach chāvahāsārtham asat-kṛito "si
vihāra-śhayyāsana-bhojaneṣhu

eko "tha vāpy achyuta tat-samakṣhaṁ
tat kṣhāmaye tvām aham aprameyam

And that You have been discourteously treated out of fun–while walking, while on a bed, while on a seat, while eating, in privacy, or, O Acyuta, even in public, for that I beg pardon of You, the incomprehensible One.

ଓ 43 ଡ଼

पितासि लोकस्य चराचरस्य त्वमस्य पूज्यश्च गुरुर्गरीयान् ।
न त्वत्समोऽस्त्यभ्यधिकः कुतोऽन्यो लोकत्रयेऽप्यप्रतिमप्रभाव ।।

pitāsi lokasya charācharasya
tvam asya pūjyaśh cha gurur garīyān
na tvat-samo "sty abhyadhikaḥ kuto "nyo
loka-traye "py apratima-prabhāva

You are the Father of all beings moving and non-moving; to this (world) You are worthy of worship, the Teacher, and greater (than a teacher). There is none equal to You; how at all can there be anyone greater even in all the three worlds, O You or unrivalled power?

☙ 44 ❧

तस्मात्प्रणम्य प्रणिधाय कायं प्रसादये त्वामहमीशमीड्यम् ।
पितेव पुत्रस्य सखेव सख्युः प्रियः प्रियायार्हसि देव सोढुम् ।।

tasmāt praṇamya praṇidhāya kāyaṁ
prasādaye tvām aham īśham īḍyam
piteva putrasya sakheva sakhyuḥ
priyaḥ priyāyārhasi deva soḍhum

Therefore, by bowing down and prostrating the body, I seek to propitiate You who are God and are adorable. O Lord, You should forgive (my faults) as would a father (the faults) of a son, as a friend, of a friend, and as a lover of a beloved.

☙ 45 ❧

अदृष्टपूर्वं हृषितोऽस्मि दृष्ट्वा भयेन च प्रव्यथितं मनो मे ।
तदेव मे दर्शय देवरूपं प्रसीद देवेश जगन्निवास ।।

adṛiṣhṭa-pūrvaṁ hṛiṣhito "smi dṛiṣhṭvā
bhayena cha pravyathitaṁ mano me
tad eva me darśhaya deva rūpaṁ
prasīda deveśha jagan-nivāsa

I am delighted by seeing something not seen heretofore, and my mind is stricken with fear. O Lord, show me that very form; O supreme God, O Abode of the Universe, be gracious!

☙ 46 ❧

किरीटिनं गदिनं चक्रहस्त. मिच्छामि त्वां द्रष्टुमहं तथैव ।
तेनैव रूपेण चतुर्भुजेन सहस्रबाहो भव विश्वमूर्ते ।।

kirīṭinaṁ gadinaṁ chakra-hastam
ichchhāmi tvāṁ draṣhṭum ahaṁ tathaiva
tenaiva rūpeṇa chatur-bhujena
sahasra-bāho bhava viśhva-mūrte

I want to see You just as before, wearing a crown, wielding a mace, and holding a disc in hand. O You with thousand arms, O You of Cosmic form, appear with that very form with four hands.

☙ 47 ❧

श्रीभगवानुवाच ।
मया प्रसन्नेन तवार्जुनेदं रूपं परं दर्शितमात्मयोगात् ।
तेजोमयं विश्वमनन्तमाद्यं यन्मे त्वदन्येन न दृष्टपूर्वम् ।।

śhrī-bhagavān uvācha
mayā prasannena tavārjunedaṁ
rūpaṁ paraṁ darśhitam ātma-yogāt

tejo-mayaṁ viśhvam anantam ādyaṁ
yan me tvad anyena na dṛiṣhṭa-pūrvam

The Blessed Lord said: Out of grace, O Arjuna, this supreme, radiant, Cosmic, infinite, primeval form- which (form) of Mine has not been seen before by anyone other than you, has been shown to you by Me through the power of My Own Yoga.

48

न वेदयज्ञाध्ययनैर्न दानै. र्न च क्रियाभिर्न तपोभिरुग्रैः ।
एवंरूपः शक्य अहं नृलोके द्रष्टुं त्वदन्येन कुरुप्रवीर ॥

na veda-yajñādhyayanair na dānair
na cha kriyābhir na tapobhir ugraiḥ
evaṁ-rūpaḥ śhakya ahaṁ nṛi-loke
draṣhṭuṁ tvad anyena kuru-pravīra

Not by the study of the Vedas and sacrifices, not by gifts, not even by rituals, not by severe austerities can I, in this form, be perceived in the human world by anyone other than you, O most valiant among the Kurus.

☙ 49 ❧

मा ते व्यथा मा च विमूढभावो दृष्ट्वा रूपं घोरमीदृङ्ममेदम् ।
व्यपेतभीः प्रीतमनाः पुनस्त्वं तदेव मेः पमिदं प्रपश्य ।।

mā te vyathā mā cha vimūḍha-bhāvo
dṛiṣhṭvā rūpaṁ ghoram īdṛiṅ mamedam
vyapeta-bhīḥ prīta-manāḥ punas tvaṁ
tad eva me rūpam idaṁ prapaśhya

May you have no fear, and may not there be bewilderment by seeing this form of Mine so terrible Becoming free from fear and gladdened in mind again, see this very earlier form of Mine.

☙ 50 ❧

सञ्जय उवाच ।
इत्यर्जुनं वासुदेवस्तथोक्त्वा स्वकंरूपं दर्शयामास भूयः ।
आश्वासयामास च भीतमेनं भूत्वा पुनः सौम्यवपुर्महात्मा ।।

sañjaya uvācha
ity arjunaṁ vāsudevas tathoktvā
svakaṁ rūpaṁ darśhayām āsa bhūyaḥ
āśhvāsayām āsa cha bhītam enaṁ
bhūtvā punaḥ saumya-vapur mahātmā

Sanjaya said: Thus, having spoken to Arjuna in that manner, Vasudeva showed His own form again. And He, the exalted One, reassured this terrified one by again becoming serene in form.

☙ 51 ❧

अर्जुन उवाच ।
दृष्ट्वेदं मानुषं पं तव सौम्यं जनार्दन ।
इदानीमस्मि संवृत्तः सचेताः प्रकृतिं गतः ।।

arjuna uvācha
dṛiṣhṭvedaṁ mānuṣhaṁ rūpaṁ tava saumyaṁ janārdana
idānīm asmi saṁvṛittaḥ sa-chetāḥ prakṛitiṁ gataḥ

Arjuna said: O Janardana, having seen this serene human form of Yours, I have now become calm in mind and restored to my own nature.

☙ 52 ❧

श्रीभगवानुवाच ।
सुदुर्दर्शमिदं रूपं दृष्टवानसि यन्मम ।
देवा अप्यस्य रूपस्य नित्यं दर्शनकाङ्क्षिणः ।।

śhrī-bhagavān uvācha
su-durdarśham idaṁ rūpaṁ dṛiṣhṭavān asi yan mama
devā apy asya rūpasya nityaṁ darśhana-kāṅkṣhiṇaḥ

The Blessed Lord said: This form of Mine which you have seen is very difficult to see; even the gods are ever desirous of a vision of this form.

ᘓ 53 ᘐ

नाहं वेदैर्न तपसा न दानेन न चेज्यया ।
शक्य एवंविधो द्रष्टुं दृष्टवानसि मां यथा ।।

nāhaṁ vedair na tapasā na
dānena na chejyayā
śhakya evaṁ-vidho drașhṭuṁ
dṛișhṭavān asi māṁ yathā

Not through the Vedas, not by austerity, not by gifts, nor even by sacrifice can I be seen in this form as you have seen Me.

ᘓ 54 ᘐ

भक्त्या त्वनन्यया शक्य अहमेवंविधोऽर्जुन ।
ज्ञातुं द्रष्टुं च तत्वेन प्रवेष्टुं च परन्तप ।।

bhaktyā tv ananyayā śhakya
aham evaṁ-vidho "rjuna
jñātuṁ drașhṭuṁ cha tattvena
praveșhṭuṁ cha parantapa

But, O Arjuna, by single-minded devotion am I, in this form, able to be known and seen in reality, and also be entered into, O destroyer of foes.

55

मत्कर्मकृन्मत्परमो मद्भक्तः सङ्गवर्जितः ।
निर्वैरः सर्वभूतेषु यः स मामेति पाण्डव ॥

mat-karma-kṛin mat-paramo
mad-bhaktaḥ saṅga-varjitaḥ
nirvairaḥ sarva-bhūteṣhu yaḥ
sa mām eti pāṇḍava

O son of Pandu, he who works for Me, accepts Me as the supreme Goal, is devoted to Me, is devoid of attachment and free from enmity towards all beings-he attains Me.

Chapter 12

Bhakti Yoga
The Yoga of Devotion

ꕥ 1 ꕥ

अर्जुन उवाच ।
एवं सततयुक्ता ये भक्तास्त्वां पर्युपासते ।
ये चाप्यक्षरमव्यक्तं तेषां के योगवित्तमाः ।।

arjuna uvācha
evaṁ satata-yuktā ye bhaktās tvāṁ paryupāsate
ye chāpy akṣharam avyaktaṁ teṣhāṁ ke yoga-vittamāḥ

Arjuna said: Those devotees who, being thus ever dedicated, meditate on You, and those again (who meditate) on the Immutable, the Unmanifested of them, who are the best experiencers of yoga.

ꕥ 2 ꕥ

श्रीभगवानुवाच ।
मय्यावेश्य मनो ये मां नित्ययुक्ता उपासते ।
श्रद्धया परयोपेतास्ते मे युक्ततमा मताः ।।

śhrī-bhagavān uvācha
mayy āveśhya mano ye māṁ nitya-yuktā upāsate
śhraddhayā parayopetās te me yuktatamā matāḥ

The Blessed Lord said: Those who meditate on Me by fixing their minds on Me with steadfast devotion (and) being endowed with supreme faith–they are considered to be the most perfect yogis according to Me.

ଓ 3 ଃ

ये त्वक्षरमनिर्देश्यमव्यक्तं पर्युपासते ।
सर्वत्रगमचिन्त्यञ्च कूटस्थमचलन्ध्रुवम् ।।

ଓ 4 ଃ

सन्नियम्येन्द्रियग्रामं सर्वत्र समबुद्धयः ।
ते प्राप्नुवन्ति मामेव सर्वभूतहिते रताः ।।

ye tv akṣharam anirdeśhyam avyaktaṁ paryupāsate
sarvatra-gam achintyañcha kūṭa-stham achalandhruvam

sanniyamyendriya-grāmaṁ sarvatra sama-buddhayaḥ
te prāpnuvanti mām eva sarva-bhūta-hite ratāḥ

Those, however, who meditate in every way on the Immutable, the Indefinable, the Unmanifest, which is all-pervading, incomprehensible, change-less, immovable and constant. By fully controlling all the organs and always being even-minded, they, engaged in the welfare of all beings, attain Me alone.

☙ 5 ❧

क्लेशोऽधिकतरस्तेषामव्यक्तासक्तचेतसाम् ।
अव्यक्ता हि गतिर्दुखं देहवद्भिरवाप्यते ।।

kleśho "dhikataras teṣhām
avyaktāsakta-chetasām
avyaktā hi gatir duḥkhaṁ
dehavadbhir avāpyate

For them who have their minds attached to the Unmanifested the struggle is greater; for, the Goal which is the Unmanifest is attained with difficulty by the embodied ones.

☙ 6 ❧

ये तु सर्वाणि कर्माणि मयि संन्यस्य मत्परः ।
अनन्येनैव योगेन मां ध्यायन्त उपासते ।।

ye tu sarvāṇi karmāṇi mayi
sannyasya mat-paraḥ
ananyenaiva yogena
māṁ dhyāyanta upāsate

As for those who, having dedicated all actions to Me and accepted Me as the supreme, meditate by thinking of Me with single-minded concentration only.

☙ 7 ❧

तेषामहं समुद्धर्ता मृत्युसंसारसागरात् ।
भवामि नचिरात्पार्थ मय्यावेशितचेतसाम् ।।

teṣhām ahaṁ samuddhartā
mṛityu-saṁsāra-sāgarāt
bhavāmi na chirāt pārtha
mayy āveśhita-chetasām

O son of Partha, for them who have their minds absorbed in Me, I become, without delay, the Deliverer from the sea of the world which is fraught with death.

☙ 8 ❧

मय्येव मन आधत्स्व मयि बुद्धिं निवेशय ।
निवसिष्यसि मय्येव अत ऊर्ध्वं न संशयः ।।

mayy eva mana ādhatsva
mayi buddhiṁ niveśhaya
nivasiṣhyasi mayy eva ata
ūrdhvaṁ na sanśhayaḥ

Fix the mind on Me alone; in Me alone rest the intellect. There is no doubt that hereafter you will dwell in Me alone.

ଓ 9 ଷ

अथ चित्तं समाधातुं न शक्नोषि मयि स्थिरम् ।
अभ्यासयोगेन ततो मामिच्छाप्तुं धनञ्जय ॥

atha chittaṁ samādhātuṁ na śhaknoṣhi mayi sthiram
abhyāsa-yogena tato mām ichchhāptuṁ dhanañjaya

If, however, you are unable to establish the mind steadily on Me, then, O Dhananjaya, seek to attain Me through the Yoga of Practice.

ଓ 10 ଷ

अभ्यासेऽप्यसमर्थोऽसि मत्कर्मपरमो भव ।
मदर्थमपि कर्माणि कुर्वन्सिद्धिमवाप्स्यसि ॥

abhyāse "py asamartho "si mat-karma-paramo bhava
mad-artham api karmāṇi kurvan siddhim avāpsyasi

If you are unable even to practise, be intent on works for Me. By undertaking works for Me as well, you will attain perfection.

11

अथैतदप्यशक्तोऽसि कर्तुं मद्योगमाश्रितः ।
सर्वकर्मफलत्यागं ततः कुरु यतात्मवान् ॥

athaitad apy aśhakto "si k
artuṁ mad-yogam āśhritaḥ
sarva-karma-phala-tyāgaṁ tataḥ
kuru yatātmavān

If you are unable to do even this, in that case, having resorted to the Yoga for Me, thereafter renounce the results of all works by becoming controlled in mind.

12

श्रेयो हि ज्ञानमभ्यासाज्ज्ञानाद्ध्यानं विशिष्यते ।
ध्यानात्कर्मफलत्यागस्त्यागाच्छान्तिरनन्तरम् ॥

śhreyo hi jñānam abhyāsāj
jñānād dhyānaṁ viśhiṣhyate
dhyānāt karma-phala-tyāgas
tyāgāch chhāntir anantaram

Knowledge is surely superior to practice; meditation surpasses knowledge. The renunciation of the results of works (excels) meditation. From renunciation, Peace follows immediately.

13

अद्वेष्टा सर्वभूतानां मैत्रः करुण एव च ।
निर्ममो निरहङ्कारः समदुःखसुखः क्षमी ।।

adveṣhṭā sarva-bhūtānāṁ maitraḥ karuṇa eva cha
nirmamo nirahankāraḥ sama-duḥkha-sukhaḥ kṣhamī

He who is not hateful towards any creature, who is friendly and compassionate, who has no idea of 'mine' and the idea of egoism, who is the same under sorrow and happiness, who is forgiving.

14

सन्तुष्टः सततं योगी यतात्मा दृढनिश्चयः ।
मय्यर्पितमनोबुद्धिर्यो मद्भक्तः स मे प्रियः ।।

santuṣhṭaḥ satataṁ yogī
yatātmā dṛiḍha-niśhchayaḥ
mayy arpita-mano-buddhir yo
mad-bhaktaḥ sa me priyaḥ

He who is ever content, who is a yogi, who has self-control, who has firm conviction, who has dedicated his mind and intellect to Me–he who is such a devotee of Mine is dear to Me.

ঌ 15 ৡ

यस्मान्नोद्विजते लोको लोकान्नोद्विजते च यः ।
हर्षामर्षभयोद्वेगैर्मुक्तो यः स च मे प्रियः ।।

yasmān nodvijate loko
lokān nodvijate cha yaḥ
harṣhāmarṣha-bhayodvegair mukto
yaḥ sa cha me priyaḥ

He, too, owing to whom the world is not disturbed, and who is not disturbed by the world, who is free from joy, impatience, fear and anxiety, is dear to Me.

ঌ 16 ৡ

अनपेक्षः शुचिर्दक्ष उदासीनो गतव्यथः ।
सर्वारम्भपरित्यागी यो मद्भक्तः स मे प्रियः ।।

anapekṣhaḥ śhuchir dakṣha
udāsīno gata-vyathaḥ
sarvārambha-parityāgī yo
mad-bhaktaḥ sa me priyaḥ

He who has no desires, who is pure, who is dextrous, who is impartial, who is free from fear, who has renounced every undertaking–he who is (such) a devotee of Mine is dear to Me.

☙ 17 ❧

योो न हृष्यति न द्वेष्टि न शोचति न काङ्क्षति ।
शुभाशुभपरित्यागी भक्तिमान्यः स मे प्रियः ।।

yo na hṛiṣhyati na dveṣhṭi
na śhochati na kāṅkṣhati
śhubhāśhubha-parityāgī
bhaktimān yaḥ sa me priyaḥ

He who does not rejoice, does not fret, does not lament, does not hanker; who gives up good and bad, who is filled with devotion–he is dear to Me.

☙ 18 ❧

समः शत्रौ च मित्रे च तथा मानापमानयोः ।
शीतोष्णसुखदुःखेषु समः सङ्गविवर्जितः ।।

samaḥ śhatrau cha mitre cha
tathā mānāpamānayoḥ
śhītoṣhṇa-sukha-duḥkheṣhu
samaḥ saṅga-vivarjitaḥ

He who is the same towards friend and foe, and so also in honour and dishonour; who is the same under cold, heat, happiness and sorrow, who is free from attachment to everything.

19

तुल्यनिन्दास्तुतिर्मौनी सन्तुष्टो येन केनचित् ।
अनिकेतः स्थिरमतिर्भक्तिमान्मे प्रियो नरः ॥

tulya-nindā-stutir maunī santuṣhṭo yena kenachit
aniketaḥ sthira-matir bhaktimān me priyo naraḥ

The person to whom denunciation and praise are the same, who is silent, content with anything, homeless, steady-minded, and full of devotion is dear to Me.

20

ये तु धर्म्यामृतमिदं यथोक्तं पर्युपासते ।
श्रद्दधाना मत्परमा भक्तास्तेऽतीव मे प्रियाः ॥

ye tu dharmyāmṛitam idaṁ yathoktaṁ paryupāsate
śhraddadhānā mat-paramā bhaktās te "tīva me priyāḥ

But [Tu (but) is used to distinguish those who have attained the highest Goal from the aspirants.] those devotees who accept Me as the supreme Goal, and with faith seek for this ambrosia which is indistinguishable from the virtues as stated above, they are very dear to Me.

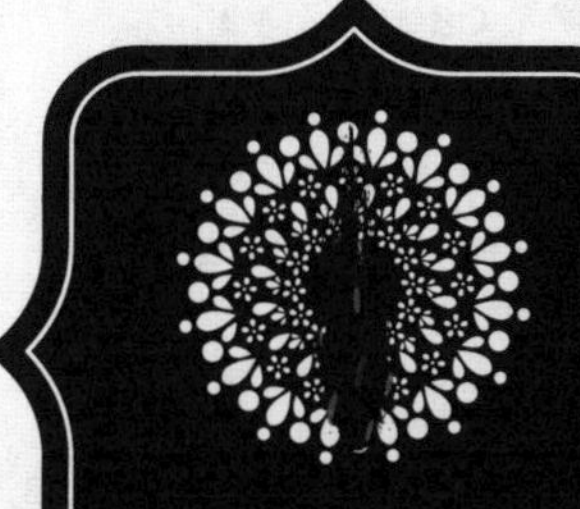

Chapter 13

Ksetra Ksetrajna Vibhaga Yoga

Yoga through Distinguishing the Field and the Knower of the Field

ꕥ 1 ꕥ

अर्जुन उवाच ।
प्रकृतिं पुरुषं चैव क्षेत्रं क्षेत्रज्ञमेव च ।
एतद्वेदितुमिच्छामि ज्ञानं ज्ञेयं च केशव ।।

arjuna uvācha
prakṛitiṁ puruṣhaṁ chaiva
kṣhetraṁ kṣhetra-jñam eva cha
etad veditum ichchhāmi jñānaṁ
jñeyaṁ cha keśhava

Arjun said: O Keshav, I wish to understand what are prakriti and purush, and what are kshetra and kshetrayajna (knower of the field)? I also wish to know what true knowledge is, and what is the goal of this knowledge?

ꕥ 2 ꕥ

श्रीभगवानुवाच ।
इदं शरीरं कौन्तेय क्षेत्रमित्यभिधीयते ।
एतद्यो वेत्ति तं प्राहुः क्षेत्रज्ञ इति तद्विदः ।।

śhrī-bhagavān uvācha
idaṁ śharīraṁ kaunteya kṣhetram ity abhidhīyate
etad yo vetti taṁ prāhuḥ kṣhetra-jña iti tad-vidaḥ

The Blessed Lord said: O son of Kunti, this body is referred to as the 'field'. Those who are versed in this call him who is conscious of it as the 'knower of the field.'

∞ 3 ∞

क्षेत्रज्ञं चापि मां विद्धि सर्वक्षेत्रेषु भारत ।
क्षेत्रक्षेत्रज्ञयोर्ज्ञानं यत्तज्ज्ञानं मतं मम ।।

kṣhetra-jñaṁ chāpi māṁ viddhi
sarva-kṣhetreṣhu bhārata
kṣhetra-kṣhetrajñayor jñānaṁ
yat taj jñānaṁ mataṁ mama

And, O scion of the Bharata dynasty, understand Me to be the 'Knower of the field' in all the fields. In My opinion, that is Knowledge which is the knowledge of the field and the knower of the field.

ଓ 4 ଌ

तत्क्षेत्रं यच्च यादृक्च यद्विकारि यतश्च यत् ।
स च यो यत्प्रभावश्च तत्समासेन मे शृणु ।।

tat kṣhetraṁ yach cha yādṛik cha
yad-vikāri yataśh cha yat
sa cha yo yat-prabhāvaśh cha
tat samāsena me śhṛiṇu

Hear from Me in brief about (all) that as to what that field is and how it is; what its changes are, and from what cause arises what effect; and who He is, and what His powers are.

ଓ 5 ଌ

ऋषिभिर्बहुधा गीतं छन्दोभिर्विविधैः पृथक् ।
ब्रह्मसूत्रपदैश्चैव हेतुमद्भिर्विनिश्चितैः ।।

ṛiṣhibhir bahudhā gītaṁ
chhandobhir vividhaiḥ pṛithak
brahma-sūtra-padaiśh chaiva
hetumadbhir viniśhchitaiḥ

It has been sung of in various ways by the Rishis, separately by the different kinds [the different branches of Vedic texts] of Vedic texts, and also by the rational and convincing sentences themselves which are indicative of and lead to Brahman.

ꕤ 6 ꕤ

महाभूतान्यङ्ककारो बुद्धिरव्यक्त मेव च ।
इन्द्रियाणि दशैकं च पञ्च चेन्द्रियगोचराः ।।

mahā-bhūtāny ahankāro
buddhir avyaktam eva cha
indriyāṇi daśhaikaṁ cha
pañcha chendriya-gocharāḥ

The great elements, egoism, intellect and the Unmanifest itself; the ten organs and the one, and the five objects of the senses;

ꕤ 7 ꕤ

इच्छा द्वेषः सुखं दुःखं सङ्घातश्चेतना धृतिः ।
एतत्क्षेत्रं समासेन सविकारमुदाहृतम् ।।

ichchhā dveṣhaḥ sukhaṁ duḥkhaṁ
saṅghātaśh chetanā dhṛitiḥ
etat kṣhetraṁ samāsena
sa-vikāram udāhṛitam

Desire, repulsion, happiness, sorrow, the aggregate (of body and organs), sentience, fortitude– this field, together with its modifications, has been spoken of briefly.

ᗢ 8 ᗣ

अमानित्वमदम्भित्वमहिंसा क्षान्तिरार्जवम् ।
आचार्योपासनं शौचं स्थैर्यमात्मविनिग्रहः ॥

amānitvam adambhitvam ahinsā kṣhāntir ārjavam
āchāryopāsanaṁ śhauchaṁ sthairyam ātma-vinigrahaḥ

Humility, unpretentiousness, non-injury, for–bearance, sincerity, service of the teacher, cleanliness, steadiness, control of body and organs;

ᗢ 9 ᗣ

इन्द्रियार्थेषु वैराग्यमनहङ्कार एव च ।
जन्ममृत्युजराव्याधिदुःखदोषानुदर्शनम् ॥

indriyārtheṣhu vairāgyam anahankāra eva cha
janma-mṛityu-jarā-vyādhi-duḥkha-doṣhānudarśhanam

Non-attachment with regard to objects of the senses, and also absence of egotism; seeing the evil in birth, death, old age, diseases and miseries;

☙ 10 ❧

असक्तिरनभिष्वङ्गः पुत्रदारगृहादिषु ।
नित्यं च समचित्तत्वमिष्टानिष्टोपपत्तिषु ।।

asaktir anabhiṣhvaṅgaḥ
putra-dāra-gṛihādiṣhu
nityaṁ cha sama-chittatvam
iṣhṭāniṣhṭopapattiṣhu

Non-attachment and absence of fondness with regard to sons, wives, homes, etc., and constant equanimity of the mind with regard to the attainment of the desirable and the undesirable;

☙ 11 ❧

मयि चानन्ययोगेन भक्तिरव्यभिचारिणी ।
विविक्तदेशसेवित्वमरतिर्जनसंसदि ।।

mayi chānanya-yogena
bhaktir avyabhichāriṇī
vivikta-deśha-sevitvam
aratir jana-sansadi

And unwavering devotion to Me with single-minded concentration; inclination to repair into a clean place; lack of delight in a crowd of people;

☙ 12 ❧

अध्यात्मज्ञाननित्यत्वं तत्वज्ञानार्थदर्शनम् ।
एतज्ज्ञानमिति प्रोक्तमज्ञानं यदतोऽन्यथा ।।

adhyātma-jñāna-nityatvaṁ
tattva-jñānārtha-darśhanam
etaj jñānam iti proktam ajñānaṁ
yad ato "nyathā

Steadfastness in the knowledge of the Self, contemplation on the Goal of the knowledge of Reality–this is spoken of as Knowledge. Ignorance is that which is other than this.

☙ 13 ❧

ज्ञेयं यत्तत्प्रवक्ष्यामि यज्ज्ञात्वामृतमश्नुते ।
अनादिमत्परं ब्रह्म न सत्तन्नासदुच्यते ।।

jñeyaṁ yat tat pravakṣhyāmi yaj jñātvāmṛitam aśhnute
anādi mat-paraṁ brahma na sat tan nāsad uchyate

I shall speak of that which is to be known, by realizing which one attains Immortality. The supreme Brahman is without any beginning. That is called neither being nor non-being.

∽ 14 ∼

सर्वतः पाणिपादं तत्सर्वतोऽक्षिशिरोमुखम् ।
सर्वतः श्रुतिमल्लोके सर्वमावृत्य तिष्ठति ।।

sarvataḥ pāṇi-pādaṁ tat
sarvato "kṣhi-śhiro-mukham
sarvataḥ śhrutimal loke
sarvam āvṛitya tiṣhṭhati

That (Knowable), which has hands and feet everywhere, which has eyes, heads and mouths everywhere, which has ears everywhere, exists in creatures by pervading them all.

∽ 15 ∼

सर्वेन्द्रियगुणाभासं सर्वेन्द्रियविवर्जितम् ।
असक्तं सर्वभृच्चैव निर्गुणं गुणभोक्तृ च ।।

sarvendriya-guṇābhāsaṁ sarvendriya-vivarjitam
asaktaṁ sarva-bhṛich chaiva nirguṇaṁ guṇa-bhoktṛi cha

Shining through the functions of all the organs, (yet) devoid of all the organs; unattached, and verily the supporter of all; without quality, and the perceiver of qualities;

☙ 16 ❧

बहिरन्तश्च भूतानामचरं चरमेव च ।
सूक्ष्मत्वात्तदविज्ञेयं दूरस्थं चान्तिके च तत् ॥

bahir antaśh cha bhūtānām
acharaṁ charam eva cha
sūkṣhmatvāt tad avijñeyaṁ
dūra-sthaṁ chāntike cha tat

Existing outside and inside all beings; moving as well as non-moving, It is incomprehensible due to subtleness. So also, It is far away, and yet near.

☙ 17 ❧

अविभक्तं च भूतेषु विभक्तमिव च स्थितम् ।
भूतभर्तृ च तज्ज्ञेयं ग्रसिष्णु प्रभविष्णु च ॥

avibhaktaṁ cha bhūteṣhu
vibhaktam iva cha sthitam
bhūta-bhartṛi cha taj jñeyaṁ
grasiṣhṇu prabhaviṣhṇu cha

And the Knowable, though undivided, appears to be existing as divided in all beings, and It is the sustainer of all beings as also the devourer and originator.

☙ 18 ❧

ज्योतिषामपि तज्ज्योतिस्तमसः परमुच्यते ।
ज्ञानं ज्ञेयं ज्ञानगम्यं हृदि सर्वस्य विष्ठितम् ।।

jyotiṣhām api taj jyotis
tamasaḥ param uchyate
jñānaṁ jñeyaṁ jñāna-gamyaṁ
hṛidi sarvasya viṣhṭhitam

That is the Light even of the lights; It is spoken of as beyond darkness. It is Knowledge, the Knowable, and the Known. It exists specially in the hearts of all.

☙ 19 ❧

इति क्षेत्रं तथा ज्ञानं ज्ञेयं चैक्तं समासतः ।
मद्भक्त एतद्विज्ञाय मद्भावायोपपद्यते ।।

iti kṣhetraṁ tathā jñānaṁ
jñeyaṁ choktaṁ samāsataḥ
mad-bhakta etad vijñāya
mad-bhāvāyopapadyate

Thus has been spoken of in brief the field as also Knowledge and the Knowable. By understanding this My devotee becomes qualified for My state.

☙ 20 ❧

प्रकृतिं पुरुषं चैव विद्ध्यनादी उभावपि ।
विकारांश्च गुणांश्चैव विद्धि प्रकृतिसम्भवान् ।।

prakṛitiṁ puruṣhaṁ chaiva
viddhy anādī ubhāv api
vikārānśh cha guṇānśh chaiva
viddhi prakṛiti-sambhavān

Know both Nature and also the individual soul to be verily without beginning; know the modifications as also the qualities as born of Nature.

☙ 21 ❧

कार्यकारणकर्तृत्वे हेतुः प्रकृतिरुच्यते ।
पुरुषः सुखदुःखानां भोक्तृत्वे हेतुरुच्यते ।।

kārya-kāraṇa-kartṛitve
hetuḥ prakṛitir uchyate
puruṣhaḥ sukha-duḥkhānāṁ
bhoktṛitve hetur uchyate

With regard to the source of body and organs, Nature is said to be the cause. The soul is the cause so far as enjoyer-ship of happiness and sorrow is concerned.

☙ 22 ❧

पुरुषः प्रकृतिस्थो हि भुङ्क्ते प्रकृतिजान्गुणान् ।
कारणं गुणसङ्गोऽस्य सदसद्योनिजन्मसु ॥

puruṣhaḥ prakṛiti-stho hi
bhuṅkte prakṛiti-jān guṇān
kāraṇaṁ guṇa-saṅgo "sya
sad-asad-yoni-janmasu

Since the soul is seated in Nature, therefore it experiences the qualities born of Nature. Contact with the qualities is the cause of its births in good and evil wombs.

☙ 23 ❧

उपद्रष्टानुमन्ता च भर्ता भोक्ता महेश्वरः ।
परमात्मेति चाप्युक्तो देहेऽस्मिन्पुरुषः परः ॥

upadraṣhṭānumantā cha bhartā
bhoktā maheśhvaraḥ
paramātmeti chāpy ukto
dehe "smin puruṣhaḥ paraḥ

He who is the Witness, the Permitter, the Sustainer, the Experiencer, the great Lord, and who is also spoken of as the transcendental Self is the supreme Person in this body.

∽ 24 ∾

य एवं वेत्ति पुरुषं प्रकृतिं च गुणैः सह ।
सर्वथा वर्तमानोऽपि न स भूयोऽभिजायते ।।

ya evaṁ vetti puruṣhaṁ
prakṛitiṁ cha guṇaiḥ saha
sarvathā vartamāno "pi
na sa bhūyo "bhijāyate

He who knows thus the Person and Nature along with the qualities will not be born again, in whatever way he may live.

∽ 25 ∾

ध्यानेनात्मनि पश्यन्ति केचिदात्मानमात्मना ।
अन्ये साङ् ख्येन योगेन कर्मयोगेन चापरे ।।

dhyānenātmani paśhyanti
kechid ātmānam ātmanā
anye sānkhyena yogena
karma-yogena chāpare

Through meditation some realize the Self in (their) intellect with the help of the internal organs; others through Sankhya-yoga, and others through Karma-yoga.

26

अन्ये त्वेवमजानन्तः श्रुत्वान्येभ्य उपासते ।
तेऽपि चातितरन्त्येव मृत्युं श्रुतिपरायणाः ।।

anye tv evam ajānantaḥ
śhrutvānyebhya upāsate
te "pi chātitaranty eva
mṛityuṁ śhruti-parāyaṇāḥ

Others, again, who do not know thus, take to thinking after hearing from others; they, too, who are devoted to hearing, certainly overcome death.

27

यावत्सञ्जायते किञ्चित्सत्त्वं स्थावरजङ्गमम् ।
क्षेत्रक्षेत्रज्ञसंयोगात्तद्विद्धि भरतर्षभ ।।

yāvat sañjāyate kiñchit sattvaṁ
sthāvara-jaṅgamam
kṣhetra-kṣhetrajña-sanyogāt
tad viddhi bharatarṣhabha

O scion of the Bharata dynasty, whatever object, moving or non-moving, comes into being, know that to be from the association of the field and the Knower of the field!

28

समं सर्वेषु भूतेषु तिष्ठन्तं परमेश्वरम् ।
विनश्यत्स्वविनश्यन्तं यः पश्यति स पश्यति ।।

samaṁ sarveṣhu bhūteṣhu
tiṣhṭhantaṁ parameśhvaram
vinaśhyatsv avinaśhyantaṁ
yaḥ paśhyati sa paśhyati

He sees who sees the supreme Lord as existing equally in all beings, and as the Imperishable among the perishable.

29

समं पश्यन्हि सर्वत्र समवस्थितमीश्वरम् ।
न हिनस्त्यात्मनात्मानं ततो याति परां गतिम् ।।

samaṁ paśhyan hi sarvatra
samavasthitam īśhvaram
na hinasty ātmanātmānaṁ
tato yāti parāṁ gatim

Since by seeing equally God who is present alike everywhere he does not injure the Self by the Self, therefore he attains the supreme Goal.

◌ 30 ◌

प्रकृत्यैव च कर्माणि क्रियमाणानि सर्वशः ।
यः पश्यति तथात्मानमकर्तारं स पश्यति ।।

prakṛityaiva cha karmāṇi
kriyamāṇāni sarvaśhaḥ
yaḥ paśhyati tathātmānam
akartāraṁ sa paśhyati

And he who sees actions as being done in various ways by Nature itself, and also the Self as the non-agent, he sees.

◌ 31 ◌

यदा भूतपृथग्भावमेकस्थमनुपश्यति ।
तत एव च विस्तारं ब्रह्म सम्पद्यते तदा ।।

yadā bhūta-pṛithag-bhāvam
eka-stham anupaśhyati
tata eva cha vistāraṁ
brahma sampadyate tadā

When one realizes that the state of diversity of living things is rooted in the One, and that their manifestation is also from That, then one becomes identified with Brahman.

ଓ 32 ଛ

अनादित्वान्निर्गुणत्वात्परमात्मायमव्ययः ।
शरीरस्थोऽपि कौन्तेय न करोति न लिप्यते ।।

anāditvān nirguṇatvāt
paramātmāyam avyayaḥ
śharīra-stho "pi kaunteya
na karoti na lipyate

Being without beginning and without qualities, O son of Kunti, this immutable, supreme Self does not act nor is It affected, although existing in the body.

ଓ 33 ଛ

यथा सर्वगतं सौक्ष्म्यादाकाशं नोपलिप्यते ।
सर्वत्रावस्थितो देहे तथात्मा नोपलिप्यते ।।

yathā sarva-gataṁ saukṣhmyād
ākāśhaṁ nopalipyate
sarvatrāvasthito dehe
tathātmā nopalipyate

As the all-pervading space is not defiled, because of its subtlety, similarly the Self, present everywhere in the body, is not defiled.

ॐ 34 ॐ

यथा प्रकाशयत्येकः कृत्स्नं लोकमिमं रविः ।
क्षेत्रं क्षेत्री तथा कृत्स्नं प्रकाशयति भारत ।।

yathā prakāśhayaty ekaḥ kṛitsnaṁ lokam imaṁ raviḥ
kṣhetraṁ kṣhetrī tathā kṛitsnaṁ prakāśhayati bhārata

As the single sun illumines this whole world, similarly, O descendant of the Bharata dynasty, the Knower of the field illumines the whole field.

ॐ 35 ॐ

क्षेत्रक्षेत्रज्ञयोरेवमन्तरं ज्ञानचक्षुषा ।
भूतप्रकृतिमोक्षं च ये विदुर्यान्ति ते परम् ।।

kṣhetra-kṣhetrajñayor evam
antaraṁ jñāna-chakṣhuṣhā
bhūta-prakṛiti-mokṣhaṁ cha
ye vidur yānti te param

Those who know thus through the eye of wisdom the distinction between the field and the Knower of the field, and the annihilation of the Matrix of beings, they reach the Supreme.

Chapter 14

Gunatraya Vibhaga Yoga Three Modes of Material Nature and Yoga

ꕥ 1 ꕥ

श्रीभगवानुवाच ।
परं भूयः प्रवक्ष्यामि ज्ञानानां ज्ञानमुत्तमम् ।
यज्ज्ञात्वा मुनयः सर्वे परां सिद्धिमितो गताः ।।

śhrī-bhagavān uvācha
paraṁ bhūyaḥ pravakṣhyāmi
jñānānāṁ jñānam uttamam
yaj jñātvā munayaḥ sarve
parāṁ siddhim ito gatāḥ

The Blessed Lord said: I shall speak again of the supreme Knowledge, the best of all knowledges, by realizing which all the contemplatives reached the highest Perfection from here.

ꕥ 2 ꕥ

इदं ज्ञानमुपाश्रित्य मम साधर्म्यमागताः ।
सर्गेऽपि नोपजायन्ते प्रलये न व्यथन्ति च ।।

idaṁ jñānam upāśhritya mama sādharmyam āgatāḥ
sarge "pi nopajāyante pralaye na vyathanti cha

Those who attain identity with Me by resorting of this Knowledge are not born even during creation, nor do they suffer pain during dissolution.

☙ 3 ❧

मम योनिर्महद् ब्रह्म तस्मिन्गर्भं दधाम्यहम् ।
सम्भवः सर्वभूतानां ततो भवति भारत ।।

mama yonir mahad brahma
tasmin garbhaṁ dadhāmy aham
sambhavaḥ sarva-bhūtānāṁ
tato bhavati bhārata

My womb is the great-sustainer. In that I place the seed. From that, O scion of the Bharata dynasty, occurs the birth of all things.

☙ 4 ❧

सर्वयोनिषु कौन्तेय मूर्तयः सम्भवन्ति याः ।
तासां ब्रह्म महद्योनिरहं बीजप्रदः पिता ।।

sarva-yoniṣhu kaunteya
mūrtayaḥ sambhavanti yāḥ
tāsāṁ brahma mahad yonir ahaṁ
bīja-pradaḥ pitā

O son of Kunti, whatever forms are born from all the wombs, of them the great-sustainer is the womb; I am the father who deposits the seed.

☙ 5 ❧

सत्वं रजस्तम इति गुणाः प्रकृतिसम्भवाः ।
निबध्नन्ति महाबाहो देहे देहिनमव्ययम् ।।

sattvaṁ rajas tama iti guṇāḥ
prakṛiti-sambhavāḥ
nibadhnanti mahā-bāho
dehe dehinam avyayam

O mighty-armed one, the qualities, viz sattva, rajas and tamas, born of Nature, being the immutable embodies being to the body.

☙ 6 ❧

तत्र सत्वं निर्मलत्वात्प्रकाशकमनामयम् ।
सुखसङ्गेन बध्नाति ज्ञानसङ्गेन चानघ ।।

tatra sattvaṁ nirmalatvāt
prakāśhakam anāmayam
sukha-saṅgena badhnāti
jñāna-saṅgena chānagha

Among them, sattva, being pure is an illuminator and is harmless. O sinless one, it binds through attachment to happiness and attachment to knowledge.

☙ 7 ❧

रजो रागात्मकं विद्धि तृष्णासङ्गसमुद्भवम् ।
तन्निबध्नाति कौन्तेय कर्मसङ्गेन देहिनम् ।।

rajo rāgātmakaṁ viddhi
tṛiṣhṇā-saṅga-samudbhavam
tan nibadhnāti kaunteya
karma-saṅgena dehinam

Know rajas to be of the nature of passion, born of hankering and attachment. O son of Kunti, that binds the embodied one through attachment to action.

☙ 8 ❧

तमस्त्वज्ञानजं विद्धि मोहनं सर्वदेहिनाम् ।
प्रमादालस्यनिद्राभिस्तन्निबध्नाति भारत ।।

tamas tv ajñāna-jaṁ viddhi
mohanaṁ sarva-dehinām
pramādālasya-nidrābhis
tan nibadhnāti bhārata

On the other hand, know tamas, which deludes all embodied beings, to be born of ignorance. O scion of the Bharata dynasty, that binds through inadvertence, laziness and sleep.

ᨖ 9 ᨗ

सत्वं सुखे सञ्जयति रजः कर्मणि भारत ।
ज्ञानमावृत्य तु तमः प्रमादे सञ्जयत्युत ।।

sattvaṁ sukhe sañjayati
rajaḥ karmaṇi bhārata
jñānam āvṛitya tu tamaḥ
pramāde sañjayaty uta

O scion of the Bharata dynasty, sattva attaches one to happiness, rajas to action, while tamas, covering up knowledge, leads to inadvertence also.

ᨖ 10 ᨗ

रजस्तमश्चाभिभूय सत्वं भवति भारत ।
रजः सत्वं तमश्चैव तमः सत्वं रजस्तथा ।।

rajas tamaśh chābhibhūya
sattvaṁ bhavati bhārata
rajaḥ sattvaṁ tamaśh chaiva
tamaḥ sattvaṁ rajas tathā

O scion of the Bharata dynasty, sattva increases by subduing rajas and tamas, rajas by overpowering sattva and tamas, and tamas by dominating over sattva and rajas.

௸ 11 ௸

सर्वद्वारेषु देहेऽस्मिन्प्रकाश उपजायते ।
ज्ञानं यदा तदा विद्याद्विवृद्धं सत्वमित्युत ।।

sarva-dvāreṣhu
dehe "smin prakāśha upajāyate
jñānaṁ yadā tadā vidyād
vivṛiddhaṁ sattvam ity uta

When the illumination that is knowledge radiates in this body through all the doors (of the senses), then one should know that sattva has increased greatly.

௸ 12 ௸

लोभः प्रवृत्तिरारम्भः कर्मणामशमः स्पृहा ।
रजस्येतानि जायन्ते विवृद्धे भरतर्षभ ।।

lobhaḥ pravṛittir ārambhaḥ
karmaṇām aśhamaḥ spṛihā
rajasy etāni jāyante
vivṛiddhe bharatarṣhabha

O best of the Bharata dynasty, when rajas becomes predominant, these come into being: avarice, movement, undertaking of actions, unrest and hankering.

☙ 13 ❧

अप्रकाशोऽप्रवृत्तिश्च प्रमादो मोह एव च ।
तमस्येतानि जायन्ते विवृद्धे कुरुनन्दन ।।

aprakāśho "pravṛittiśh cha
pramādo moha eva cha
tamasy etāni jāyante
vivṛiddhe kuru-nandana

O descendant of the Kuru dynasty, when tamas predominates these surely come into being: non-discrimination and inactivity, inadvertence and delusion.

☙ 14 ❧

यदा सत्वे प्रवृद्धे तु प्रलयं याति देहभृत् ।
तदोत्तमविदां लोकानमलान्प्रतिपद्यते ।।

yadā sattve pravṛiddhe tu
pralayaṁ yāti deha-bhṛit
tadottama-vidāṁ lokān
amalān pratipadyate

When an embodied one undergoes death while sattva is exclusively predominant, then he attains the taintless worlds of those who know the highest (entities).

☙ 15 ❧

रजसि प्रलयं गत्वा कर्मसङ्गिषु जायते ।
तथा प्रलीनस्तमसि मूढयोनिषु जायते ॥

rajasi pralayaṁ gatvā
karma-saṅgiṣhu jāyate
tathā pralīnas tamasi
mūḍha-yoniṣhu jāyate

When one dies while rajas predominates, he is born among people attached to activity. Similarly, when one dies while tamas predominates, he takes birth among the stupid species.

☙ 16 ❧

कर्मणः सुकृतस्याहुः सात्विकं निर्मलं फलम् ।
रजसस्तु फलं दुःखमज्ञानं तमसः फलम् ॥

karmaṇaḥ sukṛitasyāhuḥ
sāttvikaṁ nirmalaṁ phalam
rajasa tu phalaṁ duḥkham
ajñānaṁ tamasaḥ phalam

They say that the result of good work is pure and is born of sattva. But the result of rajas is sorrow; the result of tamas is ignorance.

ଓ 17 ଃ

सत्वात्सञ्जायते ज्ञानं रजसो लोभ एव च ।
प्रमादमोहौ तमसो भवतोऽज्ञानमेव च ॥

sattvāt sañjāyate jñānaṁ rajaso lobha eva cha
pramāda-mohau tamaso bhavato "kzñānam eva cha

From sattva is born knowledge [knowledge acquired through the sense-organs], and from rajas, verily, avarice. From tamas are born inadvertence and delusion as also ignorance, to be sure.

ଓ 18 ଃ

ऊर्ध्वं गच्छन्ति सत्वस्था मध्ये तिष्ठन्ति राजसाः ।
जघन्यगुणवृत्तिस्था अधो गच्छन्ति तामसाः ॥

ūrdhvaṁ gachchhanti sattva-sthā
madhye tiṣhṭhanti rājasāḥ
jaghanya-guṇa-vṛitti-sthā
adho gachchhanti tāmasāḥ

People who conform to sattva go higher up; those who conform to rajas stay in the middle; those who conform to tamas, who conform to the actions of the lowest quality, go down.

ଔ 19 ଓ

नान्यं गुणेभ्यः कर्तारं यदा द्रष्टानुपश्यति ।
गुणेभ्यश्च परं वेत्ति मद्भावं सोऽधिगच्छति ।।

nānyaṁ guṇebhyaḥ kartāraṁ
yadā draṣhṭānupaśhyati
guṇebhyaśh cha paraṁ vetti
mad-bhāvaṁ so "dhigachchhati

When the witness sees none other than the qualities as the agent, and knows that which is superior to the qualities, he attains My nature.

ଔ 20 ଓ

गुणानेतानतीत्य त्रीन्देही देहसमुद्भवान् ।
जन्ममृत्युजरादुःखैर्विमुक्तोऽमृतमश्नुते ।।

guṇān etān atītya trīn dehī
deha-samudbhavān
janma-mṛityu-jarā-duḥkhair
vimukto "mṛitam aśhnute

Having transcended these three qualities which are the origin of the body, the embodied one, becoming free from birth, death, old age and sorrows, experiences Immortality.

☙ 21 ❧

अर्जुन उवाच ।
कैर्लिङ्गैस्त्रीन्गुणानेतानतीतो भवति प्रभो ।
किमाचारः कथं चैतांस्त्रीन्गुणानतिवर्तते ।।

arjuna uvācha
kair liṅgais trīn guṇān etān atīto bhavati prabho
kim āchāraḥ kathaṁ chaitāns trīn guṇān ativartate

Arjuna said: O Lord, by what signs is one (known) who has gone beyond these three qualities? What is his behaviour, and how does he transcend these three qualities?

☙ 22 ❧

श्रीभगवानुवाच ।
प्रकाशं च प्रवृत्तिं च मोहमेव च पाण्डव ।
न द्वेष्टि सम्प्रवृत्तानि न निवृत्तानि काङ् क्षति ।।

śhrī-bhagavān uvācha
prakāśhaṁ cha pravṛittiṁ cha moham eva cha pāṇḍava
na dveṣhṭi sampravṛittāni na nivṛittāni kāṅkṣhati

The Blessed Lord said: O son of Pandu, he neither dislikes illumination (knowledge), activity and delusion when they appear, nor does he long for them when they disappear.

ᘛ 23 ᘚ

उदासीनवदासीनो गुणैर्यो न विचाल्यते ।
गुणा वर्तन्त इत्येवं योऽवतिष्ठति नेङ्गते ॥

udāsīna-vad āsīno guṇair yo na vichālyate
guṇā vartanta ity evaṁ yo "vatiṣhṭhati neṅgate

He who, sitting like one indifferent, is not distracted by the three qualities; he who, thinking that the qualities alone act, remains firm and surely does not move;

ᘛ 24 ᘚ

समदुःखसुखः स्वस्थः समलोष्टाश्मकाञ्चनः ।
तुल्यप्रियाप्रियो धीरस्तुल्यनिन्दात्मसंस्तुतिः ॥

sama-duḥkha-sukhaḥ sva-sthaḥ
sama-loṣhṭāśhma-kāñchanaḥ
tulya-priyāpriyo dhīras
tulya-nindātma-sanstutiḥ

He to whom sorrow and happiness are alike, who is established in his own Self, to whom a lump of earth, iron and gold are the same, to whom the agreeable and the disagreeable are the same, who is wise, to whom censure and his own praise are the same;

☙ 25 ❧

मानापमानयोस्तुल्यस्तुल्यो मित्रारिपक्षयोः ।
सर्वारम्भपरित्यागी गुणातीतः स उच्यते ।।

mānāpamānayos tulyas
tulyo mitrāri-pakṣhayoḥ
sarvārambha-parityāgī
guṇātītaḥ sa uchyate

He who is the same under honour and dishonour, who is equally disposed both towards the side of the friend and of the foe, who has renounced all enterprise–he is said to have gone beyond the qualities.

☙ 26 ❧

मां च योऽव्यभिचारेण भक्तियोगेन सेवते ।
स गुणान्समतीत्यैतान्ब्रह्मभूयाय कल्पते ।।

māṁ cha yo "vyabhichāreṇa
bhakti-yogena sevate
sa guṇān samatītyaitān
brahma-bhūyāya kalpate

And he who serves Me through the unswerving Yoga of Devotion, he, having gone beyond these qualities, qualifies for becoming Brahman.

♥ 27 ♥

ब्रह्मणो हि प्रतिष्ठाहममृतस्याव्ययस्य च ।
शाश्वतस्य च धर्मस्य सुखस्यैकान्तिकस्य च ॥

brahmaṇo hi pratiṣhṭhāham
amṛitasyāvyayasya cha
śhāśhvatasya cha dharmasya
sukhasyaikāntikasya cha

For I am the Abode of Brahman–the indestructible and immutable, the eternal, the Dharma and absolute Bliss.

Chapter 15

Purushottama Yoga
The Timeless and Transcendental Person

ଓ 1 ଡ଼

श्रीभगवानुवाच ।
ऊर्ध्वमूलमधःशाखमश्वत्थं प्राहुरव्ययम् ।
छन्दांसि यस्य पर्णानि यस्तं वेद स वेदवित् ।।

śhrī-bhagavān uvācha
ūrdhva-mūlam adhaḥ-śhākham
aśhvatthaṁ prāhur avyayam
chhandānsi yasya parṇāni
yas taṁ veda sa veda-vit

The Blessed Lord said: They say that the peepul Tree, which has its roots upward and the branches downward, and of which the Vedas are the leaves, is imperishable. He who realizes it is knower of the Vedas.

ଓ 2 ଡ଼

अधश्चैर्ध्वं प्रसृतास्तस्य शाखा गुणप्रवृद्धा विषयप्रवालाः ।
अधश्च मूलान्यनुसन्ततानि कर्मानुबन्धीनि मनुष्यलोके ।।

adhaśh chordhvaṁ prasṛitās tasya śhākhā
guṇa-pravṛiddhā viṣhaya-pravālāḥ
adhaśh cha mūlāny anusantatāni
karmānubandhīni manuṣhya-loke

The branches of that (Tree), extending downwards and upwards, are strengthened by the qualities and have sense objects, as their shoots. And the roots, which are followed by actions, spread downwards in the human world.

☙ 3 ❧

न रूपमस्येह तथोपलभ्यते नान्तो न चादिर्न च सम्प्रतिष्ठा ।
अश्वत्थमेनं सुविरूढमूल मसङ्गशस्त्रेण दृढेन छित्वा ।।

na rūpam asyeha tathopalabhyate
nānto na chādir na cha sampratiṣhṭhā
aśhvatthaṁ enaṁ su-virūḍha-mūlam
asaṅga-śhastreṇa dṛiḍhena chhittvā

Its form is not perceived here in that way; nor its end, nor beginning, nor continuance, after felling this Peepul whose roots are well developed, with the strong sword of detachment;

ᘓ 4 ᘐ

ततः पदं तत्परिमार्गितव्यं यस्मिन्गता न निवर्तन्ति भूयः ।
तमेव चाद्यं पुरुषं प्रपद्ये यतः प्रवृत्तिः प्रसृता पुराणी ।।

tataḥ padaṁ tat parimārgitavyaṁ
yasmin gatā na nivartanti bhūyaḥ
tam eva chādyaṁ puruṣhaṁ prapadye
yataḥ pravṛittiḥ prasṛitā purāṇī

Thereafter, that State has to be sought for, going where they do not return again: I take refuge in that Primeval Person Himself, from whom has ensued the eternal Manifestation.

ᘓ 5 ᘐ

निर्मानमोहा जितसङ्गदोषा अध्यात्मनित्या विनिवृत्तकामाः ।
द्वन्द्वैर्विमुक्ताः सुखदुःखसंज्ञै गच्छन्त्यमूढाः पदमव्ययं तत् ।।

nirmāna-mohā jita-saṅga-doṣhā
adhyātma-nityā vinivṛitta-kāmāḥ
dvandvair vimuktāḥ sukha-duḥkha-sanjñair
gachchhanty amūḍhāḥ padam avyayaṁ tat

The wise ones who are free from pride and non-discrimination, who have conquered the evil of association, who are ever devoted to spirituality, completely free from desires, free from the dualities called happiness and sorrow, reach that undecaying State.

6

न तद्भासयते सूर्यो न शशाङ्को न पावकः ।
यद्गत्वा न निवर्तन्ते तद्धाम परमं मम ।।

na tad bhāsayate sūryo na śhaśhāṅko na pāvakaḥ
yad gatvā na nivartante tad dhāma paramaṁ mama

Neither the sun nor the moon nor fire illumines That. That is My Supreme Abode, reaching which they do not return.

7

ममैवांशो जीवलोके जीवभूतः सनातनः ।
मनःषष्ठानीन्द्रियाणि प्रकृतिस्थानि कर्षति ।।

mamaivānśho jīva-loke jīva-bhūtaḥ sanātanaḥ
manaḥ-ṣhaṣhṭhānīndriyāṇi prakṛiti-sthāni karṣhati

It is verily a part of Mine which, becoming the eternal individual soul in the region of living beings, draws (to itself) the organs which have the mind as their sixth, and which abide in Nature.

⁂ 8 ⁂

शरीरं यदवाप्नोति यच्चाप्युत्क्रामतीश्वरः ।
गृहीत्वैतानि संयाति वायुर्गन्धानिवाशयात् ।।

śharīraṁ yad avāpnoti
yach chāpy utkrāmatīśhvaraḥ
gṛihītvaitāni sanyāti
vāyur gandhān ivāśhayāt

When the master leaves it and even when he assumes a body, he departs taking these, as wind (carries away) odours from their receptacles.

⁂ 9 ⁂

श्रोत्रं चक्षुः स्पर्शनं च रसनं घ्राणमेव च ।
अधिष्ठाय मनश्चायं विषयानुपसेवते ।।

śhrotraṁ chakṣhuḥ sparśhanaṁ cha
rasanaṁ ghrāṇam eva cha
adhiṣhṭhāya manaśh chāyaṁ
viṣhayān upasevate

This one enjoys the objects by presiding over the ear, eyes, skin and tongue as also the nose and the mind.

☙ 10 ❧

उत्क्रामन्तं स्थितं वापि भुञ्जानं वा गुणान्वितम् ।
विमूढा नानुपश्यन्ति पश्यन्ति ज्ञानचक्षुषः ।।

utkrāmantaṁ sthitaṁ vāpi
bhuñjānaṁ vā guṇānvitam
vimūḍhā nānupaśhyanti
paśhyanti jñāna-chakṣhuṣhaḥ

Persons who are diversely deluded do not see it even when it is leaving or residing (in this body), or experiencing, or in association with the qualities. Those with the eye of knowledge see.

☙ 11 ❧

यतन्तो योगिनश्चैनं पश्यन्त्यात्मन्यवस्थितम् ।
यतन्तोऽप्यकृतात्मानो नैनं पश्यन्त्यचेतसः ।।

yatanto yoginaśh chainaṁ
paśhyanty ātmany avasthitam
yatanto "py akṛitātmāno nainaṁ
paśhyanty achetasaḥ

And the yogis who are diligent see this one as existing in themselves. The non-discriminating ones who lack self-control do not see this one, though (they be) diligent.

☙ 12 ❧

यदादित्यगतं तेजो जगद्भासयतेऽखिलम् ।
यच्चन्द्रमसि यच्चाग्नौ तत्तेजो विद्धि मामकम् ।।

yad āditya-gataṁ tejo
jagad bhāsayate "khilam
yach chandramasi yach chāgnau
tat tejo viddhi māmakam

That light in the sun which illumines the whole world, that which is in the moon, and that which is in fire, know that light to be Mine.

☙ 13 ❧

गामाविश्य च भूतानि धारयाम्यहमोजसा ।
पुष्णामि चैषधीः सर्वाः सोमो भूत्वा रसात्मकः ।।

gām āviśhya cha bhūtāni
dhārayāmy aham ojasā
puṣhṇāmi chauṣhadhīḥ sarvāḥ
somo bhūtvā rasātmakaḥ

And entering the earth I sustain the beings through (My) power; and nourish all the plants by becoming Soma which is of the nature of sap.

☙ 14 ❧

अहं वैश्वानरो भूत्वा प्राणिनां देहमाश्रितः ।
प्राणापानसमायुक्तः पचाम्यन्नं चतुर्विधम् ।।

ahaṁ vaiśhvānaro bhūtvā
prāṇināṁ deham āśhritaḥ
prāṇāpāna-samāyuktaḥ
pachāmy annaṁ chatur-vidham

Taking the form of Vaisvanara and residing in the bodies of creatures, I, in association with Prana and Apana, digest the four kinds of food.

☙ 15 ❧

सर्वस्य चाहं हृदि सन्निविष्टो मत्तः स्मृतिर्ज्ञानमपोहनं च ।
वेदैश्च सर्वैरहमेव वेद्यो वेदान्तकृद्वेदविदेव चाहम् ।।

sarvasya chāhaṁ hṛidi sanniviṣhṭo
mattaḥ smṛitir jñānam apohanaṁ cha
vedaiśh cha sarvair aham eva vedyo
vedānta-kṛid veda-vid eva chāham

And I am seated in the hearts of all. From Me are memory, knowledge and their loss. I alone am the object to be known through all the Vedas; I am also the originator of the Vedanta, and I Myself am the knower of the Vedas.

☙ 16 ❧

द्वाविमौ पुरुषौ लोके क्षरश्चाक्षर एव च ।
क्षरः सर्वाणि भूतानि कूटस्थोऽक्षर उच्यते ।।

dvāv imau puruṣhau loke
kṣharaśh chākṣhara eva cha
kṣharaḥ sarvāṇi bhūtāni
kūṭa-stho "kṣhara uchyate

There are these two persons in the world–the mutable and the immutable. The mutable consists of all things; the one existing as Maya is called the immutable.

☙ 17 ❧

उत्तमः पुरुषस्त्वन्यः परमात्मेत्युदाहृतः ।
यो लोकत्रयमाविश्य बिभर्त्यव्यय ईश्वरः ।।

uttamaḥ puruṣhas tv anyaḥ
paramātmety udāhṛitaḥ
yo loka-trayam āviśhya
bibharty avyaya īśhvaraḥ

But different is the supreme Person who is spoken of as the transcendental Self, who, permeating the three worlds, upholds (them), and is the imperishable God.

☙ 18 ❧

यस्मात्क्षरमतीतोऽहमक्षरादपि चैत्तमः ।
अतोऽस्मि लोके वेदे च प्रथितः पुरुषोत्तमः ।।

yasmāt kṣharam atīto "ham
akṣharād api chottamaḥ
ato "smi loke vede cha
prathitaḥ puruṣhottamaḥ

Since I am transcendental to the mutable and above even the immutable, hence I am well known in the world and in the Vedas as the supreme Person.

☙ 19 ❧

यो मामेवमसम्मूढो जानाति पुरुषोत्तमम् ।
स सर्वविद्भजति मां सर्वभावेन भारत ।।

yo mām evam asammūḍho
jānāti puruṣhottamam
sa sarva-vid bhajati māṁ
sarva-bhāvena bhārata

O scion of the Bharata dynasty, he who, being free from delusion, knows Me the supreme Person thus, he is all-knowing and adores Me with his whole being.

❧ 20 ☙

इति गुह्यतमं शास्त्रमिदमुक्तं मयानघ ।
एतद्बुद्ध्वा बुद्धिमान्स्यात्कृतकृत्यश्च भारत ।।

iti guhyatamaṁ
śhāstram idam uktaṁ mayānagha
etad buddhvā
buddhimān syāt kṛita-kṛityaśh cha bhārata

O sinless one, this most secret scripture has thus been uttered by Me. Understanding this, one becomes wise and has his duties fulfilled, O scion of the Bharata dynasty.

Chapter
16

Daivasura Sampad Vibhaga Yoga
Dissecting the Divine and Demoniac

☙ 1 ❧

श्रीभगवानुवाच ।
अभयं सत्वसंशुद्धिर्ज्ञानयोगव्यवस्थितिः ।
दानं दमश्च यज्ञश्च स्वाध्यायस्तप आर्जवम् ।।

śhrī-bhagavān uvācha
abhayaṁ sattva-sanśhuddhir jñāna-yoga-vyavasthitiḥ
dānaṁ damaśh cha yajñaśh cha svādhyāyas tapa ārjavam

The Blessed Lord said: Fearlessness, purity of mind, persistence in knowledge and yoga, charity and control of the external organs, sacrifice, (scriptural) study, austerity and rectitude;

☙ 2 ❧

अहिंसा सत्यमक्रोधस्त्यागः शान्तिरपैशुनम् ।
दया भूतेष्वलोलुप्त्वं मार्दवं ह्रीरचापलम् ।।

ahinsā satyam akrodhas tyāgaḥ śhāntir apaiśhunam
dayā bhūteṣhv aloluptvaṁ mārdavaṁ hrīr achāpalam

Non-injury, truthfulness, absence of anger, renunciation, control of the internal organ, absence of vilification, kindness to creatures, non-covetousness, gentleness, modesty, freedom from restlessness;

ଔ 3 ଝ

तेजः क्षमा धृतिः शौचमद्रोहोनातिमानिता ।
भवन्ति सम्पदं दैवीमभिजातस्य भारत ।।

tejaḥ kṣhamā dhṛitiḥ śhaucham adroho nāti-mānitā
bhavanti sampadaṁ daivīm abhijātasya bhārata

Vigour, forgiveness, fortitude, purity, freedom from malice, absence of haughtiness–these, O scion of the Bharata dynasty, are (the qualities) of one born destined to have the divine nature.

ଔ 4 ଝ

दम्भो दर्पोऽभिमानश्च क्रोधः पारुष्यमेव च ।
अज्ञानं चाभिजातस्य पार्थ सम्पदमासुरीम् ।।

dambho darpo "bhimānaśh cha
krodhaḥ pāruṣhyam eva cha
ajñānaṁ chābhijātasya pārtha
sampadam āsurīm

O son of Partha, (the attributes) of one destined to have the demoniacal nature are religious ostentation, pride and haughtiness, anger as also rudeness and ignorance.

ꕥ 5 ꕥ

दैवी सम्पद्विमोक्षाय निबन्धायासुरी मता ।
मा शुचः सम्पदं दैवीमभिजातोऽसि पाण्डव ।।

daivī sampad vimokṣhāya
nibandhāyāsurī matā
mā śhuchaḥ sampadaṁ
daivīm abhijāto "si pāṇḍava

The divine nature is the Liberation, the demoniacal is considered to be for inevitable bondage. Do not grieve, O son of Pandu! You are destined to have the divine nature.

ꕥ 6 ꕥ

द्वौ भूतसर्गौ लोकेऽस्मिन्दैव आसुर एव च ।
दैवो विस्तरशः प्रोक्त आसुरं पार्थ मे शृणु ।।

dvau bhūta-sargau loke "smin daiva āsura eva cha
daivo vistaraśhaḥ prokta āsuraṁ pārtha me śhṛiṇu

In this world there are two (kinds of) creation of beings: the divine and the demoniacal. The divine has been spoken of elaborately. Hear about the demoniacal from Me, O son of Partha.

☙ 7 ❧

प्रवृत्तिं च निवृत्तिं च जना न विदुरासुराः ।
न शौचं नापि चाचारो न सत्यं तेषु विद्यते ॥

pravṛittiṁ cha nivṛittiṁ cha
janā na vidur āsurāḥ
na śhauchaṁ nāpi chāchāro
na satyaṁ teṣhu vidyate

Neither do the demoniacal persons understand what is to be done and what is not to be done; nor does purity, or even good conduct or truthfulness exist in them.

☙ 8 ❧

असत्यमप्रतिष्ठं ते जगदाहुरनीश्वरम् ।
अपरस्परसम्भूतं किमन्यत्कामहैतुकम् ॥

asatyam apratiṣhṭhaṁ te jagad āhur anīśhvaram
aparaspara-sambhūtaṁ kim anyat kāma-haitukam

They say that the world is unreal, it has no basis, it is without a God. It is born of mutual union brought about by passion! What other (cause can there be)?

☙ 9 ❧

एतां दृष्टिमवष्टभ्य नष्टात्मानोऽल्पबुद्धयः ।
प्रभवन्त्युग्रकर्माणः क्षयाय जगतोऽहिताः ।।

etāṁ dṛishṭim avashṭabhya
nashṭātmāno "lpa-buddhayaḥ
prabhavanty ugra-karmāṇaḥ
kshayāya jagato "hitāḥ

Holding on to this view, (these people) who are of depraved character, of poor intellect, given to fearful actions and harmful, wax strong for the ruin of the world.

☙ 10 ❧

काममाश्रित्य दुष्पूरं दम्भमानमदान्विताः ।
मोहाद्गृहीत्वासद्ग्राहान्प्रवर्तन्तेऽशुचिव्रताः ।।

kāmam āśhritya dushpūraṁ
dambha-māna-madānvitāḥ
mohād gṛihītvāsad-grāhān
pravartante "śhuchi-vratāḥ

Giving themselves up to insatiable passion, filled with vanity, pride and arrogance, adopting bad objectives due to delusion, and having impure resolves, they engage in actions.

☙ 11 ❧

चिन्तामपरिमेयां च प्रलयान्तामुपाश्रिताः ।
कामोपभोगपरमा एतावदिति निश्चिताः ।।

chintām aparimeyāṁ cha
pralayāntām upāśhritāḥ
kāmopabhoga-paramā
etāvad iti niśhchitāḥ

Beset with innumerable cares which end (only) with death, holding that the enjoyment of desirable objects is the highest goal, feeling sure that this is all.

☙ 12 ❧

आशापाशशतैर्बद्धाः कामक्रोधपरायणाः ।
ईहन्ते कामभोगार्थमन्यायेनार्थसञ्जयान् ।।

āśhā-pāśha-śhatair baddhāḥ
kāma-krodha-parāyaṇāḥ
īhante kāma-bhogārtham
anyāyenārtha-sañchayān

Bound by hundreds of shackles in the form of hope, giving themselves wholly to passion and anger, they endeavour to amass wealth through foul means for the enjoyment of desirable objects.

☙ 13 ❧

इदमद्य मया लब्धमिमं प्राप्स्ये मनोरथम् ।
इदमस्तीदमपि मे भविष्यति पुनर्धनम् ।।

idam adya mayā labdham
imaṁ prāpsye manoratham
idam astīdam api me
bhaviṣhyati punar dhanam

This has been gained by me today; I shall acquire this desired object. This is in hand; again, this wealth also will come to me.

☙ 14 ❧

असौ मया हतः शत्रुर्हनिष्ये चापरानपि ।
ईश्वरोऽहमहं भोगी सिद्धोऽहं बलवान्सुखी ।।

asau mayā hataḥ śhatrur
haniṣhye chāparān api
īśhvaro "ham ahaṁ bhogī
siddho "haṁ balavān sukhī

That enemy has been killed by me, and I shall kill others as well. I am the lord, I am the enjoyer, I am well-established, mighty and happy.

☙ 15 ❧

आढ्योऽभिजनवानस्मि कोऽन्योऽस्ति सदृशो मया ।
यक्ष्ये दास्यामि मोदिष्य इत्यज्ञानविमोहिताः ॥

☙ 16 ❧

अनेकचित्तविभ्रान्ता मोहजालसमावृताः ।
प्रसक्ताः कामभोगेषु पतन्ति नरकेऽशुचै ॥

āḍhyo "bhijanavān asmi
ko "nyo "sti sadṛiśho mayā
yakṣhye dāsyāmi modiṣhya
ity ajñāna-vimohitāḥ

aneka-chitta-vibhrāntā
moha-jāla-samāvṛitāḥ
prasaktāḥ kāma-bhogeṣhu
patanti narake "śhuchau

I am rich and high-born; who else is there similar to me? I shall perform sacrifices; I shall give, I shall rejoice, thus they are diversely deluded by non-discrimination. Bewildered by numerous thoughts, caught in the net of delusion, (and) engrossed in the enjoyment of desirable objects, they fall into a foul hell.

☙ 17 ❧

आत्मसम्भाविताः स्तब्धा धनमानमदान्विताः ।
यजन्ते नामयज्ञैस्ते दम्भेनाविधिपूर्वकम् ।।

ātma-sambhāvitāḥ stabdhā
dhana-māna-madānvitāḥ
yajante nāma-yajñais te
dambhenāvidhi-pūrvakam

Self-conceited, haughty, filled with pride and intoxication of wealth, they perform sacrifices which are so in name only, with ostentation and regardless of the injunctions.

☙ 18 ❧

अहङ्कारं बलं दर्पं कामं क्रोधं च संश्रिताः ।
मामात्मपरदेहेषु प्रद्विषन्तोऽभ्यसूयकाः ।।

ahankāraṁ balaṁ darpaṁ
kāmaṁ krodhaṁ cha sanśhritāḥ
māṁ ātma-para-deheṣhu
pradviṣhanto "bhyasūyakāḥ

Resorting to egotism, power, arrogance, passion and anger, hating Me in their own and others' bodies, (they become) envious by nature.

☙ 19 ❧

तानहं द्विषतः क्रूरान्संसारेषु नराधमान् ।
क्षिपाम्यजस्रमशुभानासुरीष्वेव योनिषु ।।

tān ahaṁ dviṣhataḥ krūrān
sansāreṣhu narādhamān
kṣhipāmy ajasram aśhubhān
āsurīṣhv eva yoniṣhu

I cast for ever those hateful, cruel, evil-doers in the worlds, the vilest of human beings, verily into the demoniacal classes.

☙ 20 ❧

आसुरीं योनिमापन्ना मूढा जन्मनि जन्मनि ।
मामप्राप्यैव कौन्तेय ततो यान्त्यधमां गतिम् ।।

āsurīṁ yonim āpannā
mūḍhā janmani janmani
mām aprāpyaiva kaunteya
tato yānty adhamāṁ gatim

Being born among the demoniacal species in births after births, the foods, without ever reaching Me, O son of Kunti, attain conditions lower than that.

☙ 21 ❧

त्रिविधं नरकस्येदं द्वारं नाशनमात्मनः ।
कामः क्रोधस्तथा लोभस्तस्मादेतत्त्रयं त्यजेत् ।।

tri-vidhaṁ narakasyedaṁ
dvāraṁ nāśhanam ātmanaḥ
kāmaḥ krodhas tathā
lobhas tasmād etat trayaṁ tyajet

This door of hell, which is the destroyer of the soul, is of three kinds–passion, anger and also greed. Therefore, one should forsake these three.

☙ 22 ❧

एतैर्विमुक्तः कौन्तेय तमोद्वारैस्त्रिभिर्नरः ।
आचरत्यात्मनः श्रेयस्ततो याति परां गतिम् ।।

etair vimuktaḥ kaunteya
tamo-dvārais tribhir naraḥ
ācharaty ātmanaḥ śhreyas tato
yāti parāṁ gatim

O son of Kunti, a person who is free from these three doors to darkness strives for the good of the soul. Then, he attains the highest Goal.

☙ 23 ❧

यः शास्त्रविधिमुत्सृज्य वर्तते कामकारतः ।
न स सिद्धिमवाप्नोति न सुखं न परां गतिम् ।।

yaḥ śhāstra-vidhim utsṛijya vartate kāma-kārataḥ
na sa siddhim avāpnoti na sukhaṁ na parāṁ gatim

Ignoring the precept of the scriptures, he who acts under the impulsion of passion, he does not attain perfection, nor happiness, nor the supreme Goal.

☙ 24 ❧

तस्माच्छास्त्रं प्रमाणं ते कार्याकार्यव्यवस्थितौ ।
ज्ञात्वा शास्त्रविधानोक्तं कर्म कर्तुमिहार्हसि ।।

tasmāch chhāstraṁ pramāṇaṁ
te kāryākārya-vyavasthitau
jñātvā śhāstra-vidhānoktaṁ
karma kartum ihārhasi

Therefore, the scripture is your authority as regards the determination of what is to be done and what is not to be done. After understanding (your) duty as presented by scriptural injunction, you ought to perform (your duty) here.

Chapter

17

Sraddhatraya
Vibhaga Yoga
Three Forms of Faith

ଓ 1 ଓ

अर्जुन उवाच ।
ये शास्त्रविधिमुत्सृज्य यजन्ते श्रद्धयान्विताः ।
तेषां निष्ठा तु का कृष्ण सत्वमाहो रजस्तमः ।।

arjuna uvācha
ye śhāstra-vidhim utsṛijya yajante śhraddhayānvitāḥ
teṣhāṁ niṣhṭhā tu kā kṛiṣhṇa sattvam āho rajas tamaḥ

Arjuna said: But, O Krishna, what is the state of those who, endued with faith, adore by ignoring the injunctions of the scriptures? Is it sattva, rajas or tamas?

ଓ 2 ଓ

श्रीभगवानुवाच ।
त्रिविधा भवति श्रद्धा देहिनां सा स्वभावजा ।
सात्विकी राजसी चैव तामसी चेति तां शृणु ।।

śhrī-bhagavān uvācha
tri-vidhā bhavati śhraddhā dehināṁ sā svabhāva-jā
sāttvikī rājasī chaiva tāmasī cheti tāṁ śhṛiṇu

The Blessed Lord said: That faith of the embodied beings, born of their own nature, is threefold–born of sattva, rajas and tamas. Hear about it.

∞ 3 ∞

सत्वानुरूपा सर्वस्य श्रद्धा भवति भारत ।
श्रद्धामयोऽयं पुरुषो यो यच्छ्रद्धः स एव सः ॥

sattvānurūpā sarvasya
śhraddhā bhavati bhārata
śhraddhā-mayo "yaṁ puruṣho yo
yach-chhraddhaḥ sa eva saḥ

O scion of the Bharata dynasty, the faith of all beings is in accordance with their minds. This person is made up of faith as the dominant factor. He is verily what his faith is.

∞ 4 ∞

यजन्ते सात्विका देवान्यक्षरक्षांसि राजसाः ।
प्रेतान्भूतगणांश्चान्ये यजन्ते तामसा जनाः ॥

yajante sāttvikā devān yakṣha-rakṣhānsi rājasāḥ
pretān bhūta-gaṇānśh chānye yajante tāmasā janāḥ

Those having the sattva quality worship the gods; those having rajas, the demi-gods and ogres; and other people possessed of tamas worship ghosts and the hosts of spirits.

ও 5 ৩

अशास्त्रविहितं घोरं तप्यन्ते ये तपो जनाः ।
दम्भाहङ्कारसंयुक्ताः कामरागबलान्विताः ।।

aśhāstra-vihitaṁ ghoraṁ tapyante ye tapo janāḥ
dambhāhankāra-sanyuktāḥ kāma-rāga-balānvitāḥ

Those persons who, given to ostentation and pride, and possessed of passion, attachment and strength, undertake severe austerities not sanctioned in the scriptures;

ও 6 ৩

कर्षयन्तः शरीरस्थं भूतग्राममचेतसः ।
मां चैवान्तःशरीरस्थं तान्विद्ध्यासुरनिश्चयान् ।।

karṣhayantaḥ śharīra-sthaṁ
bhūta-grāmam achetasaḥ
māṁ chaivāntaḥ śharīra-sthaṁ
tān viddhy āsura-niśhchayān

(And who,) being non-discriminating, torture, all the organs in the body as also even Me who reside in the body, know them as possessed of demoniacal conviction.

☙ 7 ❧

आहारस्त्वपि सर्वस्य त्रिविधो भवति प्रियः ।
यज्ञस्तपस्तथा दानं तेषां भेदमिमं शृणु ।।

āhāras tv api sarvasya
tri-vidho bhavati priyaḥ
yajñas tapas tathā dānaṁ
teṣhāṁ bhedam imaṁ śhṛiṇu

Food also, which is dear to all, is of three kinds; and so also are sacrifices, austerity and charity. Listen to this classification of them.

☙ 8 ❧

आयुःसत्वबलारोग्यसुखप्रीतिविवर्धनाः ।
रस्याः स्निग्धाः स्थिरा हृद्या आहाराः सात्विकप्रियाः ।।

āyuḥ-sattva-balārogya-sukha-prīti-vivardhanāḥ
rasyāḥ snigdhāḥ sthirā hṛidyā āhārāḥ sāttvika-priyāḥ

Foods that augment life, firmness of mind, strength, health, happiness and delight, and which are succulent, oleaginous, substantial and agreeable, are dear to one endowed with sattva.

☙ 9 ❧

कट्वम्ललवणात्युष्णतीक्ष्णःक्षविदाहिनः ।
आहारा राजसस्येष्टा दुःखशोकामयप्रदाः ।।

kaṭv-amla-lavaṇāty-uṣhṇa- tīkṣhṇa-rūkṣha-vidāhinaḥ
āhārā rājasayeṣhṭā duḥkha-śhokāmaya-pradāḥ

Foods that are bitter, sour, salty, very hot, pungent, dry and burning, and which production pain, sorrow and disease, are dear to one having rajas.

☙ 10 ❧

यातयामं गतरसं पूति पर्युषितं च यत् ।
उच्छिष्टमपि चामेध्यं भोजनं तामसप्रियम् ।।

yāta-yāmaṁ gata-rasaṁ
pūti paryuṣhitaṁ cha yat
uchchhiṣhṭam api chāmedhyaṁ
bhojanaṁ tāmasa-priyam

Food which is not properly cooked, lacking in essence, putrid and stale, and even ort and that which is unfit for sacrifice, is dear to one possessed of tamas.

☙ 11 ❧

अफलाकाङ्क्षिभिर्यज्ञो विधिदृष्टो य इज्यते ।
यष्टव्यमेवेति मनः समाधाय स सात्त्विकः ।।

aphalākāṅkṣhibhir yajño
vidhi-driṣhṭo ya ijyate
yaṣhṭavyam eveti manaḥ
samādhāya sa sāttvikaḥ

That sacrifice which is in accordance with the injunctions, (and is) performed by persons who do not hanker after results, and with the mental conviction that it is surely obligatory, is done through sattva.

☙ 12 ❧

अभिसन्धाय तु फलं दम्भार्थमपि चैव यत् ।
इज्यते भरतश्रेष्ठ तं यज्ञं विद्धि राजसम् ।।

abhisandhāya tu phalaṁ dambhārtham api chaiva yat
ijyate bharata-śhreṣhṭha taṁ yajñaṁ viddhi rājasam

But that sacrifice which is performed having in view a result, as also for ostentation, know that sacrifice to be done through rajas, O greatest among the descendants of Bharata.

☙ 13 ❧

विधिहीनमसृष्टान्नं मन्त्रहीनमदक्षिणम् ।
श्रद्धाविरहितं यज्ञं तामसं परिचक्षते ।।

vidhi-hīnam asṛiṣhṭānnaṁ
mantra-hīnam adakṣhiṇam
śhraddhā-virahitaṁ yajñaṁ
tāmasaṁ parichakṣhate

They declare that sacrifice as 'done through tamas' which is contrary to injunction, in which food is not distributed, in which mantras are not used, in which offerings are not made to priests, and which is devoid of faith.

☙ 14 ❧

देवद्विजगुरुप्राज्ञपूजनं शौचमार्जवम् ।
ब्रह्मचर्यमहिंसा च शारीरं तप उच्यते ।।

deva-dwija-guru-prājña- pūjanaṁ
śhaucham ārjavam
brahmacharyam ahinsā cha
śhārīraṁ tapa uchyate

The worship of gods, twice-born, venerable persons and the wise; purity, straightforwardness, celibacy and non-injury, are said to be bodily austerity.

☙ 15 ❧

अनुद्वेगकरं वाक्यं सत्यं प्रियहितं च यत् ।
स्वाध्यायाभ्यसनं चैव वाङ्मयं तप उच्यते ॥

anudvega-karaṁ vākyaṁ
satyaṁ priya-hitaṁ cha yat
svādhyāyābhyasanaṁ chaiva
vāṅ-mayaṁ tapa uchyate

That speech which causes no pain, which is true, agreeable and beneficial; as well as the practice of study of the scriptures, is said to be austerity of speech.

☙ 16 ❧

मनः प्रसादः सौम्यत्वं मौनमात्मविनिग्रहः ।
भावसंशुद्धिरित्येतत्तपो मानसमुच्यते ॥

manaḥ-prasādaḥ saumyatvaṁ
maunam ātma-vinigrahaḥ
bhāva-sanśhuddhir ity etat tapo
mānasam uchyate

Tranquillity of mind, gentleness, reticence, withdrawal of the mind, purity of heart, these are what is called mental austerity.

ଓ 17 ଡ

श्रद्धया परया तप्तं तपस्तत्त्रिविधं नरैः ।
अफलाकाङ्क्षिभिर्युक्तैः सात्विकं परिचक्षते ।।

śhraddhayā parayā taptaṁ tapas
tat tri-vidhaṁ naraiḥ
aphalākāṅkṣhibhir yuktaiḥ
sāttvikaṁ parichakṣhate

When that threefold austerity is undertaken with supreme faith by people who do not hanker after results and are self-controlled, they speak of it as born of sattva.

ଓ 18 ଡ

सत्कारमानपूजार्थं तपो दम्भेन चैव यत् ।
क्रियते तदिह प्रोक्तं राजसं चलमध्रुवम् ।।

satkāra-māna-pūjārthaṁ
tapo dambhena chaiva yat
kriyate tad iha proktaṁ
rājasaṁ chalam adhruvam

That austerity which is undertaken for earning a name, being honoured and worshipped, and also ostentatiously, that is spoken of as born of rajas, belonging to this world, uncertain and transitory.

ଓ 19 ଐ

मूढग्राहेणात्मनो यत्पीडया क्रियते तपः ।
परस्योत्सादनार्थं वा तत्तामसमुदाहृतम् ।।

mūḍha-grāheṇātmano
yat pīḍayā kriyate tapaḥ
parasyotsādanārthaṁ vā
tat tāmasam udāhṛitam

That austerity which is undertaken with a foolish intent, by causing pain to oneself, or for the destruction of others that is said to be born of tamas.

ଓ 20 ଐ

दातव्यमिति यद्दानं दीयतेऽनुपकारिणे ।
देशे काले च पात्रे च तद्दानं सात्विकं स्मृतम् ।।

dātavyam iti yad dānaṁ
dīyate "nupakāriṇe
deśhe kāle cha pātre cha
tad dānaṁ sāttvikaṁ smṛitam

That gift is referred to as born of sattva which gift is given with the idea that it ought to be given, to one who will not serve in return, and at the (proper) place, (proper) time and to a (proper) person.

ꕥ 21 ꕥ

यत्तु प्रत्युपकारार्थं फलमुद्दिश्य वा पुनः ।
दीयते च परिक्लिष्टं तद्दानं राजसं स्मृतम् ।।

yat tu pratyupakārārthaṁ
phalam uddiśhya vā punaḥ
dīyate cha parikliṣhṭaṁ
tad dānaṁ rājasaṁ smṛitam

But the gift which is given expecting reciprocation, or again, with a desire for its result, and which is given grudgingly, that is considered to be born of rajas.

ꕥ 22 ꕥ

अदेशकाले यद्दानमपात्रेभ्यश्च दीयते ।
असत्कृतमवज्ञातं तत्तामसमुदाहृतम् ।।

adeśha-kāle yad dānam
apātrebhyaśh cha dīyate
asat-kṛitam avajñātaṁ
tat tāmasam udāhṛitam

The gift which is made at an improper place and time, and to undeserving persons, without proper treatment and with disdain, is declared to be born of tamas.

☙ 23 ❧

ॐ तत्सदिति निर्देशो ब्रह्मणस्त्रिविधः स्मृतः ।
ब्राह्मणास्तेन वेदाश्च यज्ञाश्च विहिताः पुरा ।।

oṁ tat sad iti nirdeśho
brahmaṇas tri-vidhaḥ smṛitaḥ
brāhmaṇās tena vedāśh cha
yajñāśh cha vihitāḥ purā

'Om-tat-sat' is considered to be the threefold designation of Brahman. The Brahmanas and Vedas and the sacrifices were ordained by that in the days of yore.

☙ 24 ❧

तस्माद् ॐ इत्युदाहृत्य यज्ञदानतपःक्रियाः ।
प्रवर्तन्ते विधानोक्ताः सततं ब्रह्मवादिनाम् ।।

tasmād oṁ ity udāhṛitya yajña-dāna-tapaḥ-kriyāḥ
pravartante vidhānoktāḥ satataṁ brahma-vādinām

Therefore, acts of sacrifice, charity and austerity as prescribed through injunctions, of those who study and expound the Vedas, always commence after uttering the syllable Om.

ଓ 25 ଡ

तदित्यनभिसन्धाय फलं यज्ञतपःक्रियाः ।
दानक्रियाश्च विविधाः क्रियन्ते मोक्षकाङ्क्षिभिः ।।

tad ity anabhisandhāya
phalaṁ yajña-tapaḥ-kriyāḥ
dāna-kriyāśh cha vividhāḥ
kriyante mokṣha-kāṅkṣhibhiḥ

After (uttering) the word tat, acts of sacrifice and austerity as also the various acts of charity are performed without regard for results by persons aspiring for Liberation.

ଓ 26 ଡ

सद्भावे साधुभावे च सदित्येतत्प्रयुज्यते ।
प्रशस्ते कर्मणि तथा सच्छब्दः पार्थ युज्यते ।।

sad-bhāve sādhu-bhāve cha sad ity etat prayujyate
praśhaste karmaṇi tathā sach-chhabdaḥ pārtha yujyate

This word sat is used with regard to (something) coming into being and with regard to (someone) becoming good. So also, O son of the word sat is used with regard to an auspicious rite.

☙ 27 ❧

यज्ञे तपसि दाने च स्थितिः सदिति चैच्यते ।
कर्म चैव तदर्थीयं सदित्येवाभिधीयते ।।

yajñe tapasi dāne cha sthitiḥ sad iti chochyate
karma chaiva tad-arthīyaṁ sad ity evābhidhīyate

And the steadfastness in sacrifice, austerity and charity is spoken of as sat. And even the action meant for these is, verily, called as sat (good).

☙ 28 ❧

अश्रद्धया हुतं दत्तं तपस्तप्तं कृतं च यत् ।
असदित्युच्यते पार्थ न च तत्प्रेत्य नो इह ।।

aśhraddhayā hutaṁ dattaṁ tapas taptaṁ kṛitaṁ cha yat
asad ity uchyate pārtha na cha tat pretya no iha

O son of Partha, whatever is offered in sacrifice and given in charity, as also whatever austerity is undertaken or whatever is done without, faith, is said to be of on avail. And it is of no conscience after death, nor here.

Chapter 18

Moksha Sanyas Yoga
Achieving Perfection through Renunciation and Surrender

ꟹ 1 ꟹ

अर्जुन उवाच ।
सन्न्यासस्य महाबाहो तत्वमिच्छामि वेदितुम् ।
त्यागस्य च हृषीकेश पृथक्केशिनिषूदन ।।

arjuna uvācha
sannyāsaya mahā-bāho
tattvam ichchhāmi veditum
tyāgasya cha hṛiṣhīkeśha
pṛithak keśhi-niṣhūdana

Arjuna said: O mighty-armed Hrsikesa, O slayer of (the demon) Kesi, I want to know severally the truth about sannyasa as also about tyaga.

ꟹ 2 ꟹ

श्रीभगवानुवाच ।
काम्यानां कर्मणां न्यासं सन्न्यासं कवयो विदुः ।
सर्वकर्मफलत्यागं प्राहुस्त्यागं विचक्षणाः ।।

śhrī-bhagavān uvācha
kāmyānāṁ karmaṇāṁ nyāsaṁ
sannyāsaṁ kavayo viduḥ
sarva-karma-phala-tyāgaṁ
prāhus tyāgaṁ vichakṣhaṇāḥ

The Blessed Lord said: The learned ones know sannyasa to be the giving up of actions done with a desire for reward. The adepts call the abandonment of the results of all works as tyaga.

ଓ 3 ଌ

त्याज्यं दोषवदित्येके कर्म प्राहुर्मनीषिणः ।
यज्ञदानतपःकर्म न त्याज्यमिति चापरे ॥

tyājyaṁ doṣha-vad ity eke karma prāhur manīṣhiṇaḥ
yajña-dāna-tapaḥ-karma na tyājyam iti chāpare

Some learned persons say that action, beset with evil (as it is), should be given up, and others (say) that the practice of sacrifice, charity and austerity should not be given up.

ଓ 4 ଌ

निश्चयं शृणु मे तत्र त्यागे भरतसत्तम ।
त्यागो हि पुरुषव्याघ्र त्रिविधः सम्प्रकीर्तितः ॥

niśhchayaṁ śhṛiṇu me tatra tyāge bharata-sattama
tyāgo hi puruṣha-vyāghra tri-vidhaḥ samprakīrtitaḥ

O the most excellent among the descendants of Bharata, hear from Me the firm conclusion regarding that tyaga. For, O greatest among men, tyaga has been clearly declared to be of three kinds.

ଓ 5 ଌ

यज्ञदानतपःकर्म न त्याज्यं कार्यमेव तत् ।
यज्ञो दानं तपश्चैव पावनानि मनीषिणाम् ।।

yajña-dāna-tapaḥ-karma na tyājyaṁ kāryam eva tat
yajño dānaṁ tapaśh chaiva pāvanāni manīṣhiṇām

The practice of sacrifice, charity and austerity is not to be abandoned; it is surely to be undertaken. Sacrifice, charity and austerity are verily the purifiers of the wise.

ଓ 6 ଌ

एतान्यपि तु कर्माणि सङ्गं त्यक्त्वा फलानि च ।
कर्तव्यानीति मे पार्थ निश्चितं मतमुत्तमम् ।।

etāny api tu karmāṇi saṅgaṁ
tyaktvā phalāni cha
kartavyānīti me pārtha
niśhchitaṁ matam uttamam

But even these actions have to be undertaken by renouncing attachment and (hankering for) results. This is My firm and best conclusion, O Partha.

☙ 7 ❧

नियतस्य तु सन्न्यासः कर्मणो नोपपद्यते ।
मोहात्तस्य परित्यागस्तामसः परिकीर्तितः ।।

niyatasya tu sannyāsaḥ
karmaṇo nopapadyate
mohāt tasya parityāgas
tāmasaḥ parikīrtitaḥ

The abandoning of daily obligatory acts (nityakamas) is not justifiable. Giving up that through delusion is declared to be based on tamas.

☙ 8 ❧

दुःखमित्येव यत्कर्म कायक्लेशभयात्यजेत् ।
स कृत्वा राजसं त्यागं नैव त्यागफलं लभेत् ।।

duḥkham ity eva yat karma
kāya-kleśha-bhayāt tyajet
sa kṛitvā rājasaṁ tyāgaṁ n
aiva tyāga-phalaṁ labhet

Whatever action one may relinquish merely as being painful, from fear of physical suffering, he, having resorted to renunciation based on rajas, will surely not acquire the fruits of renunciation.

~ 9 ~

कार्यमित्येव यत्कर्म नियतं क्रियतेऽर्जुन ।
सङ्गं त्यक्त्वा फलं चैव स त्यागः सात्विको मतः ।।

kāryam ity eva yat karma niyataṁ kriyate "rjuna
saṅgaṁ tyaktvā phalaṁ chaiva sa tyāgaḥ sāttviko mataḥ

Whatever obligatory duty is performed just because it is a bounden duty, O Arjuna, by giving up attachment and the result as well, that renunciation is considered to be based on sattva.

~ 10 ~

न द्वेष्ट्यकुशलं कर्म कुशले नानुषज्जते ।
त्यागी सत्वसमाविष्टो मेधावी छिन्नसंशयः ।।

na dveṣhṭy akuśhalaṁ karma
kuśhale nānuṣhajjate
tyāgī sattva-samāviṣhṭo
medhāvī chhinna-sanśhayaḥ

The man of renunciation who has become imbued with sattva, who is wise and freed from doubts, does not hate unbefitting action, nor does he become attached to befitting activity.

೧ 11 ೨

न हि देहभृता शक्यं त्यक्तुं कर्माण्यशेषतः ।
यस्तु कर्मफलत्यागी स त्यागीत्यभिधीयते ।।

na hi deha-bhṛitā śhakyaṁ tyaktuṁ karmāṇy aśheṣhataḥ
yas tu karma-phala-tyāgī sa tyāgīty abhidhīyate

Since it is not possible for one who holds on to a body to give up actions entirely, therefore he, on the other hand, who renounces results on actions is called a man of renunciation.

೧ 12 ೨

अनिष्टमिष्टं मिश्रं च त्रिविधं कर्मणः फलम् ।
भवत्यत्यागिनां प्रेत्य न तु सन्न्यासिनां क्वचित् ।।

aniṣhṭam iṣhṭaṁ miśhraṁ cha
tri-vidhaṁ karmaṇaḥ phalam
bhavaty atyāgināṁ pretya na tu
sannyāsināṁ kvachit

The threefold results of actions–the undesirable, the desirable, and the mixed accrues after death to those who do not resort to renunciation, but never to those who resort to monasticism.

꧁ 13 ꧂

पञ्चैतानि महाबाहो कारणानि निबोध मे ।
साङ्ख्ये कृतान्ते प्रोक्तानि सिद्धये सर्वकर्मणाम् ।।

pañchaitāni mahā-bāho
kāraṇāni nibodha me
sānkhye kṛitānte proktāni
siddhaye sarva-karmaṇām

O mighty-armed one, learned from Me these five factors for the accomplishment of all actions, which have been spoken of in the Vedanta in which actions terminate.

꧁ 14 ꧂

अधिष्ठानं तथा कर्ता करणं च पृथग्विधम् ।
विविधाश्च पृथक्चेष्टा दैवं चैवात्र पञ्चमम् ।।

adhiṣhṭhānaṁ tathā kartā
karaṇaṁ cha pṛithag-vidham
vividhāśh cha pṛithak cheṣhṭā
daivaṁ chaivātra pañchamam

The locus as also the agent, the kinds of organs, the many and distinct activities, and, the divine is here the fifth.

☙ 15 ❧

शरीरवाङ्मनोभिर्यत्कर्म प्रारभते नरः ।
न्याय्यं वा विपरीतं वा पञ्चैते तस्य हेतवः ।।

śharīra-vāṅ-manobhir yat karma
prārabhate naraḥ
nyāyyaṁ vā viparītaṁ vā
pañchaite tasya hetavaḥ

Whatever action a man performs with the body, speech and mind, be it just or its reverse, of it these five are the causes.

☙ 16 ❧

तत्रैवं सति कर्तारमात्मानं केवलं तु यः ।
पश्यत्यकृतबुद्धित्वान्न स पश्यति दुर्मतिः ।।

tatraivaṁ sati kartāram ātmānaṁ
kevalaṁ tu yaḥ
paśhyaty akṛita-buddhitvān na sa
paśhyati durmatiḥ

This being the case, anyone, who, owing to the imperfection of his intellect, perceives the absolute Self as the agent, that man does not perceive (properly), and has a perverted intellect.

☙ 17 ❧

यस्य नाहङ्कृतो भावो बुद्धिर्यस्य न लिप्यते ।
हत्वाऽपि स इमाँल्लोकान्न हन्ति न निबध्यते ।।

yasya nāhankṛito bhāvo
buddhir yasya na lipyate
hatvā "pi sa imāl lokān na
hanti na nibadhyate

He who has not the feeling of egoism, whose intellect is not tainted, he does not kill, nor does he become bound even by killing these creatures!

☙ 18 ❧

ज्ञानं ज्ञेयं परिज्ञाता त्रिविधा कर्मचैदना ।
करणं कर्म कर्तेति त्रिविधः कर्मसंग्रहः ।।

jñānaṁ jñeyaṁ parijñātā
tri-vidhā karma-chodanā
karaṇaṁ karma karteti
tri-vidhaḥ karma-saṅgrahaḥ

Knowledge, the object the knowledge and the knower –this is the threefold inducement to action. The comprehension of actions comes under three heads –the instruments, the object and the subject.

☙ 19 ❧

ज्ञानं कर्म च कर्ता च त्रिधैव गुणभेदतः ।
प्रोच्यते गुणसङ्ख्याने यथावच्छृणु तान्यपि ।।

jñānaṁ karma cha kartā cha
tridhaiva guṇa-bhedataḥ
prochyate guṇa-saṅkhyāne
yathāvach chhṛiṇu tāny api

Knowledge, action and agent are stated in the teaching about the gunas to be only of three kinds according to the dffierences of the gunas. Hear about them also as they are.

☙ 20 ❧

सर्वभूतेषु येनैकं भावमव्ययमीक्षते ।
अविभक्तं विभक्तेषु तज्ज्ञानं विद्धि सात्विकम् ।।

sarva-bhūteṣhu yenaikaṁ
bhāvam avyayam īkṣhate
avibhaktaṁ vibhakteṣhu
taj jñānaṁ viddhi sāttvikam

Know that knowledge to be originating from sattva through which one sees a single, undecaying, undivided Entity in all the diversified things.

☙ 21 ❧

पृथक्त्वेन तु यज्ज्ञानं नानाभावान्पृथग्विधान् ।
वेत्ति सर्वेषु भूतेषु तज्ज्ञानं विद्धि राजसम् ॥

pṛithaktvena tu yaj jñānaṁ
nānā-bhāvān pṛithag-vidhān
vetti sarveṣhu bhūteṣhu
taj jñānaṁ viddhi rājasam

But know that knowledge to be originating from rajas which, amidst all things, apprehends the entities of various kinds as distinct.

☙ 22 ❧

यत्तु कृत्स्नवदेकस्मिन्कार्ये सक्तमहैतुकम् ।
अतत्वार्थवदल्पं च तत्तामसमुदाहृतम् ॥

yat tu kṛitsna-vad ekasmin kārye
saktam ahaitukam
atattvārtha-vad alpaṁ cha
tat tāmasam udāhṛitam

But that (knowledge) is said to be born of tamas which is confined to one form as though it were all, which is irrational, not concern with truth and trivial.

❧ 23 ❧

नियतं सङ्गरहितमरागद्वेषतः कृतम् ।
अफलप्रेप्सुना कर्म यतत्सात्त्विकमुच्यते ।।

niyataṁ saṅga-rahitam
arāga-dveṣhataḥ kṛitam
aphala-prepsunā karma
yat tat sāttvikam uchyate

The daily obligatory action which is performed without attachment and without likes or dislikes by one who does not hanker for rewards, that is said to be born of sattva.

❧ 24 ❧

यत्तु कामेप्सुना कर्म साहङ्कारेण वा पुनः ।
क्रियते बहुलायासं तद्राजसमुदाहृतम् ।।

yat tu kāmepsunā karma
sāhankāreṇa vā punaḥ
kriyate bahulāyāsaṁ
tad rājasam udāhṛitam

But that action is said to be born of rajas which is done by one desirous of results or by one who is egotistic, and which is highly strenuous.

✥ 25 ✥

अनुबन्धं क्षयं हिंसामनपेक्ष्य च पौरुषम् ।
मोहादारभ्यते कर्म यत्तत्तामसमुच्यते ॥

anubandhaṁ kṣhayaṁ
hinsām anapekṣhya cha paurușham
mohād ārabhyate karma
yat tat tāmasam uchyate

That action is said to be born of tamas which is undertaken out of delusion, (and) without consideration of its conscience, loss, harm and ability.

✥ 26 ✥

मुक्तसङ्गोऽनहंवादी धृत्युत्साहसमन्वितः ।
सिद्ध्यसिद्ध्योर्निर्विकारः कर्ता सात्त्विक उच्यते ॥

mukta-saṅgo "nahaṁ-vādī
dhṛity-utsāha-samanvitaḥ
siddhy-asiddhyor nirvikāraḥ
kartā sāttvika uchyate

The agent who is free from attachment not egotistic, endowed with fortitude and diligence, and unperturbed by success and failure is said to be possessed of sattva.

☙ 27 ❧

रागी कर्मफलप्रेप्सुर्लुब्धो हिंसात्मकोऽशुचिः ।
हर्षशोकान्वितः कर्ता राजसः परिकीर्तितः ।।

rāgī karma-phala-prepsur lubdho
hinsātmako "śhuchiḥ
harṣha-śhokānvitaḥ kartā
rājasaḥ parikīrtitaḥ

The agent who has attachment, who is desirous of the results of actions, covetous, cruel by nature, unclean and subject to joy and sorrow is declared to be possessed of rajas.

☙ 28 ❧

अयुक्तः प्राकृतः स्तब्धः शठो नैष्कृतिकोऽलसः ।
विषादी दीर्घसूत्री च कर्ता तामस उच्यते ।।

ayuktaḥ prākṛitaḥ stabdhaḥ
śhaṭho naiṣhkṛitiko "lasaḥ
viṣhādī dīrgha-sūtrī cha
kartā tāmasa uchyate

The agent who is unsteady, naive, unbending, deceitful, wicked, lazy, morose and procrastinating is said to be possessed of tamas.

꧁ 29 ꧂

बुद्धेर्भेदं धृतेश्चैव गुणतस्त्रिविधं शृणु ।
प्रोच्यमानमशेषेण पृथक्त्वेन धनञ्जय ।।

buddher bhedaṁ dhṛiteśh chaiva
guṇatas tri-vidhaṁ śhṛiṇu
prochyamānam aśheṣheṇa
pṛithaktvena dhanañjaya

O Dhananjaya, listen to the classification of the intellect as also of fortitude, which is threefold according to the gunas, while it is being stated elaborately and severely.

꧁ 30 ꧂

प्रवृत्तिंच निवृत्तिं च कार्याकार्ये भयाभये ।
बन्धं मोक्षं च या वेत्तिबुद्धिः सा पार्थ सात्विकी ।।

pravṛittiṁ cha nivṛittiṁ cha
kāryākārye bhayābhaye
bandhaṁ mokṣhaṁ cha yā
vetti buddhiḥ sā pārtha sāttvikī

O Partha, that intellect is born of sattva which understands action and withdrawal, duty and what is not duty, the sources of fear and fearlessness, and bondage and freedom.

31

यया धर्ममधर्मं च कार्यं चाकार्यमेव च ।
अयथावत्प्रजानाति बुद्धिः सा पार्थ राजसी ।।

yayā dharmam adharmaṁ cha
kāryaṁ chākāryam eva cha
ayathāvat prajānāti buddhiḥ
sā pārtha rājasī

O Partha, that intellect is born of rajas with which one wrongly understands virtue and vice as also what ought to be done and ought not to be done.

32

अधर्मं धर्ममिति या मन्यते तमसावृता ।
सर्वार्थान्विपरीतांश्च बुद्धिः सा पार्थ तामसी ।।

adharmaṁ dharmam iti yā
manyate tamasāvṛitā
sarvārthān viparītānśh cha
buddhiḥ sā pārtha tāmasī

O Partha, that intellect is born of tamas which, being covered by darkness, considers vice as virtue, and verily perceives all things contrary to what they are.

☙ 33 ❧

धृत्या यया धारयते मनःप्राणेन्द्रियक्रियाः ।
योगेनाव्यभिचारिण्या धृतिः सा पार्थ सात्विकी ।।

dhṛityā yayā dhārayate manaḥ-prāṇendriya-kriyāḥ
yogenāvyabhichāriṇyā dhṛitiḥ sā pārtha sāttvikī

O Partha, the firmness that is unfailing through concentration, with which one restrains the functions of the mind, vital forces and the organs, that firmness is born of sattva.

☙ 34 ❧

यया तु धर्मकामार्थान्धृत्या धारयतेऽर्जुन ।
प्रसङ्गेन फलाकाङ् क्षी धृतिः सा पार्थ राजसी ।।

yayā tu dharma-kāmārthān dhṛityā
dhārayate "rjuna
prasaṅgena phalākāṅkṣhī dhṛitiḥ
sā pārtha rājasī

But, O Partha, the firmness with which one holds on to righteousness, covetable things and wealth, being desirous of their fruits as the occasion for each arises, that firmness is born of rajas.

☙ 35 ❧

यया स्वप्नं भयं शोकं विषादं मदमेव च ।
न विमुञ्चति दुर्मेधा धृतिः सा पार्थ तामसी ।।

yayā svapnaṁ bhayaṁ śhokaṁ
viṣhādaṁ madam eva cha
na vimuñchati durmedhā dhṛitiḥ
sā pārtha tāmasī

That firmness is considered to be born of tamas due to which a person with a corrupt intellect does not give up sleep, fear, sorrow, despondency as also sensuality.

☙ 36 ❧

सुखं त्विदानीं त्रिविधं शृणु मे भरतर्षभ ।
अभ्यासाद्रमते यत्र दुःखान्तं च निगच्छति ।।

☙ 37 ❧

यत्तदग्रे विषमिव परिणामेऽमृतोपमम् ।
तत्सुखं सात्विकं प्रोक्तमात्मबुद्धिप्रसादजम् ।।

sukhaṁ tv idānīṁ tri-vidhaṁ
śhṛiṇu me bharatarṣhabha
abhyāsād ramate yatra
duḥkhāntaṁ cha nigachchhati

yat tad agre viṣham iva
pariṇāme "mṛitopamam
tat sukhaṁ sāttvikaṁ
proktam ātma-buddhi-prasāda-jam

Now hear from Me, O scion of the Bharata dynasty, as regards the three kinds of joy: That in which one delights owing to habit, and certainly attains the cessation of sorrows; That which is like poison in the beginning, but comparable to nectar in the end, and which, arises from the purity of one's intellect–that joy is spoken of as born of sattva.

৩ 38 ৪

विषयेन्द्रियसंयोगाद्यत्तदग्रेऽमृतोपमम् ।
परिणामे विषमिव तत्सुखं राजसं स्मृतम् ॥

viṣhayendriya-sanyogād
yat tad agre "mṛitopamam
pariṇāme viṣham iva
tat sukhaṁ rājasaṁ smṛitam

That joy is referred to as born of rajas which, arising from the contact of the organs and (their) objects, is like nectar in the beginning, but like poison at the end.

☙ 39 ❧

यदग्रे चानुबन्धे च सुखं मोहनमात्मनः ।
निद्रालस्यप्रमादोत्थं तत्तामसमुदाहृतम् ।।

yad agre chānubandhe cha
sukhaṁ mohanam ātmanaḥ
nidrālasya-pramādotthaṁ
tat tāmasam udāhṛitam

That joy is said to be born of tamas which, both in the beginning and in the end, is delusive to oneself and arises from sleep, laziness and inadvertence.

☙ 40 ❧

न तदस्ति पृथिव्यां वा दिवि देवेषु वा पुनः ।
सत्वं प्रकृतिजैर्मुक्तं यदेभिः स्यात्त्रिभिर्गुणैः ।।

na tad asti pṛithivyāṁ vā
divi deveṣhu vā punaḥ
sattvaṁ prakṛiti-jair muktaṁ
yad ebhiḥ syāt tribhir guṇaiḥ

There is no such entity in the world or, again, among the gods in heaven, which can be free from these three gunas born of Nature.

☙ 41 ❧

ब्राह्मणक्षत्रियविशां शूद्राणां च परन्तप ।
कर्माणि प्रविभक्तानि स्वभावप्रभवैर्गुणैः ।।

brāhmaṇa-kṣhatriya-viśhāṁ śhūdrāṇāṁ cha parantapa
karmāṇi pravibhaktāni svabhāva-prabhavair guṇaiḥ

O scorcher of enemies, the duties of the Brahmanas, the Ksatriyas and the Vaisyas, as also of the Sudras have been fully classified according to the gunas born from Nature.

☙ 42 ❧

शमो दमस्तपः शौचं क्षान्तिरार्जवमेव च ।
ज्ञानं विज्ञानमास्तिक्यं ब्रह्मकर्म स्वभावजम् ।।

śhamo damas tapaḥ śhauchaṁ
kṣhāntir ārjavam eva cha
jñānaṁ vijñānam āstikyaṁ
brahma-karma svabhāva-jam

The natural duties of the Brahmanas are the control of the internal and external organs, austerity, purity, forgiveness, straightforwardness, knowledge as also wisdom and faith.

ও 43 ঌ

शौर्यं तेजो धृतिर्दाक्ष्यं युद्धे चाप्यपलायनम् ।
दानमीश्वरभावश्च क्षात्रं कर्म स्वभावजम् ।।

śhauryaṁ tejo dhṛitir dākṣhyaṁ
yuddhe chāpy apalāyanam
dānam īśhvara-bhāvaśh cha
kṣhātraṁ karma svabhāva-jam

The natural duties of the Ksatriyas are heroism, boldness, fortitude, capability, and also not retreating from battle, generosity and lordliness.

ও 44 ঌ

कृषिगौरक्ष्यवाणिज्यं वैश्यकर्म स्वभावजम् ।
परिचर्यात्मकं कर्म शूद्रस्यापि स्वभावजम् ।।

kṛiṣhi-gau-rakṣhya-vāṇijyaṁ
vaiśhya-karma svabhāva-jam
paricharyātmakaṁ karma
śhūdrasyāpi svabhāva-jam

The natural duties of the Vaisyas are agriculture, cattle-rearing and trade. Of the Sudras, too, the natural duty is in the form of service.

☙ 45 ❧

स्वे स्वे कर्मण्यभिरतः संसिद्धिं लभते नरः ।
स्वकर्मनिरतः सिद्धिं यथा विन्दति तच्छृणु ।।

sve sve karmaṇy abhirataḥ
sansiddhiṁ labhate naraḥ
sva-karma-nirataḥ siddhiṁ
yathā vindati tach chhṛiṇu

Being devoted to his own duty, man attains complete success. Hear that as to how one devoted to his own duty achieves success.

☙ 46 ❧

यतः प्रवृत्तिर्भूतानां येन सर्वमिदं ततम् ।
स्वकर्मणा तमभ्यर्च्य सिद्धिं विन्दति मानवः ।।

yataḥ pravṛittir bhūtānāṁ
yena sarvam idaṁ tatam
sva-karmaṇā tam abhyarchya
siddhiṁ vindati mānavaḥ

A human being achieves success by adoring through his own duties Him from whom is the origin of creatures, and by whom is all this pervaded.

ও 47 ৩

श्रेयान्स्वधर्मो विगुणः परधर्मात्स्वनुष्ठितात् ।
स्वभावनियतं कर्म कुर्वन्नाप्नोति किल्बिषम् ॥

śhreyān swa-dharmo viguṇaḥ
para-dharmāt sv-anuṣhṭhitāt
svabhāva-niyataṁ karma
kurvan nāpnoti kilbiṣham

One's own duty, (though) defective, is superior to another's duty well performed. By performing a duty as dictated by one's own nature, one does not incur sin.

ও 48 ৩

सहजं कर्म कौन्तेय सदोषमपि न त्यजेत् ।
सर्वारम्भा हि दोषेण धूमेनाग्निरिवावृताः ॥

saha-jaṁ karma kaunteya
sa-doṣham api na tyajet
sarvārambhā hi doṣheṇa
dhūmenāgnir ivāvṛitāḥ

O son of Kunti, one should not give up the duty to which one is born, even though it be faulty. For all undertakings are surrounded with evil, as fire is with smoke.

೧ 49 ೨

असक्तबुद्धिः सर्वत्र जितात्मा विगतस्पृहः ।
नैष्कर्म्यसिद्धिं परमां सन्न्यासेनाधिगच्छति ॥

asakta-buddhiḥ sarvatra
jitātmā vigata-spṛihaḥ
naiṣhkarmya-siddhiṁ paramāṁ
sannyāsenādhigachchhati

He whose intellect remains unattached to everything, who has conquered his internal organs and is desire-less, attains through monasticism the supreme perfection consisting in the state of one free from duties.

೧ 50 ೨

सिद्धिं प्राप्तो यथा ब्रह्म तथाप्नोति निबोध मे ।
समासेनैव कौन्तेय निष्ठा ज्ञानस्य या परा ॥

siddhiṁ prāpto yathā brahma tathāpnoti nibodha me
samāsenaiva kaunteya niṣhṭhā jñānasya yā parā

Understand for certain from Me, in brief indeed, O son of Kunti, that process by which one who has achieved success attains Brahman, which is the supreme consummation of Knowledge.

☙ 51 ❧

बुद्ध्या विशुद्धया युक्तो धृत्यात्मानं नियम्य च ।
शब्दादीन्विषयांस्त्यक्त्वा रागद्वेषौ व्युदस्य च ।।

buddhyā viśhuddhayā yukto
dhṛityātmānaṁ niyamya cha
śhabdādīn viṣhayāns tyaktvā
rāga-dveṣhau vyudasya cha

Being endowed with a pure intellect, and controlling oneself with fortitude, rejecting the objects beginning from sound, and eliminating attachment and hatred;

☙ 52 ❧

विविक्तसेवी लघ्वाशी यतवाक्कायमानसः ।
ध्यानयोगपरो नित्यं वैराग्यं समुपाश्रितः ।।

vivikta-sevī laghv-āśhī
yata-vāk-kāya-mānasaḥ
dhyāna-yoga-paro nityaṁ
vairāgyaṁ samupāśhritaḥ

One who resorts to solitude, eats sparingly, has speech, body and mind under control, to whom meditation and concentration are ever the highest (duty), and who is possessed of dispassion;

∞ 53 ∞

अहङ्कारं बलं दर्पं कामं क्रोधं परिग्रहम् ।
विमुच्य निर्ममः शान्तो ब्रह्मभूयाय कल्पते ।।

ahankāraṁ balaṁ darpaṁ
kāmaṁ krodhaṁ parigraham
vimuchya nirmamaḥ śhānto
brahma-bhūyāya kalpate

(That person,) having discarded egotism, force, pride, desire, anger and superfluous possessions, free from the idea of possession, and serene, is fit for becoming Brahman.

∞ 54 ∞

ब्रह्मभूतः प्रसन्नात्मा न शोचति न काङ्क्षति ।
समः सर्वेषु भूतेषु मद्भक्तिं लभते पराम् ।।

brahma-bhūtaḥ prasannātmā na śhochati na kāṅkṣhati
samaḥ sarveṣhu bhūteṣhu mad-bhaktiṁ labhate parām

One who has become Brahman and has attained the blissful Self does not grieve or desire. Becoming the same towards all beings, he attains supreme devotion to Me.

꧁ 55 ꧂

भक्त्या मामभिजानाति यावान्यश्चास्मि तत्वतः ।
ततो मां तत्वतो ज्ञात्वा विशते तदनन्तरम् ।।

bhaktyā mām abhijānāti
yāvān yaśh chāsmi tattvataḥ
tato māṁ tattvato jñātvā
viśhate tad-anantaram

Through devotion he knows Me in reality, as to what and who I am. Then, having known Me in truth, he enters (into Me) immediately after that (Knowledge).

꧁ 56 ꧂

सर्वकर्माण्यपि सदा कुर्वाणो मद्व्यपाश्रयः ।
मत्प्रसादादवाप्नोति शाश्वतं पदमव्ययम् ।।

sarva-karmāṇy api sadā
kurvāṇo mad-vyapāśhrayaḥ
mat-prasādād avāpnoti
śhāśhvataṁ padam avyayam

Ever engaging even in all actions, one to whom I am the refuge, attains the eternal, immutable State through My grace.

꧁ 57 ꧂

चेतसा सर्वकर्माणि मयि सन्न्यस्य मत्परः ।
बुद्धियोगमुपाश्रित्य मच्चित्तः सततं भव ।।

chetasā sarva-karmāṇi
mayi sannyasya mat-paraḥ
buddhi-yogam upāśhritya
mach-chittaḥ satataṁ bhava

Mentally surrendering all actions to Me and accepting Me as the supreme, have your mind ever fixed on Me by resorting to the concentration of your intellect.

꧁ 58 ꧂

मच्चित्तः सर्वदुर्गाणि मत्प्रसादात्तरिष्यसि ।
अथ चेत्त्वमहङ्कारान्न श्रोष्यसि विनङ्क्ष्यसि ।।

mach-chittaḥ sarva-durgāṇi
mat-prasādāt tariṣhyasi
atha chet tvam ahankārān na
śhroṣhyasi vinaṅkṣhyasi

Having your mind fixed on Me, you will cross over all difficulties through My grace. If, on the other hand, you do not listen out of egotism, you will get destroyed.

☙ 59 ❧

यदहङ्कारमाश्रित्य न योत्स्य इति मन्यसे ।
मिथ्यैष व्यवसायस्ते प्रकृतिस्त्वां नियोक्ष्यति ।।

yad ahankāram āśhritya na
yotsya iti manyase
mithyaiṣha vyavasāyas te
prakṛitis tvāṁ niyokṣhyati

That you think 'I shall not fight', by relying on egotism, vain is this determination of yours. (Your) nature impel you!

☙ 60 ❧

स्वभावजेन कौन्तेय निबद्धः स्वेन कर्मणा ।
कर्तुं नेच्छसि यन्मोहात्करिष्यस्यवशोऽपि तत् ।।

swbhāva-jena kaunteya
nibaddhaḥ svena karmaṇā
kartuṁ nechchhasi yan mohāt
kariṣhyasy avaśho "pi tat

Being bound by your own duty born of nature, O son of Kunti, you, being helpless, will verily do that which you do not wish to do owing to indiscrimination.

☙ 61 ❧

ईश्वरः सर्वभूतानां हृद्देशेऽर्जुन तिष्ठति ।
भ्रामयन्सर्वभूतानि यन्त्राऽऽरूढानि मायया ।।

īśhvaraḥ sarva-bhūtānāṁ
hṛid-deśhe "rjuna tiṣhṭhati
bhrāmayan sarva-bhūtāni
yantrārūḍhāni māyayā

O Arjuna, the Lord resides in the region of the heart of all creatures, revolving through Maya all the creatures (appearing as) mounted on a machine!

☙ 62 ❧

तमेव शरणं गच्छ सर्वभावेन भारत ।
तत्प्रसादात्परां शान्तिं स्थानं प्राप्स्यसि शाश्वतम् ।।

tam eva śharaṇaṁ gachchha
sarva-bhāvena bhārata
tat-prasādāt parāṁ śhāntiṁ sthānaṁ
prāpsyasi śhāśhvatam

Take refuge in Him alone with your whole being, O scion of the Bharata dynasty. Through His grace you will attain the supreme Peace and the eternal Abode.

ଔ 63 ର

इति ते ज्ञानमाख्यातं गुह्याद्गुह्यतरं मया ।
विमृश्यैतदशेषेण यथेच्छसि तथा कुरु ॥

iti te jñānam ākhyātaṁ
guhyād guhyataraṁ mayā
vimṛiśhyaitad aśheṣheṇa
yathechchhasi tathā kuru

To you has been imparted by Me this knowledge which is more secret than any secret. Pondering over this as a whole, do as you like.

ଔ 64 ର

सर्वगुह्यतमं भूयः शृणु मे परमं वचः ।
इष्टोऽसि मे दृढमिति ततो वक्ष्यामि ते हितम् ॥

sarva-guhyatamaṁ bhūyaḥ
śhṛiṇu me paramaṁ vachaḥ
iṣhṭo "si me dṛiḍham iti
tato vakṣhyāmi te hitam

Listen again to My highest utterance which is the profoundest of all. Since you are ever dear to Me, therefore I shall speak what is beneficial to you.

☙ 65 ❧

मन्मना भव मद्भक्तो मद्याजी मां नमस्कुरु ।
मामेवैष्यसि सत्यं ते प्रतिजाने प्रियोऽसि मे ।।

man-manā bhava mad-bhakto
mad-yājī māṁ namaskuru
mām evaiṣhyasi satyaṁ te
pratijāne priyo "si me

Have your mind fixed on Me, be My devotee, be a sacrificer to Me and bow down to Me. (Thus) you will come to Me alone. (This) truth do I promise to you. (For) you are dear to Me.

☙ 66 ❧

सर्वधर्मान्परित्यज्य मामेकं शरणं व्रज ।
अहं त्वां सर्वपापेभ्यो मोक्षयिष्यामि मा शुचः ।।

sarva-dharmān parityajya
mām ekaṁ śharaṇaṁ vraja
ahaṁ tvāṁ sarva-pāpebhyo
mokṣhayiṣhyāmi mā śhuchaḥ

Abandoning all forms of rites and duties, take refuge in Me alone. I shall free you from all sins. (Therefore) do not grieve.

ॡ 67 ॡ

इदं ते नातपस्काय नाभक्ताय कदाचन ।
न चाशुश्रूषवे वाच्यं न च मां योऽभ्यसूयति ।।

idaṁ te nātapaskyāya
nābhaktāya kadāchana
na chāśhuśhruṣhave vāchyaṁ na cha
māṁ yo "bhyasūtayi

This (that I have taught) you should not ever be taught to one who is devoid of austerities and to one who is not a devotee; also, neither to one who does not render service, nor as well to one who cavils at Me.

ॡ 68 ॡ

य इदं परमं गुह्यं मद्भक्तेष्वभिधास्यति ।
भक्तिं मयि परां कृत्वा मामेवैष्यत्यसंशयः ।।

ya idaṁ paramaṁ guhyaṁ
mad-bhakteṣhv abhidhāsyati
bhaktiṁ mayi parāṁ kṛitvā
mām evaiṣhyaty asanśhayaḥ

He who, entertaining supreme devotion to Me, will speak of this highest secret, to My devotees will without doubt reach Me alone.

☙ 69 ❧

न च तस्मान्मनुष्येषु कश्चिन्मे प्रियकृत्तमः ।
भविता न च मे तस्मादन्यः प्रियतरो भुवि ॥

na cha tasmān manuṣhyeṣhu
kaśhchin me priya-kṛittamaḥ
bhavitā na cha me tasmād anyaḥ
priyataro bhuvi

And as compared with him, none else among human beings is the best accomplisher of what is dear to Me. Moreover, nor will there be anyone else in the world dearer to Me than he.

☙ 70 ❧

अध्येष्यते च य इमं धर्म्यं संवादमावयोः ।
ज्ञानयज्ञेन तेनाहमिष्टः स्यामिति मे मतिः ॥

adhyeṣhyate cha ya imaṁ dharmyaṁ saṁvādam āvayoḥ
jñāna-yajñena tenāham iṣhṭaḥ syām iti me matiḥ

And he who will study this sacred conversation between us two, which is conducive to virtue, by him I shall be adored through the Sacrifice in the form of Knowledge. This is My judgement.

☙ 71 ❧

श्रद्धावाननसूयश्च शृणुयादपि यो नरः ।
सोऽपि मुक्तः शुभाँल्लोकान्प्राप्नुयात्पुण्यकर्मणाम् ॥

śhraddhāvān anasūyaśh cha
śhṛiṇuyād api yo naraḥ
so "pi muktaḥ śhubhāl lokān
prāpnuyāt puṇya-karmaṇām

Any man who, being reverential and free from cavilling, might even hear (this), he too, becoming free, shall attain the blessed worlds of those who perform virtuous deeds.

☙ 72 ❧

कच्चिदेतच्छ्रुतं पार्थ त्वयैकाग्रेण चेतसा ।
कच्चिदज्ञानसम्मोहः प्रनष्टस्ते धनञ्जय ॥

kachchid etach chhrutaṁ pārtha
tvayaikāgreṇa chetasā
kachchid ajñāna-sammohaḥ
pranaṣhṭas te dhanañjaya

O Partha, has this been listened to by you with a one-pointed mind? O Dhananjaya, has your delusion caused by ignorance been destroyed?

∞ 73 ∞

अर्जुन उवाच ।
नष्टो मोहः स्मृतिर्लब्धा त्वत्प्रसादान्मयाच्युत ।
स्थितोऽस्मि गतसन्देहः करिष्ये वचनं तव ॥

arjuna uvācha
naṣhṭo mohaḥ smṛitir labdhā
tvat-prasādān mayāchyuta
sthito "smi gata-sandehaḥ
kariṣhye vachanaṁ tava

Arjuna said: O Acyuta, (my) delusion has been destroyed and memory has been retained by me through Your grace. I stand with my doubt removed; I shall follow Your instruction.

∞ 74 ∞

सञ्जय उवाच ।
इत्यहं वासुदेवस्य पार्थस्य च महात्मनः ।
संवादमिममश्रौषमद्भुतं रोमहर्षणम् ॥

sañjaya uvācha
ity ahaṁ vāsudevasya
pārthasya cha mahātmanaḥ
saṁvādam imam aśhrauṣham adbhutaṁ
roma-harṣhaṇam

Sanjaya said: I thus heard this conversation of Vasudeva and of the great-souled Partha, which is unique and makes one's hair stand on end.

☙ 75 ❧

व्यासप्रसादाच्छ्रुतवानेतद्गुह्यमहं परम् ।
योगं योगेश्वरात्कृष्णात्साक्षात्कथयतः स्वयम् ॥

vyāsa-prasādāch chhrutavān
etad guhyam ahaṁ param
yogaṁ yogeśhvarāt kṛiṣhṇāt
sākṣhāt kathayataḥ svayam

Through the favour of Vyasa I heard this secret concerning the supreme Yoga from Krishna, the Lord of yogas, while He Himself was actually speaking!

☙ 76 ❧

राजन्संस्मृत्य संस्मृत्य संवादमिममद्भुतम् ।
केशवार्जुनयोः पुण्यं हृष्यामि च मुहुर्मुहुः ॥

rājan sansmṛitya sansmṛitya
saṁvādam imam adbhutam
keśhavārjunayoḥ puṇyaṁ
hṛiṣhyāmi cha muhur muhuḥ

And, O king, while repeatedly remembering this unique, sacred dialogue between Kesava and Arjuna, I rejoice every moment.

☙ 77 ❧

तच्च संस्मृत्य संस्मृत्य रूपमत्यद्भुतं हरेः ।
विस्मयो मे महानराजन्हृष्यामि च पुनः पुनः ॥

tach cha sansmṛitya saṁsmṛitya
rūpam aty-adbhutaṁ hareḥ
vismayo ye mahān rājan hṛiṣhyāmi cha
punaḥ punaḥ

O king, repeatedly recollecting that greatly extraordinary form of Hari, I am struck with wonder. And I rejoice again and again.

78

यत्र योगेश्वरः कृष्णो यत्र पार्थो धनुर्धरः ।
तत्र श्रीर्विजयो भूतिर्ध्रुवा नीतिर्मतिर्मम ॥

yatra yogeśhvaraḥ kṛiṣhṇo
yatra pārtho dhanur-dharaḥ
tatra śhrīr vijayo bhūtir
dhruvā nītir matir mama

Where there is Krishna, the Lord of yogas, and where there is Partha, the wielder of the bow, there are fortune, victory, prosperity and unfailing prudence. Such is my conviction.